A PASSION FOR SPEED

Victor and Mildred Bruce reunited at Croydon. (Courtesy of Caroline Gough-Cooper)

A PASSION FOR SPEED

THE DARING LIFE OF MILDRED, THE HONOURABLE MRS VICTOR BRUCE

PAUL SMIDDY

The History Press

Cover illustrations
Front: Mildred's Blackburn Bluebird; Mildred with her habitual string of pearls. (BAe Heritage) *Back:* Painting her steed's name for the benefit of journalists just before departure on her round-the-world flight. (BAe Heritage)

First published 2017

The History Press
The Mill, Brimscombe Port
Stroud, Gloucestershire, GL5 2QG
www.thehistorypress.co.uk

British Library Cataloguing in Publication Data.
A catalogue record for this book is available from the British Library.

ISBN 978-0-7509-8366-2

Typesetting and origination by The History Press
Printed in Great Britain

CONTENTS

FOREWORD

It is rare to find anyone who embraces all disciplines of speed, let alone a woman! The Hon. Mrs Victor Bruce, who began her addiction to speed before women had the vote in this country, is definitely the exception. This is the story of an incredible woman who lived life on the edge and yet managed to survive into her nineties.

In this biography, Paul Smiddy grips one's imagination with a roller coaster of accidents, fights with bureaucracy and the sheer guts and courage of an Edwardian woman who defied all the conventions of her time. Paul's meticulous research and attention to detail brings alive the spirit of a woman who coped with her car landing in a ditch and catching fire, flying over jungles, becoming engulfed in monsoons and landing in a muddy field and turning upside down.

Follow this intrepid lady as she pushes all boundaries in what was then a 'man's world'. Undeterred by setbacks, she ventures into the business world and drives herself at a pace which makes one quite breathless. Her focus, endurance, stamina and confidence are carried by her immense ability to charm her way out of any situation.

This is an incredible read as you journey through the life of a truly indomitable spirit.

Polly Vacher (aviatrix)
April 2017

A pensive Mildred and Victor before departure. (BAe Heritage)

ACKNOWLEDGEMENTS

I am grateful I have managed to find many people who share my interest in Mildred and, in some cases, Blackburn Aircraft. My deep thanks go to: Paul Lawson and his colleagues at the BAe Systems Heritage Centre at Brough, for sharing their archive and knowledge so enthusiastically; Alan Wynn and his colleagues at the Brooklands Museum – a time capsule and jewel to be preserved, one hopes, from further industrial and housing encroachment; the staff at The National Archives in Kew – which is quite simply a national treasure; the management and staff at the RAF Museum at Hendon (which also houses some of the Royal Aeronautical Society's archive material), who are enthusiastic and helpful; Wendy Grimmond, for generously sharing her memories of her father and her father's collection; Caroline Brown, for showing me her Mildred material (and how to ski); Stuart McCrudden, for his reminiscences; John Davies, for his insight into life at Babdown; Peter Amos, the acknowledged guru of Miles Aircraft; The Orion Publishing Group for material reproduced from *Montlhéry, the Story of the Paris Autodrome* by William Boddy – I acknowledge that all other attempts at contacting the copyright holder of *Montlhéry* were unsuccessful; Amy Rigg and her colleagues at The History Press, for their faith, patience and wisdom; and finally my wife Tina for her long-suffering support.

Every effort has been made to trace all copyright holders and to obtain their permission for the use of copyright material. To rectify any omissions, please contact the author care of the publisher so that we can incorporate such corrections in future reprints or editions.

Paul Smiddy
February 2017

INTRODUCTION

This book owes its genesis to my grandmother – a very sweet lady, who was the cousin of Robert and Norman Blackburn, the founders of Blackburn Aircraft (if I ever meet you, I shall share one or two of her stories …). It must have been this that sparked my desire to fly. It certainly sparked my lifelong interest in the Blackburn Aircraft Company, and many years ago I had begun to attend auctions of aeronautica, and had started to purchase the odd artefact connected with Blackburn's.

I heard of a forthcoming sale of the archive of a lady who had achieved great things in a Blackburn Bluebird – one Hon. Mrs Victor Bruce. The more I delved into her story, the more intriguing it became. Sadly, I was outbid at the auction by a determined (and presumably wealthier!) woman. Some years passed before, one day, I was chatting to a fellow aviator and skier and we established that we were both interested in Mrs Bruce. She, Caroline Gough-Cooper, had been my outbidder, and could not have been more helpful in showing me the archive she had purchased that day. It convinced me that a book just had to be written.

The days chasing Mildred's story in the archives of Hendon, Kew, Wiltshire and BAe were very absorbing. Separating the fact from the fiction was better than doing any crossword. Some call our heroine 'Mary Petre'; her husband called her 'Jane' – for what reason no one knows, since it was not one of her given names. I have chosen 'Mildred', as that seems to have been the most popular in her family. For the world at large, she was known as the Hon. Mrs Victor Bruce: this became her brand, and one that she refused to relinquish, even after divorce. Here is a lady whose story bears telling …

LIVING THE NOVEL: RESCUE FROM THE BRIGANDS

Mildred's dream is not supposed to end like this, but at least she has someone in whom to confide her mounting fear – herself, as she has taken the novel step of installing a primitive dictating machine on the passenger seat to her left in the open-cockpit biplane. The petite 34-year-old Englishwoman is trying to reach her destination at Jask in Persia before the full heat of the day. Even at 5 a.m., four hours earlier, when she had taken off, it had been hot enough, but now she has left behind the comfort of supportive RAF officers at Bushire.

The geography of the littoral below is entrancing, 'Wonderful, weird rock formations, which extend for miles with precise regularity,' with 'some wonderful oxide formations, mountains and hills of varying hues, such as the sugar-loaf formation towering up several hundred feet, of a brilliant turquoise blue.'[1] The old river beds appear like silver ribbons leading from her left wing. It is desolate country, devoid of vegetation apart from occasional clumps of palms on the coastline. From time to time, dive boats from the pearl fisheries pass underneath.

She confides to the dictating machine, 'I am losing a great deal of oil from my engine and am very anxious about it.' Because of the time pressure and numbed with fatigue, instead of following the coast, Mildred has decided to cut a corner by flying straight across the 100-mile wide Straits of Hormuz. It should save her an hour or so because at 6,000ft in her single-engine, heavily laden Blackburn Bluebird, progress is slow.

A few minutes earlier, she has been cheered by the sight of two warships of the Royal Navy passing through the straits and has swooped low and returned the waves of the ratings on deck. Alan Cobham, on his famous proving flight to Australia in 1926, had been flying a seaplane so he was more attuned to the state of the sea than Mildred. He noted that there were permanent rollers on this part of the Gulf, so a ditching in the sea would make short shrift of Mildred's Bluebird.[2]

Her de Havilland Gipsy engine has been proving incontinent since leaving England, and has required the attentions of Imperial Airways engineers several times along the route. A wiser soul would have awaited the arrival of spares at Bushire to replace the offending parts, but her schedule is overbearing, Mildred having been advised that it is imperative to cross the tropics before the onset of the monsoon season. Instead, she has made a temporary repair.

Now that oil is spewing across the windscreen, she is beginning to rue that decision. Her engineering background enables her to discern that it is coming from the thrust race housing – as if that knowledge is a help. A very bad vibration increases her anxiety. It has only been a matter of weeks since she has learned to fly and her experience in the air is negligible – nothing has prepared her for this.

It is late summer in 1930. Amy Johnson has only just returned to Great Britain from her record-breaking flight to Australia, having become the nation's sweetheart and attracted admirers from around the globe. Mildred has less to prove. She has already won prizes for her motor racing, and broken records on land and sea. More to the point, she is not like Amy – a young, single woman trying to overcome the legacy of spurned love. When she took off from Croydon Airport four days earlier, Mildred left behind a husband and a young son. Nonetheless, her attempt to fly around the world is driven by the same compulsion and confidence that has attended all her previous expeditions.

At the beginning of the 1920s, the British Government had begun to scatter military bases around the Middle East to defend the Empire – but more particularly to protect trading and oil interests. Through the nineteenth century and up to the First World War, the region had seen Britain in direct competition with Germany for trading contracts and influence. Marshal of the Royal Air Force Lord Trenchard had successfully concluded an experiment in Somaliland in 1920 which had proved that RAF bombers were an exceedingly cost-efficient way of containing tribal threats and maintaining British control.

So now, the Gulf States are littered with RAF airfields. Conditions for the airmen tasked with flying the flag are harsh. Women, apart from the wife or daughters of the officer commanding and a handful of nurses, are notable by their absence (the conditions considered deleterious to the health of other females). The heat is exhausting, the postings long. One airman wrote to his wife, 'Darling; for God's sake have the bedroom ceiling painted a colour you like, because it's all you're going to see for a couple of months when I get back.'[3] For the sweating men in shorts at the RAF base of Bushire, a diminutive female in pearls alighting from her Bluebird is a heavenly apparition.

At 11.45 a.m., Mildred speaks to her dictating machine, 'This may be my end, as the oil pressure is down to nought. See land in distance, but fear engine will fail before I reach it.' The sea below, she is later to learn, is well stocked with sharks, sting rays and poisonous sea snakes. If she could now only reach the coast, her plan is to land on the beach and top up the engine oil.

By the time the pressure has fallen to 5–10lb per square inch, she has managed to pass the coast. But it is difficult terrain: all the way down from Bandar Abbas ('*Bandar*' being 'port' in Persian) there are no major settlements, no harbours, little fresh water and pitfalls of swamps and quicksands.[4] A sandstorm provides another distraction, 'making the surface of the desert look as smooth as a golden billiard table'. Mildred almost pulls off the landing at Kuh Mobarak, a desolate area just inland, some 25 miles short of her destination at Jask. But the Bluebird noses in and 'amid a deafening sound of splintering wood, and a smell of escaping petrol, I found myself hanging in the straps, the tail of the aircraft bolt upright in the air, and the engine buried in the soft sands'.[5] The impact bruises her chin and legs, but she leaps out as fast as she can in her dazed state, aware of the risk of fire. 'I hit my head but was only stunned for a moment.'[6] It is one o'clock in the afternoon, and she needs to shelter from the oppressive heat under the wing.

Some Belushi tribesmen arrive, their children beat her with sticks until they are chastised by the elders and charmed by her. 'I knew to show fear was fatal so went and shook hands with them and laughed. This changed them and they seemed more friendly.'[7] Mildred's only food is some dates and a small tin of biscuits, her refreshment only half a bottle of water and some Ovaltine. Soon, the tribesmen and children encircle her and try to eat one of her precious Dictaphone records, believing it to be chocolate. They show particular interest in her alarm clock, which she has to set off a few times for their amusement. She gives them some of her 'treasured' Ovaltine to drink. Shahmorad bin Salla, the tribal chief, begins to dance, gesturing that she must do the same. She soon exhausts herself and her water, but is resupplied by the tribesman. Bin Salla tells her that if she will sleep under the wing, he himself will mount guard to ensure her safety. Sleep does not come easily.

Feeling a little better the following day, when the tribesmen return she gives one a hastily scribbled message to take to the British outpost in Jask, 'Please send help. Crashed – Mrs Bruce.' After dusk, the undaunted Mildred sets to with her machine which, with local help, is soon put back on an even keel. When she examines the Bluebird, she finds that only the propeller is broken, and her spare prop, strapped underneath the fuselage, is quite unharmed. Having lost most of her tools, she has to resort to cleaning the sand-filled engine with her toothbrush. She removes the sharded propeller and fits the spare.

The toil is rewarded and the Gipsy engine bursts into life, but the Bluebird will not pull itself out of the soft ground – she has to confront the fact that she is stranded until outside help arrives. While temporarily alone, she goes down to the shore for a wash and bathe. 'I heard a splash behind me and turned to find a horrible black native, nearly naked, leaping towards me. He seized me around the waist, and in a frantic struggle we both fell into the water. Somehow I managed to slip from his grasp.'[8] She runs back to her aircraft to consult the chapter in her notebook entitled 'Treatment of Savages'. (Perhaps at the back of Mildred's mind was Edith Maude Hull's 1919 novel, *The Sheik*, in which 'an English girl was kidnapped in the desert by an Arab Sheik and repeatedly raped, but grew to enjoy it after five pages. "Oh you brute, you brute," complained the heroine until his knees silenced her'.[9])

Before leaving England, Mildred has astutely stimulated press interest by refusing to reveal her intended final destination; journalists therefore have termed it a 'mystery flight'. At her Esher home, the file of press cuttings is already thick. Her non-arrival at Jask has, of course, been noted, and the following day the British papers pick up on her disappearance. Mildred's fame has even spread to Australia, where the *Melbourne Herald* fears she has fallen into the sea between Henjam and the mainland and been lost:

> Mrs Victor Bruce [titles apparently carrying little weight in Australia] is a product of her time. A restless, adventurous spirit, with a talent for mechanics, she comes from one of the most distinguished Catholic families in England, and by her marriage is connected with half the aristocracy of England. [They might have added 'and Wales too'.]

Henjam is the island in the middle of the straits, which she has been observed overflying safely. Victor and her 10-year-old son will no doubt find the morning papers unhelpful to digesting their breakfast back at home in Esher.

Her tribal protectors grow increasingly nervous on the second night, looking towards the mountains to the north, and making gestures towards her throat with knives. Their fears are well-founded. It is all so reminiscent of a 1920s silent film, one almost expects Errol Flynn or Beau Geste to ride over the horizon. Indeed, three brigands arrive on horseback, armed to the teeth, and Mildred's prose echoes a Mills & Boon novel, 'The leader was a marvellous sight, and very handsome, with swarthy aquiline features, and straight black hair, worn very long.' Mildred piles on the charm, and gives the leader £5, but he takes little notice – grabbing her leather helmet, he climbs into the cockpit to begin wiggling the controls. Unsettling enough for a pilot at any time, but for a lone woman, stranded in a very strange country with a fragile and possibly broken aircraft, one can imagine her terror.

But this roving aristocrat has been bred to stare death in the face. James Radclyffe, 3rd Earl of Derwentwater, was Mildred's five times great-grand-father (and said, by her, to be a cousin of James III). Radclyffe himself had an exotic background: his mother was a daughter of Charles II by his mistress, Moll Davis. Radclyffe was companion to James, the young prince, in his court in exile. Radclyffe returned to England in 1710 and played a central part in the Jacobite uprising of 1715, which ended in defeat at the Battle of Preston. He was dispatched to the Tower of London, and refused to renounce his allegiance to James. George I was deaf to pleas for clemency by various senior courtiers, and Radclyffe was taken to the scaffold on 24 February 1716. In Mildred's words, 'It was the custom of the condemned man to tip the gaoler who led him to the block. But this Earl said to the gaoler, "You should be tipping me!".' He, and the undoubtedly large audience on Tower Hill, first had to suffer a long and tedious sermon by Samuel Rosewell MA. Radclyffe's mind had plenty of time to wander into very dark places. According to family legend, when the preacher finally drew breath, Radclyffe examined the block and said to the executioner, 'That's too rough for my neck. Get someone to smooth it out.' After his wish was carried out, he said, 'Strike when I say "Jesus" three times.' And so his life ended.

Meanwhile, in the twentieth century, the leader of the brigands rifles through Mildred's bags and, in what might have been in other circumstances a Pythonesquely amusing move, tries on her evening frock. The ruffians try to force her on to the back of a horse, but the leader of the Belushis stands his ground and remains at her side. Before riding off in disgust, they take her Burberry coat as a final souvenir. The following day, she sets off on foot for Jask, with her guardian angel – the Belushi Chief, bin Salla. Sensibly, she has written on the Bluebird's wing a succinct message for any would-be rescuer – 'I'm walking to Jask'.

After two hours of shuffling across the desert scrub she discards her shoes:

I can't remember much about that walk; the heat was scarcely bearable. The sand seemed to be burning me up, and on two or three occasions

I fell down and couldn't go on, but every time the old man pulled me up
and shouted something in his strange language.[10]

After 5 miles they eventually arrive at a date palm oasis, to be welcomed
with traditional Arab hospitality. The tribeswomen revive her with goats'
milk. It is her first real nourishment for three days, and it sends her into a
deep sleep. Meanwhile, the Belushi tribesman who has carried her original SOS message to Jask has had a torrid time. His two-day journey has
involved swimming across seven shark-infested creeks, and he too is in
a state of collapse when he finally reaches the telegraph station. But, by
7.30 p.m. on 5 October, the British Consulate receives the crucial telegram.

Jask was just a small fishing village until, in 1869, the telegraph station
opened. It was a link for the Empire's communications between Bushire,
500 miles away, and Karachi, 685 miles to the east. In 1886 Persia had
established a customs house and garrison in the village, but the Indo-
European Telegraph Department was staffed exclusively by Britons. Murray,
its assistant superintendent, assembles a five-man search party, including
Dr H.K. James (the department's doctor), J.W. Burnie (a colleague) and
George Wilson (Imperial Airways' local ground engineer). Their departure
is seriously obstructed by the Persian authorities and 'sympathy seemed
an unknown word in their lexicon', as the consul's report drily described
it later.

This was the same sort of obstruction that Amy Johnson had encountered
a few months earlier when she had crashed on landing at the aerodrome of
Bandar Abbas on the north of the Gulf of Hormuz – the route that the less
cautious Mildred should have taken. Amy had noted that the Persians loved
to exert their authority and cause delay. She had been advised to respond
with politeness and flattery.[11]

After much discussion with local government officials and policemen,
Mildred's rescue party is eventually allowed to leave port at 9 p.m. the
following day. It sails down the coast from Jask and catches up with her at
the date grove. In her state of near exhaustion, her first words to them are,
'they've been good; they've been good'. She recalled later that someone
replied, 'Thank God!', and then, 'Never mind Mrs Bruce, we've got sausages
for tea!' She later wrote, 'I shall never forget as long as I live the exquisite
English voices of [the rescue team].'[12]

Very conscious of the threat posed by more attacks from brigands, the
search party are all for an immediate return to Jask. But Mildred stands firm
– not for the first, nor last time on this trip – and refuses to leave her beloved
Bluebird in the desert. So, she is carried in a sort of improvised sedan chair
over the 5 miles back to her aircraft. The Bluebird has some further minis-

tration from Wilson and then, with a group of twenty Baluchis and some ropes tied to the boat, it is dragged down to what they hope is firmer sand right by the water's edge. Some carrier pigeons are released, announcing that Mildred has been found. But only with Wilson lying on the fuselage can Mildred succeed in powering the Bluebird from its sandy incarceration, and make the one-hour flight to Jask. Wilson laconically tells Mildred he is used to the procedure, having undergone the same indignity during his service in the First World War. The rest of the rescue party endure a torrid sail back to Jask in heavy seas and against a strong headwind.

Imminent monsoons or no, Mildred is forced to spend eighteen days at Jask, awaiting the arrival of spare parts dispatched from Britain by airmail. She contracts dysentery, but is nonetheless described by her new British friends as ineffably jolly. J. W. Burnie later said in his report, 'We've felt the greatest admiration for Mrs Bruce, who is certainly a woman of great nerve and endurance. Few, if any, would have met these troubles with her spirit.'

However, that spirit was to be tested further.

2

PETRE AND WILLIAMS: A POTENT
GENETIC COCKTAIL

Determination and panache flowed strongly through the genes on both sides of Mildred's family. Her father was descended from Sir William Petre, one of the consummate political operators of the Tudor era. The steel magnate Andrew Carnegie pithily judged that 'notwithstanding many notable exceptions, the British aristocracy was descended from bad men who did the dirty work of kings, and women who were even worse than their lords'.[13] Had he been thinking of Sir William, Carnegie would have been a little uncharitable – but on the right track.

Born around 1505 in Devon to a yeoman cattle farmer and tanner, William graduated in law from Exeter College, Oxford, and in 1523 became a fellow of All Souls. What set him on a path to influence and fortune was his tutoring of George Boleyn, brother of Anne. This brought him to the attention of Thomas Cromwell, who dispatched him abroad for four years to serve the nation.

Petre had an almost unique ability as a courtier and civil servant to withstand the tempests of Tudor rule. A Catholic, he served not only Henry VIII, but also Edward VI, Mary Tudor and finally Elizabeth I. He was a critical examiner of one of Princess Mary's closest friends, when Henry was nervous of her ambitions for the throne. He zealously helped Henry dissolve the monasteries as one of Cromwell's flying squads, together with Leigh and Layton, Tregonwell and ap Rees. Their convoy arrived unannounced at convents and monasteries, these tyrants insisting on the best accommodation available. The impact on abbots, not used to such overt hostility, was predictable. Allegations of the 'concealment of treason' were easy to make, and difficult to deny. And it was all under the cloak of 'reform'.

Petre was personally responsible for the surrender of more than thirty monasteries in 1537–38. His enthusiastic toil benefited him a year later when he was given lands at Ingatestone in Essex, which had been appropriated from the manor of Gyng Abbess. These lands became (and remain to this day) the Petre family seat.

After Henry's death, he redeemed himself with Mary Tudor by the enthusiastic prosecution of some of the supporters of Wyatt's rebellion, which had grown out of popular disquiet about Mary's marriage to Philip of Spain (a union of which Petre was a strong advocate). Despite his role in dismantling England's abbeys (and acquiring some of their real estate), William was at ease with Mary's reintroduction of Catholic influence and he secured from the Vatican a personal papal bull confirming his right to retain that property. It also, however, stimulated William to start prodigious charitable giving, whether altruistic or not.

After Mary's death, Elizabeth reasserted the Protestant faith in England. William had a central role in organising her coronation but failing health meant he was less frequently at court. However, he carried on pulling some of the levers of state from his manor at Ingatestone. William was a mix of Blondin and Blair – dancing nimbly on the high wire of Tudor religious belief, yet as accommodating as Tony Blair in shifting his political compass in whatever direction gave him greatest preferment. In her later years, Mildred was to note sardonically, 'He was a sensitive man. Whenever someone was being burned at the stake, he always made an excuse to the Monarch that he had a sore throat and went to his home at Ingatestone to look after the plumbing. He was very interested in plumbing.'

Petre's family fully embraced Catholicism, despite Queen Elizabeth's persecution. After William's death in 1572, his widow provided shelter for many priests and missionaries. Unsurprisingly, the wonderfully Tudor Ingatestone Hall retains a warren of priest holes.

William's son, John, was made 1st Baron Petre in 1603 by James I. While James had been selling baronetcies and peerages to replenish his depleted coffers, Petre, like his father, had been sufficiently involved in state service to earn his honour. John's motto, '*Sans Dieu Rien*' ('Without God Nothing'), publicly underscored his Catholic faith. An accomplished musician, he became the patron of William Byrd, the English composer, and a Member of Parliament for Essex.

Another of Mildred's forebears found infamy by becoming the inspiration for one of English literature's iconic poems. Robert, the 7th Baron Petre, her five times great-grandfather, was a handsome Hanoverian philanderer. He was overcome by an obsession with Arabella Fermor, a distant cousin from another prominent Catholic family. Their torrid affair was wryly observed by their mutual friend, the poet Alexander Pope. After Petre had been implicated in a Jacobite plot, he was forced to marry Catherine Walmsley, whose lack of beauty was more than compensated by an abundance of wealth. As a keepsake of his rejected lover, at their last tryst he snipped a handful of Arabella's hair. The episode inspired Pope's most famous poem, *The Rape of the Lock*. Less than two years after his marriage, Robert died of smallpox, but Catherine gave birth to his heir only two weeks later, becoming a major charity benefactor in widowhood.

By 1910, the House of Lords held only fifty-four peers whose titles went back to the seventeenth century or beyond.[14] The Petres were therefore well planted in the aristocratic firmament.

Mildred's grandparents, the Hon. Arthur Charles Augustus and Lady Katherine Petre, raised their family of seven children – with the aid of a governess and seven staff – in Coptfold Hall, a large, isolated, cold mansion on one of the higher points in Essex (at 200ft above sea level), reached by a mile-long avenue of trees. The Petre dynasty had demolished a villa designed by Sir Robert Taylor in 1751, erecting their brick Gothic house a century later. The Coptfold estate was heavily wooded right up to the drive leading to the house's ivy-clad western frontage. (Edwin Lutyens and Gertrude Jekyll had met in 1889 and begun their liberation of English architecture and garden design, but Coptfold had not seen their horticultural liberation.) Swathes of dense, tall rhododendrons, such a favourite of Victorian estate owners, added to its dark Gothic feel. In the grounds, the Petres built a little Roman Catholic chapel – a small-scale replica of Boulogne Cathedral.

Mildred's father, Lawrence, was the sixth child and only son, born in 1864. There had been scant opportunity for him to escape the confines of Catholic doctrine during his education, as first he was sent to St Stanislaus College, Beaumont, a recently established Catholic boarding school at Old Windsor. From there, he moved to St Mary's College, Oscott – a Catholic seminary in the Midlands. His father, Arthur, died in 1882 at Coptfold, but Lawrence spent holidays and later much of his bachelorhood at Thorndon Hall, a magnificent Palladian mansion near Brentwood (10 miles from Coptfold). At Thorndon Lawrence was, in effect, lodging with his uncle, William Joseph Petre, the 13th Baron, who was also a Monsignor of the Vatican and unmarried. These two bachelors rattled around in the gorgeous house, with only a brigade of staff and Lawrence's fifteen pointer dogs for company.

Lawrence must have subsequently found living in a much less grand house – with a woman – something of a shock. That she was an extrovert American must have given even more of a start to his palate.

In the dying years of the nineteenth century, Lawrence would still have been expected to assume a role in the squirearchical rule of Essex – if not lord lieutenant, then perhaps master of the local hunt, or chairman of the Quarter Sessions, or at the very least a Justice of the Peace. But no, at Coptfold, having been elected a fellow of the Royal Meteorological Society in 1886, Lawrence contented himself with taking the Englishman's obsession with the weather to an extreme. After pottering to his rain gauge at 9 each morning, he would record in a diary a plethora of meteorological data taken from his observatory at Hyde, on the estate. Neatly recording the readings at that time, he also noted the sky from the night before. But, 'the site was not all that could be desired as it was somewhat hemmed in by surrounding trees. It was no more than 30 yards from a large pond.' So, on 30 June he moved it to Coptfold House, and then on 20 July to a purpose-built observatory that seemed to suit the requirements of this fellow as it 'was finally placed in a very exposed situation in a large meadow, and railed off from beasts'.

On 3 October 1886 there is no reference to his birthday, which fell that day, but we learn that there were very light winds, and it was very sunny after an early morning dew. It turned overcast in the afternoon, before blue sky returned in the early evening. This fastidious Victorian would have been able to enjoy a birthday gin on the terrace or in his parterre. Detailed recordings ceased at the end of 1888, and he gave up any observations on 31 July 1889. Distraction by a star of the stage, rather than sky, had begun.

★★★

The family of Mildred's mother, Jennie, if not 'below stairs', was certainly no higher than the ground floor, and her story has faded more into the mists of time. However, it is at least as exotic. Her family had arrived on the west coast of the USA in the dramatic manner of nineteenth-century pioneers – at least in Mildred's occasionally fevered brain, Jennie's grandmother had joined a wagon train from her native Kentucky to seek gold in California. According to family legend, while under attack by Native American Indians in the Great Plains, cowering underneath a wagon she gave birth to Jennie's mother, Mary. This girl grew up to marry Alonzo Williams, who became a general in the Confederate Army in the American Civil War.

Jennie Williams became an actress, making her stage debut aged 10 as Sophie in *Led Astray* at the Baldwin Theatre in San Francisco. Six years later, she moved to the east coast to work in Minnie Maddern's company, and played some Shakespeare and Ibsen. Mildred later noted that her mother's talent could encompass both ends of the dramatic spectrum. In New York, she moved into the aegis of Tony Pastor, a highly entrepreneurial theatre impresario of Spanish descent.[15] Jenny Williams became a 'soubrette' – a flirtatious comedy character – in Pastor's troupe. Then, the *Daily Critic* (of Washington) breathlessly noted, 'Jenny Williams, a soubrette of Tony Pastor, and of late an ornament of various London concert halls, is said to be about to lead to the altar Lord [*sic*] Lawrence Petre of Coptfold Hall, Essex.' Petre's father was the Hon. Arthur Charles Augustus Petre, and well down the seniority of sons for the barony, so, while honourable, Lawrence himself was no lord. (The nuances of the English aristocracy have long been a mystery to American journalists!) However, the writer accurately reported the dynamics of the relationship.

Even at the close of the Victorian era, British aristocratic marriages were, to a greater or lesser degree, arranged. The Petre/Williams union was the antithesis and the couple had become engaged on 11 August. A New Zealand newspaper described Jennie as:

> The bright and clever little actress who made her debut in San Francisco, and who made all New York by her acting as Marie in *Mamzelle* several years ago … She was seen by a London manager, and was carried off to England to surprise the natives by her cleverness. The nobleman's full name is Lord Lawrence Petre, and his estate is Coptfold Hall, Islington, Essex County. He has immense parks, miles in length, and before the wedding ceremony, which occurs in the latter part of April, he will will a large portion of these fair lands to his still fairer bride.

Not many wires crossed there, then.

American journalists were agog at an American actress 'capturing' an English 'lord'. A New York newspaper, the *Evening World*, supplied its readers with plenty of juice. Jennie had arrived in London in spring 1890 and, according to the paper, she made her debut at the newly constructed Alhambra, and also appeared at the Pavilion and Tivoli music halls. Lawrence Petre had first become stage-struck when he saw her at the Alhambra in June, 'and was so captivated by her skirt dance, that he fell head over ears [*sic*] in love with her at once'.

Jennie did not so much take the London stage by storm, as sidle on, albeit beautifully, from the wings. She was absent from the programmes of all those London theatres, apart from the Tivoli. This music hall opened on the Strand on 25 May 1890 and Jennie was in the opening production. Charles Hürter, its manager, had attempted to suborn actors appearing at the London Pavilion into appearing at his new 1,510-seat 'theatre of varieties'. In May, the Pavilion served him an injunction thwarting his plans and Hürter had to search more widely for his launch talent. Jennie was the nineteenth act on a twenty-four-star bill. George Chirgwin the 'One-Eyed Kaffir', hid 'his white eye behind a Scotch hat as big as a dining room table', but unfortunately fell ill halfway through his act. Apart from him the playlist was devoid of the most well-known stars.[16]

Jennie was thrust into the rollicking traditions of Victorian music hall. On the opening nights:

> There were certain adventurous individuals who preferred to perch themselves on the balcony fronts ... there was a natural fear that some of them might in the course of the evening make an unwelcome dive into the stalls. Some rowdy blades in the audience continued to sing a refrain through later acts. But Jennie appeared, 'with flowing locks and pretty frocks, offered flowers for sale, and tripped merrily and gracefully on the light fantastic toe'.

The Daily News averred 'the opening night was a complete success'.

This aristocrat's courtship of an actress who was easy on his eye followed time-honoured fashion:

> The next day he sent her a bouquet containing a dazzling diamond neck-lace and soon after met her. Presents of ponies, dogcarts, phaetons, Paris bonnets and the like followed, and then the engagement ring, after he had won the consent of Miss Williams' mother, who accompanies her daughter on all professional tours.

Even if the journalist had over-burnished his story, it is clear that Petre was smitten hard and swiftly. It was all rather out of character – Lawrence was not one of the many roués who made a habit of lounging around London's West End clubs and theatres, gambling, eating, drinking and womanising his way through a trust fund. But the diamond necklace was indeed dazzling – fifty-three graduated, circular-cut diamonds of 'fine cut and brilliancy', with a diamond four-stone clasp.[17] Petre's uncharacteristic fit of largesse had to be funded somehow, and 100 head of shorthorn store cattle and some horses were sent for auction, replenishing Lawrence's bank account with nearly £1,000 – steers for diamonds, Jennie's ancestors would have chuckled.

Land had suddenly become a liability.[18] In 1877, the wheat price fell from 56s 9d per quarter to 46s 5d within twelve months. By 1886 it was down to 31s. Essex, the homeland of the Petres, was one of the worst hit counties. This was a period of retrenchment. A swathe of British aristocrats sought to bolster ailing family fortunes by marrying wealthy American women.

The list is illustrious: Winston Churchill's mother, Jennie Jerome, brought a £50,000 dowry in 1874 to Lord Randolph Churchill and the family of the impoverished Duke of Marlborough; the 9th Duke himself most notably married the coerced and heavily courted Consuelo Vanderbilt in 1895, receiving a settlement of $2.5 million for his pains. (Oxfordshire literally rolled out the red carpet for her – when she arrived at Woodstock Station for her first visit to Blenheim, she stepped on to a carpeted platform to be greeted by the mayor in full fig.)

Rudyard Kipling married Carrie Balestier in 1892; Bertrand Russell wed Alys Pearsall Smith two years later; to fill depleted coffers Lord Curzon (while Viceroy of India) in 1895 most famously married Mary Leiter, daughter of Levi Ziegler Leiter, a Chicago department store magnate. Ten per cent of all aristocratic marriages between 1870 and 1914 followed this pattern.[19]

Lawrence Petre was an exception: he was clearly driven by love, not thoughts of financial gain. Did he understand Jennie's background? Chorus girls were often wined and dined and after a few drinks, some of them would boast of their illustrious ancestry. One married a man of some standing and inflated her pedigree such that he called in a genealogist. All the latter could discover was that her grandfather had played the hind legs of an elephant in a pantomime at Margate!

Imagine the Petre family's thoughts at their only son's choice of bride. 'Quiet' and 'sensible', and at 28, old enough to know his own mind, they had expected Lawrence to take a measured decision. But his love spoke very strongly indeed. Jennie lodged at the Hotel Cecil opposite the theatre where she had been working. The marriage went ahead at the registry office on the Strand on 28 August, only seventeen days after the engagement, with Minnie as bridesmaid. None of the formidable Petre clan attended the ceremony – in their eyes, Lawrence was turning his back on his family.

Mildred (in *Nine Lives*) recognised that her mother must have been discomfited by the move from the bright lights of New York to the Coptfold estate in Essex. After their marriage, Lawrence and Jennie were installed in Furniss House, the 'secondary' house on the Coptfold estate. It was a substantial five-bedroomed farmhouse, but far from grand – there was only one servant to attend to the needs of the lovebirds.

Lady Katherine Petre (Mildred's paternal grandmother) was a lady of some stature and wealth, her father being the Earl of Wicklow. This was both a blessing and a curse. The strongly Protestant Katherine was not keen for her side of the family's wealth to disappear into the hands of papists, so she created a complicated will that prevented its capital falling into the hands of any subsequent generations who worked for Rome. This meant that Lawrence never had sufficient funds to run the large estate with any financial cushion.

His match with Jennie was unequal in many ways and, as their daughter later recognised, they were ill-suited:

> Mama used to say to me, 'Your father is a gloomy man – lugubrious'. At that time I wasn't quite sure what lugubrious meant, but I remember asking her, 'If he's gloomy why did you marry him?' Quietly, but firmly she replied, 'I married him to keep him quiet, to shut him up.'[20]

Whatever their later struggles, they buckled down to business and, on 24 June 1891, Jennie gave birth to their first born, Louis John, named after Lawrence's brother who had died aged only 17. He was baptised four weeks later at the Roman Catholic Church of St John the Evangelist and St Erconwald in nearby Ingatestone. Through her rebellious teenage years, Mildred was to find her elder brother (and in particular his motorbike) very useful. Jennie bore another son, Cecil, in 1893 but he died before his first birthday.

Mildred entered the world at Furniss House on 10 November 1895, to be christened Mildred Mary when she was two months old. Mary, an unsurprising choice for a Catholic dynasty, echoed the names of two of her aunts. Jennie then suffered the anguish of another early child death and Ronald, born eighteen months after Mildred, died before his first birthday. Finally, Mildred had a younger brother whom she could later order about when Roderick Lawrence Petre was born on 1 August 1902, after the family had left the Coptfold estate for London.[21] Lawrence installed his family, complete with a housemaid and a cook, in Holland House in Isleworth. Ironically, given her later career, nowadays this would be insufferably noisy, situated as it is underneath the approach to Heathrow's runways.

By now Lawrence had inherited Coptfold Hall, but had rented it out. The profitability of agriculture, particularly in eastern and southern England, had begun to decline markedly from around 1870. In January 1885, in nearby Ipswich, Joseph Chamberlain spelled out the underlying problem for landowners, 'I suppose that almost universally throughout England and Scotland agriculture has become a ruinous occupation.'[22] This was as a result of disease, and a great influx of cheap imports, facilitated by transport improvements.

The Petres' decamping to London coincided with the accession of Edward VII after the death of Queen Victoria. The court's tenor shifted quickly from puritanical to sybaritic. Edward's courtiers soon became more 'new money' than landed gentry. Not that he was sybaritic, but Lawrence's relinquishing rural life was of its time. Lawrence had timed the disposal of the estate well. By 1912, nineteen peers had large estates on the market.

After the First World War, death duties rose to 40 per cent: those many young sons of the landowning classes who had enlisted had become junior officers and this group suffered disproportionate fatalities. The First World War changed the British aristocracy irrevocably. The Great War inflicted losses on them not seen since the Wars of the Roses. Where two generations of a family died within a short space of time, the impact was catastrophic. Across Europe, land prices had been declining for the last two decades and by March 1919, half a million acres were up for sale, and as the sales continued until 1922, prices soon fell substantially.[23]

Joseph, the 17th Baron Petre, was only one of many English Lords to put his estate up for sale in spring 1919. In reality, it must have been Joseph's guardians since the new lord was only 5 years old, having inherited the title after his father's tragic death early in the war. Thorndon Hall, with its estate, was leased that year to a golf club, and the Petres returned to their ancient seat at Ingatestone.[24] Across Britain's aristocracy, by the end of 1919 one million acres had changed hands.

Mildred's ties to Essex had loosened; her wanderlust awakened. If Mildred gained her sense of adventure from her father's family, her mother Jennie passed on the skill to charm a crowd – which Mildred was later to use to good effect.

3

PRESSURES OF AN EDWARDIAN GIRLHOOD

In her extended family Mildred was surrounded by strong and dashing male role models. A desire to more than match up to them fuelled her drive to excel. Certainly, from a young age speed held no fear and danger was to be embraced. Jennie insisted that her husband buy a small Shetland pony once Mildred reached the age of 6 and she later recalled the animal, christened Dinky, 'was frisky and used to bolt. Everyone used to have hysterics on these occasions, I was hysterical with delight'.[25]

Three years later, the tigerish girl had yet to reform:

When my mother would go to a dealer to buy me a pony she would say at once, 'Is it quiet to ride and drive?', and if the dealer said it was, I used to nudge my mother and say, 'I don't want it, mother, I want another pony.' So that showed something – I wanted to live dangerously. I didn't want one that would just mooch along.[26]

Lawrence and Jennie relented and a Welsh pony pulled Mildred's governess cart at sufficiently exciting speeds. Following the second cart being written off after careering into a ditch, the insurance company refused to provide cover on its replacement. Luckily, there were enough acres to explore the wilder limits of pony and trap handling without injuring the public.

The budding carriage driver was also toughened up by Louis, her elder brother. A keen cricketer, he used Mildred as a target to hone his bowling skills, paying her a penny an hour to be bruised by hard cricket balls, rather than tennis balls. Louis also induced her to take up fencing so that he could have an in-house adversary. So, if only for self-defence, Mildred's hand–eye co-ordination increased apace. The Petre's household was not one where the children sat demurely in the nursery or library.

By the time Mildred was 15, Coptfold was sold and the family moved to Holland House in Spring Grove, near Osterley Park, west of London. She was dispatched to a convent education under the guidance of Theodore Ratisbonne, who had founded the Order of Sisters of Sion in France in 1842. Mildred went to its new convent school in Chepstow Villas, Bayswater, which was the order's second in the country. The very imposing red-brick building, clearly designed to convey an institution that had no doubts about the importance of its mission, had opened in 1891. Ostensibly focusing on music, Mildred did little to distinguish herself during her education there, 'I was not a scholar, being particularly bad at arithmetic.' She later ironically noted that the only prize she won during her school career was for piety.

Louis had received a small legacy and spent £120 of it to acquire an 8hp Matchless motorcycle, complete with sidecar. Nothing could have pleased his sister more – she was distracted and intrigued by the thought of eight wild horses pulling in unison. Soon afterwards, Louis went to work in Germany for a few months. Before he left he instructed his sister to 'keep it well polished'. In a calculated sisterly misinterpretation, 'I presumed that meant exercising it as well.' A 'young electrician chap' was summoned to the house to demonstrate how the brute was started and operated.

Laddie, her collie, was an involuntary passenger in the sidecar for her practice around the tennis court. One day, Jennie returned from an engagement in her horse-drawn carriage, and expressed feelings of impending doom for her daughter if she were to continue motoring. Succumbing to a dose of the growingly potent Mildred charm, Jennie replaced Laddie in the sidecar, and mother and daughter set off down a public road.

With a healthy dose of childish inquisitiveness and a developing aptitude for mechanical tinkering, over the following days Mildred found she could extract more speed from the Matchless with a series of tweaks, including removing its silencer. Soon she was tearing up the roads of nearby Hounslow at up to 60mph – a notable speed for 1911. The local citizens were less than impressed by the racket, and one day PC Parker, arm aloft, stopped Mildred and her Matchless. At the resulting court appearance, the magistrate asked the little girl in front of him, with two red ribbons in her plaits, 'How old are you, young lady?'

In an unusually shy voice, Mildred answered, 'Fifteen and three-quarters, Sir – nearly.'

'Have you a licence for this contraption?'

With bold innocence (or cheek) she replied, 'I've a licence for my dog, Sir. He's waiting for me outside.' She was banned until the age of 16, and fined

6s in costs, and Jennie left her daughter in no doubt about her mortification regarding the court appearance. But, it was the ban that hurt Mildred most.[27]

While the episode has overtones of childish naivety, it also echoes the aristocracy's aversion to what it perceived as tiresome overregulation. Mildred was a decade or two ahead of the similarly forthright Lady Helen Adare:

> Those who had ridden horses and driven motors in the Edwardian period naturally saw the imposition of speed limits and compulsory driving tests as officious and unnecessary. As late as 1939, for example, Lady Helen Adare insisted on being driven around by her maid, Sullivan, who had not passed a driving test, but was thought certain to fail one … she therefore equipped Sullivan with an envelope containing £2 to hand to the senior examiner together with a letter in which she assured him that the maid would be confined to quiet roads until she improved! For this Lady Helen was fined 50 guineas with 10 guineas costs.[28]

Mildred later claimed that she was the first Englishwoman to be charged for speeding.

It was a question of when, not whether, Mildred would have her first crash. With a girlfriend in the sidecar, she motored down to Brighton. While driving along the promenade, a rather fetching motor car parked outside the Metropole Hotel distracted her. The wheel of her sidecar touched a taxi and the ensemble cartwheeled. Crowds soon gathered and righted the tousled teenagers. By this time, she had repainted the Matchless red to match the ribbons in her hair – it probably also matched the colour of her brother's face on his return from Germany.[29]

Mildred's aristocratic upbringing was less hidebound than that of Vera Brittain, but similarly rebellious. For one of her diversions she would take her motorbike down to Sussex to race against a cousin at Storrington. She stripped the sidecar from the Matchless to compete better with his Indian.

However, when the Great War started on 28 July 1914, Mildred's indulged teenage years were drawing to a close. As an adult, the era of the carefree use of donkeys, ponies, carts, and even her brother's motorcycle, was soon to cease. However, before her father made her put away the motorbike as a war economy, she claimed to have narrowly missed several members of the army's general headquarters' staff while speeding down Whitehall.

The full horrendous impact of the war soon made itself known across the Petre clan. The mournful 16th Baron Petre had celebrated his coming of age in 1911 with a large party at Thorndon Hall. In spring 1915, he was severely wounded at the Battle of Arras as an officer in the 4th Battalion Coldstream Guards. By the end of September his life had ebbed away in a

British Army Hospital in France. His young widow and two small children watched his interment in the family vault at Ingatestone on 9 October.

Possibly it was this that encouraged Mildred's brother, Louis, to enlist. On 15 November 1915, he went to Handel House, Handel Street, in London – where any music would have been very martial. This was the recruiting office for the County of London Regiment, a Territorial Army unit. Serving less than a year before being discharged for medical reasons, Louis recovered sufficiently to try to serve his country once again and on 19 November 1917, while Winston Churchill was briefing the House of Commons on the disastrous Antwerp and Dardanelles campaigns, he enlisted once more, this time with the Royal Fusiliers. However, now aged 26, his health was not judged up to active service and he was assigned to the Officer Training Corps of the Inns of Court in London. Louis was lucky enough never to be sent to France.

The Petre family had by now fragmented: Lawrence had found life with two strong-willed females too stressful and decamped to Kensington with young Roderick, and Mildred was swept by Jennie down to Sussex. Mildred was friendly with her half second cousins (who were cousins of the 16th Baron) because they lived at Tor Bryan, on Ingatestone lands just outside the village (their house name harked back to the Petres' medieval roots in Devon). A 70-yard lime-tree-lined drive led to their Arts & Crafts house, complete with William Morris wallpaper and bounded by clipped topiary, all set out by their father, Sebastian. It was an idyllic playground for boisterous youths, and even more so after Sebastian built a workshop so that he could teach his sons woodwork and metalwork. The brothers were also crazy for the new sport of flying.

Henry Aloysius Petre was the eldest of the brothers. Together with Edward, two years his junior, he raced motorbikes along the coping of the nearby railway bridge – no wonder they and Mildred were kindred spirits. Initially Henry's father must have been content with this son's career development, since he followed him into practising law, but the aviation bug struck him early. Inspired by the first ever cross-Channel flight by Blériot, the French pioneer, Henry coerced his architect brother, Edward, to join him in designing and constructing a machine of their own in the Tor Bryan workshop.

Henry destroyed it on its first flight but, undaunted, he adopted a more sensible path and signed up to learn to fly at Brooklands. The brothers' second machine was exhibited at the Olympia Aero Show in 1910 (the embryonic industry's first sales exhibition), but it never left the ground. However, Henry's career later soared – he rose to become chief instructor of the Deperdussin School at Brooklands.

With a typical Petre sense of adventure, Henry responded to an advertisement in the *Commonwealth Gazette* by the Australian Government for an aviator and a machinist. Securing the first of those jobs, he arrived in Australia in January 1913 and created the Central Flying School at Point Cook.[30] He became one of the principal founders of the Australian Flying Corps.

On 9 March 1914, Henry suffered the school's first crash, writing off a Deperdussin. As the war intensified, Henry was sent to Mesopotamia in the Middle East. He had a torrid time, narrowly escaping imprisonment when the Ottoman Army advanced on Baghdad. Acts of bravery earned him the Military Cross and the Distinguished Service Order before he was dispatched to the Western Front. He ended the war in the RAF, and carried on flying in Britain after returning to his original trade as solicitor. Henry was to become a great supporter of Mildred when she later embarked on her own flying career.

The flying life of the next son, Edward Petre the architect, was much shorter. Like his brother, he learned to fly at Brooklands, where he was known as 'Petre the Painter' or, being 6ft tall, 'Petre the Great' (brother Henry was known as 'Petre the Monk'). He achieved some fame from being the first pilot to fly across Greater London – before such a route was banned. He was employed as chief pilot by Martin-Handasyde, one of the early pioneer manufacturers.

However, death came early at the age of only 26, on Christmas Eve 1912, at Marske in Yorkshire. In very gusty conditions, his lightly powered machine was swept into a dale while he was attempting a rather ambitious long-distance flight from Brooklands to Edinburgh. After much deliberation, the verdict at the inquest was one of accidental death.[31]

Petre the Painter was held in high regard. C.G. Grey, the highly opinionated editor of *The Aeroplane*, mourned his passing:

> He was particularly fond of flying in strong winds, and of flying high, which showed he had plenty of nerve and confidence in his machine. Personally, Edward Petre was one of the most charming of men, and his loss is deeply felt by very many of us. His exuberant spirits and keen sense of humour made him welcome wherever he went. Unfortunately for himself, he possessed a certain recklessness, which, allied to his headstrong temperament, led him to take risks which others would avoid.

Edward shared many of those characteristics with Mildred. On the other hand, Father Grant, the priest in charge at Ingatestone, unknowingly differentiated Edward from Mildred in his eulogy when he said, 'Let no one for a moment think that Edward Petre, in devoting his life to aviation, was actuated by any motive of self-glorification through beating records and the like. Nothing was further from the truth.'

John Joseph, the youngest of the air-mad brothers, signed up for the Royal Naval Air Service at the outbreak of war. He had gained his licence by October 1914 at Eastbourne, and then at that cradle of early British aviation, Eastchurch. Posted to Dunkirk in February 1915, he was mentioned in dispatches just after Christmas that year for 'his meritorious work in connection with air attack on sheds at Ostende'.

John received the same accolade two months later for more noble aggression. In June 1916, he was awarded the Distinguished Service Cross 'in recognition of his services as a pilot at Dunkirk'. The French recognised his daring with a *Croix de Guerre*. Promoted to squadron commander, his luck ran out on 13 April 1917 when he died in a flying accident in Flanders.

The final close relative of Mildred to be killed in the Great War was her cousin, Francis Ferrers. A lance corporal with the Royal West Surrey Regiment, he died on 21 March 1918, at Pozières in France. The Petres had served their nation with distinction. Mildred had witnessed the price that many paid, yet still determined to seek adventures of her own.

4

FINDING A LOVER IN POST-WAR ENGLAND

In Cities and hamlets we were born
And Little towns behind the van of time;
A closing era mocked our guileless dawn
With jingles of a military rhyme.
But in that song we heard no warning chime,
Nor visualised in hours benign and sweet
The threatening woe that our adventurous feet would starkly meet.

Thus we began, amid the echoes blown
Across our childhood from an earlier war,
To dim, too soon forgotten, to dethrone
Those dreams of happiness we thought secure:
While, imminent and fierce outside the door,
Watching a generation grow to flower,
The fate that held our youth within its power
Waited its hour.

'The War Generation: Ave', Vera Brittain, 1932

D.H. Lawrence, an author not noted for his optimism, struck a chord with many of his struggling fellow Britons when he wrote to his friend, Lady Cynthia Asquith, in November 1915 lamenting that what he saw when driving around the country was the collapse of British civilisation, the passing of an era, the crumbling of its beauty – all while a generation suffered intolerably in the trenches. He was overcome with pessimism. One assumes that Lawrence drove across the country at a more sedate

pace than Mildred, but it is inconceivable that she did not share some of
his emotions.

To restate the bald impact of the First World War on a generation, deaths
were on a previously unimagined scale. Around the world, well over 9 million young men were killed – 1.38 million Frenchmen, 1.935 million
Germans, 1.7 million Russians and 942,135 from the British Empire.
Nowadays, too easily overlooked was the whirlwind of Spanish Flu that circled the globe shortly afterwards, killing 50 million worldwide and around
200,000 in Great Britain.

So, there were many consequent and substantial pressures on Mildred's
generation. A woman placed the following classified advertisement, 'Lady,
fiancé killed, will gladly marry officer totally blinded or otherwise incapaci-
tated by the War'. The fear of a solitary life as an old spinster was extreme; in
this case, the choice of partner was instead based on those who needed her
most. Although society was worried about depopulation, the attitude of the
medical profession was, at best, unhelpful to women. Old-fashioned general
practitioners were still keen to lecture young wives that they were obliged
to repopulate the Empire and so contraception was denied. Until 1930, the
British Medical Association was steadfast in opposing birth control even
for married women.

This was a period of growth in the influence of women's magazines,
and the central creed for many was to promote a notion of romantic
love and marriage in general. They deployed a full arsenal of weapons.
Women's Own:

> … painted a stark picture of the fate awaiting a woman who was mis-
> guided enough to devote herself to a career and remain single; she would
> inevitably become a lonely, neurotic individual, 'You have only to go into
> a restaurant and note the strained, dissatisfied look on the face of a woman
> feeding alone.'[32]

The general press obsessed about the number of potentially 'surplus'
women (of whom there were 1.9 million), and urged them to emigrate to
the reaches of the Empire in order to find eligible young men. *The Times*
suggested that women who sought work abroad would not only stand
a better chance of finding a husband, but would be doing their country
a service!

Meanwhile, among the aristocracy, mothers pursued their marriage-
broking activities with undimmed zeal. Despite its potentially increasing
anachronism, the 'season' remained their focal point. Notwithstanding the

enormous expense this involved, many girls went three or four seasons without finding a husband.

Among all this ostensibly wholesome marriage hunting, the moral climate remained steamy. Adultery among the upper classes was endemic and a cause for gossip rather than adverse comment. One of the first big society weddings after the war was between Lady Diana Manners (the youngest daughter of the 8th Duke of Rutland) and Duff Cooper.[33] It was a union of two great celebrities, but it was not long before Diana, a society hostess par excellence, remarked of her husband, 'I don't mind adultery, I'm not a jealous nature.' Lady Manners had, by then, witnessed a lot for a 22-year-old. She had been a VAD (field nurse) probationer at Guy's Hospital in London and her mother, the Duchess of Rutland, had turned the family's London home, 21 Arlington Street, into a field hospital, where she eventually worked. Like Vera Brittain, she watched her circle cut down, one by one: Billy Grenfell, George Vernon, Charles Lister and Edward Horner. It was said that she only married Duff Cooper (her social inferior, and far from wealthy) because he was the only one of her pre-war friends to return from the war. Cynthia Asquith, the daughter-in-law of the prime minister, wrote, 'Soon there will be nobody left with whom one can even talk of the beloved figures of one's youth.'[34] The new Lady Duff Cooper was living for the moment.

The moral tone of the Edwardians had been directed from the top. Bertie, the Prince of Wales, considered adultery entirely normal, and becoming head of the Church of England in 1901 did nothing to change his views. In 1898, when he was 56, Bertie met the enchanting 29-year-old Mrs George Keppel, known as the 'delectable Alice'.

Margot, the second wife of Herbert Henry Asquith, prime minister from 1908 to 1916, sagely noted, 'No woman should expect to be the only woman in her husband's life.'[35] This phlegmatic approach was just as well, given Asquith's wandering eye. He was most notably obsessed with Venetia Stanley, to whom he would write love notes during cabinet meetings. A sexual obsessive, regarded as not of the greatest intellect, he was nonetheless an entertaining companion at dinner – unless you were a young woman, as he had the somewhat alarming habit of grasping their hand and pushing it down his trousers.

Asquith's successor, David Lloyd George, was an equally rampant adulterer – he had not been nicknamed 'The Goat' on account of any physical resemblance.

There was little improvement after the war. F.E. Smith (Lord Birkenhead) was the 'cleverest man in the kingdom', according to Lord Beaverbrook (the original press baron/kingmaker), but what upset his fellow MPs was his focus on the teenage daughters of his friends. One such was the beautiful Mona Dunn. Like a totem for the era, she partied through the night at the Criterion Restaurant. She died far too soon, at the age of only 26, stimulating Lord Birkenhead to pen a poem that he was keen to see in the *Sunday Express* – Beaverbrook ignored it.[36]

Sir Oswald Mosley, who had tried membership of both main political parties before later starting his own (he has been described, like Churchill, as 'an unaligned soul'), considered that high moral standards were irremediably middle class. When he met his wife, Lady Cynthia Curzon, in 1919, Mosley promised to cease his naughtiness in favour of developing into a more serious politician. In that era's equivalent of a pre-nuptial agreement, he confessed to Cynthia of all his conquests prior to their marriage. Meeting some scepticism about the totality of his new honesty, he ceded that perhaps her sister and stepmother should have been added to the list! His mistress at the time of the outbreak of the Second World War was Fay Taylour, a noted Brooklands racing driver.

Yet, it is wrong to deduce that philandering was mainly instigated by men. Edwina Mountbatten (wife of Dickie, 1st Earl Mountbatten of Burma) was a serial exponent of seduction after their marriage in 1922, while Harold Macmillan's wife, Lady Dorothy, had an affair with his colleague, Robert Boothby, after seducing him in 1929.

So the hotbed that encompassed the British aristocracy and ruling classes posed something of a dilemma for devout British Catholics. They could expect little quarter from the Pope before the Second World War: Pius X was one of the most reactionary popes ever.

With the Great War drawing to a close, Britain's women showed a huge appetite to fill the gaps in their sexual knowledge. Marie Stopes' defining volume, *Married Love*, was published in March 1918. It had six reprints that year, and had sold 400,000 copies by 1923, reaching sales of 1 million by the time the next world war started. The Establishment was fighting a rearguard action. Due to a falling birth rate – which was the pattern across Europe – the Home Office considered banning advertisements for contraceptives and all birth control literature. It was rumoured that Catholic pharmacists were putting holes in their condoms. In 1908, even the Church of England had officially pronounced that contraception was wrong on social, moral and theological grounds, reaffirming this ostrich-like stance in 1924. Unfortunately, as she left her teenage years behind, Mildred was no longer winning prizes for piety.

★★★

Two years before Mildred was born, on 23 September 1893, Stephen Easter, a builder's foreman from Shepherds Bush, had married Alice Charlotte Jane Gibbings, daughter of the owner of a building firm in London. We know from later years that this was likely a match made with financial objectives in mind as much as anything else. Easter was of a relatively humble background, never knowing his father, who died before he was born. Indeed, it seems his mother, Amy, did not know the identity of his father either, since he was noted as 'deceased, name unknown', on Stephen's marriage certificate.

Stephen and Alice started their married life in west London but soon moved to Sussex, and by 1907 were living in a fine part of fashionable Brighton. A man in a hurry to enhance his standing, Stephen acquired an accommodation address in the City of London, in order to be made a Freeman of the City in 1908. In his application, he claimed his father was Henry Easter, a builder of Tunbridge Wells – but Henry appears to be Stephen's whimsical creation.

In 1908, Alice and Stephen holidayed in Canada and New England – money was clearly not an issue. Two years later, he bought Old Salts Farm in South Lancing, on the Sussex coast. There, he started a dairy herd and lived the life of a gentleman farmer. Ironically in view of later events, in 1911 Shoreham, one of the first municipal airports in the country, opened just beyond the northern hedge of his land. In December that year the airport management issued a bold advertisement entitled 'Winter Aviation – Season now in full swing. No Fogs. Maximum Sunshine … Passengers Plentiful,' and added, 'Proprietors pay tuition fees of approved army officers.'[37]

★★★

After the young Petres had shed their blood in Flanders, we fast-forward to the summer of 1919. The Spanish Flu epidemic was still raging, rationing was still in force and the House of Commons was discussing the Sex Disqualification (Removal) Bill, which was to force universities such as Oxford to allow women to graduate in the same way as men (and to twist the arm of the legal profession into accepting female barristers). Vera Brittain had resumed her studies at Oxford:

> The various men, I thought bitterly, with whom I had come into contact since the War – men who were married already but enjoyed making use of my company for a little romantic diversion, men who imagined that I could be tempted by wealth and the promises of financial support in

politics, middle-aged men who were fussy and futile, elderly men whose avid eyes looked upon me with a narrow, appraising stare, young men who were ardent but ineffectual, men of all ages who wallowed in nauseating sentimentality and hadn't the brains of an earwig – simply provided one proof after another that the best of their sex had disappeared from a whole generation.[38]

Soon after the outbreak of war, with her relationship with Lawrence fractured, Jennie had taken Mildred with her to live in little more than a caravan on land by the Sussex coast owned by Stephen Easter. Shoreham Aerodrome had been acquired by the War Office in 1914, and became a training field for the Royal Flying Corps. A succession of reserve and training squadrons was based there for the duration. Indeed, in May 1919 the Canadian Air Force was formed there. Mildred, with her lust for speed now fully formed at the end of her teenage years, was dazzled not only by the evidence of technological advances in the air above her doorstep, but also by the constant passage of tyro (inexperienced) pilot army officers in the neighbourhood.

However, life in Sussex in this very modest accommodation was too frugal for her tastes, and the wealthy lifestyle of Easter, her mother's landlord, was in stark contrast. Now seeing much less of her own father, it is possible Easter would also have offered some paternalistic attraction. Whatever, by the summer of 1919, Mildred and Easter (twenty-one years her senior) had consummated their relationship, with predictable results.

While abortions were more readily (and healthily) available to those with money, they were still far from universally approved. Even Marie Stopes was not yet an advocate. Another family member lived a few miles inland at Storrington – Aunt Maude had bought Mulberry House in the village. A fascinating woman, a nun of sorts – modernist Catholic and deeply religious (she went on to author some serious theological tracts) – Maude would have been most disapproving of her niece's antics. Jennie's tempestuous nature meant her daughter was unlikely to find a sympathetic ear at home, and Maude was but one of several nuns in the Petre clan, so Mildred had no aunt in whom to confide.

In Mildred's defence, contraception had yet to be made more freely available to women. Marie Stopes was not to open her first family planning clinic – in Holloway, north London – for another year. Even in 1927, the annual Labour Party Conference voted by an overwhelming majority against local authorities being able to fund birth control clinics.

In 1920, Evelyn Laye first sang a tune that became very popular – 'Betty in Mayfair (Dreamland Lover)'. Was Mildred humming it when, on

1 March, she had an early Easter present? Her son was born that day at a nursing home in Teddington, near her old family home. He was registered as Anthony Billy Stephen Petre Easter. When registering his son's birth, Stephen covered his tracks somewhat, describing himself as a 'landowner', of 36 Great Tower Street, London EC3, rather than giving his actual address in Sussex. Mildred recorded her own details as 'Mildred Mary Easter, formerly Petre', implying she had married Stephen, or become his common-law wife.

However, she had not married him as Stephen would not divorce Alice. Indeed, in what can be no mere coincidence, later that year he swept Alice to Portugal on a holiday, returning to England on the SS *Asturias* in November. The jaundiced eye of the Establishment in such circumstances was spelled out by Dennis Herbert MP. On the second reading of the Matrimonial Clauses Bill in 1921, he blustered, 'Is there any man in the House who is the father of a son and a daughter, who would regard the sin of adultery on the part of his son as being as serious as the sin of adultery on the part of his daughter?'

Possibly Alice was adhering to the woman's strategy, espoused by Barbara Cartland, 'to indulge her husband and pander to his selfishness'. Behaving like the landed aristocrat he was not, Easter set aside his lover and son, arranging for a small monthly sum to be sent for Tony's maintenance.

The entire episode of the creation and arrival of her son is completely overlooked in Mildred's own writing. Instead, she focused on her wheels. Lawrence Petre had demanded that his daughter forgo the motorbike (which had been given to her by Louis when he moved up to a motor car) as a war economy, 'He said it was unpatriotic to use it ... you know, the petrol.'[39]

But with the war over:

> I decided I wanted a car – a fast car with a leather strap around the bonnet, like those they used on race tracks. From that moment on I began saving hard. By 1920 I had £75, half the price of an Enfield Allday, which could touch 75 mph; and it was then that my parents, who had been watching my efforts quietly, stepped in to help. [...] I had a lovely time with that for a long time.[40]

There is no mention of the transport needs of a young mother! Her parents had clearly not been watching *all* her efforts, quietly or no. For the 25-year-old Mildred, a newborn son threatened to be a handicap in her heady race for thrills, celebrity and fortune.[41]

5

THE NEED FOR SPEED: EDWARDIAN MOTORING, BROOKLANDS AND MEETING VICTOR

13 July 1907. Mr and Mrs Locke King came to dinner. They have been building this awful motor track and are so hated by their neighbours … that hardly anyone will speak to them. I was rather uncertain whether I had better go and see this horrid motor track, but as they offered to take me in the Fox Warren motor I thought it would be stupid of me not to go …

The motor track is a perfect nightmare. It has cost more than £150,000 to construct: a great oval of cement, 60 to 100 feet wide and more than 2.5 miles round. It is for motor races. Within it stands a ruined farm and cut down trees, mere desolation. A more unenjoyable place to come to on a hot Sunday afternoon I cannot imagine. The beautiful Surrey landscape looks down into this purgatory of motor stables and everything that motors require, seats for thousands of spectators cut in the side of the hill. There were some 20 of these snorting beasts, and Mr and Mrs Locke King were there looking most depressed. But as she offered to drive me round in her motor I got boldly in and sat by her on the 'box. She put it to 43 miles an hour – I felt my eyes pressed in by the air at that terrific speed and I could hardly breathe. I went round again in the Fox Warren motor, much slower. I find I don't care to 'go round' – what I like are the lanes and roads and views, and the getting to one's destination so quickly and easily. The enormous size of the arena, almost like a great Roman work, and the controlled strength of the motors, prevents this great horrid place from being vulgar. I might have felt differently last week when 20,000 spectators arrived and 1,200 motors.[42]

Thus spoke the diarist Lady Mary Monkswell. She was underplaying the vision and achievement of Hugh Fortescue Locke King. With bushy eyebrows and a dark moustache, he had the appearance of an avuncular owl – albeit a rich one. In 1885 he had inherited £500,000, and then proved his mettle in driving forward large projects by building the Mena House Hotel near the Cairo pyramids. But the construction of the world's first purpose-built motor-racing course was of a greater order. With the use of 2,000 labourers and world-leading concrete techniques (the Members' Banking was almost 29ft high), it took less than a year and more than £250,000 for Locke King to create the 3-mile circuit (with, it was said, no aim of making a profit). On 17 June 1907, the Earl of Lonsdale opened the track and festivities began.

If the Georgians had enjoyed the pleasure gardens at Vauxhall, Brooklands became the pleasure garden for Edwardians, or at least the many technophiles of the era. It offered all the delights a well-heeled Edwardian could desire: he could watch the duelling of the latest cars, enjoy high-quality catering, play tennis, frolic at a tea dance, or, if too exhausted, simply laze on the grass of the Members' Hill.

Its first event was a twenty-four-hour record attempt by S.F. Edge – who was later to play a major role in Mildred's life. Australian by birth, Selwyn Edge, a motoring entrepreneur, was by now a manager at Dunlop, having sold the De Dion Bouton car business that he had created to Napier. On 28 June 1907, he set off round the Brooklands track in his 7¾-litre, 60hp Napier, with a mechanic named Joseph Blackburn. They ran for 1,581 miles, achieving 65.9mph and breaking the previous record by 50 per cent. This record was to stand for seventeen years until Mildred herself broke it in 1924. But Edge's 1907 attempt had another legacy: the track's neighbours were so outraged by this assault on their night-time tranquillity that Brooklands was thereafter restricted to daytime racing. By 1910, aeroplane flights had become a feature of Brooklands' race meetings. Even on non-race days, the public flocked to the 'flying ground' where 1s admittance allowed them to witness their flying heroes, and even to rub shoulders with them at Mrs Billings' Blue Bird tea shop.

Edge alluded to the negatives of motoring, some caused by the way in which it emphasised social divisions:

On more than one occasion I have had drivers of horse-drawn vehicles slash at me with their whips as I have passed them on the road. I have had stones hurled at my head and broken glass bottles deliberately placed in front of motor tricycles ... In London one was bombarded by jeers and insults from practically every bus-driver and cab-driver one met.[43]

Moreover, the motor car was subverting the rhythms of upper-class life. Even in the latter half of the nineteenth century, landowners were still accustomed to spending at least half the year at their country estates, with a social circle defined by how far one could easily travel by carriage or horse. The car ushered in an era of weekend house parties; the London home became the primary residence and the country estate was remodelled as a place of leisure. There were many aristocrats, Lawrence Petre included, who lamented the car's noisy intrusion into their rural idylls.

But the war had demonstrated the utility of motor transport to even the most diehard Luddites. Car ownership exploded, despite the slump. The number of private cars rose from 132,000 in 1914 to 1.056 million by 1930, albeit with ownership concentrated in southern England. The positive effect of this disruption to countryside and city alike was that the motor industry employed 2 million workers by the outbreak of the Second World War. The market became much more concentrated as a raft of small manufacturers fell by the wayside and giants such as Lord Nuffield moved to the fore, bringing down prices and moving to mass-production techniques.

The downside of wider car ownership – modest competence and a widespread flouting of speed limits – was a frightening increase in the accident rate. There were 2,500 fatal and 62,000 non-fatal accidents in the early 1920s;[44] by 1930, these had risen to more than 7,000 and 150,000. The AA, the motorists' friend, aside from political lobbying, adopted the warning of motorists about nearby police patrols and speed traps as a primary role. Women enthusiastically took to motoring as another road to liberation, and Agatha Christie noted, 'I don't think anything has given me more pleasure, more joy of achievement than my dear bottle-nosed Morris Cowley.'[45]

Lady Diana Cooper, whom we have encountered before, was clearly as wayward on the road as in the bedroom. The Duff Coopers were given a car by Lord Beaverbrook in 1919. Her husband resignedly reported, 'Today Diana drove it into a milk cart on Stafford Street, upset the cart and flooded the street.' Not long afterwards, they were driving around Norfolk when she looked down for her belongings and forgot about steering – they ended up in a ditch. Edwina Mountbatten, also of that circle and of similar morals, was also known for her high accident rate (in cars).[46]

Men were sometimes concerned that this field of ostensibly technical competence had been breached by women. The waspish 1934 comment in *The Aeroplane* was not entirely untypical, 'The woman driver is generally content with half the road, but she always wants the middle half.' (The editor at the time was a noted misogynist.)

The London season of 1922 had been heralded as the best since 1914, but as an unmarried mother, Mildred could hardly have come out as a debutante. So, she carried on motoring. It is probably safe to assume that she breathed a sigh of relief that year when PC Beck retired from the Surrey Constabulary. He had garnered both plaudits (from colleagues) and brickbats (from the motoring public) for sending 10,000 drivers to the Kingston-upon-Thames bench since 1903. The A3 road was his hunting ground of choice.

Across the UK the 20mph speed limit was almost universally ignored and motoring offences were beginning to clog up magistrates' courts. The growth in motoring 'crime' was exponential: from 55,000 offences in 1910 to almost half a million by 1938. Fines of £5 were of little consequence to affluent motorists spending £1,000 or more on their transport needs (and fun). There was a disconnect in the behaviour of the British upper classes at that time. They considered themselves notably well-behaved and law-abiding people, but motoring 'had exposed the stubborn strain of recklessness bordering on anarchism, deep within the national character'.[47]

The nation's spirits were raised in September 1924 when Malcolm Campbell broke the land-speed record for the first time at Pendine Sands in Wales. Ten months later, he pushed his own record beyond 150mph.

At one level, the motor racing and the hedonistic environment of Brooklands could be viewed as a frivolous activity at a time of great economic stress in Great Britain, which held a looking glass up to the great disparities of wealth that still existed. On the other hand, as we have seen exemplified in the Petre and Bruce families, this generation had seen too many of their brothers, cousins and friends sink forever into the mud of Flanders and wither on the cliffs of Gallipoli. Having borne witness to such widespread and arguably pointless deaths, who can blame them for seeking a pastime that offered great thrills? If death was in attendance, not only would it have been preceded by more fun than their fallen friends had enjoyed, but it would in one sense enable the racers to find parity with those heroes close to them, whose names were now beginning to appear on memorials on village greens across the land.

The 19th Annual Motor Exhibition Motor Show was held in October 1925 at Olympia in London. The 120 stands saw more than 16,000 visitors on the opening day – including the Queen and Crown Prince of Norway. But the motoring correspondent of *The Times*, nose in the air, showed the same air of technical superiority as C.G. Grey at *The Aeroplane*, 'The proportion of the comparatively ignorant was probably as high as that which visits a national agricultural show.' At the end of the opening week, he snootily reported:

> The International Motor Show gives a pleasant impression of the popularity of motoring, which is all the more striking and welcome after an experience of the congested traffic of the roads that lead to Olympia.
>
> Saturday was the 'people's day', as it has always been since the Show was founded 19 years ago. But it is said by those that know that this year there was a notable change in the character or standing of visitors.
>
> In former years Saturday was regarded as the day of the driver and the mechanic, who took a professional interest in the cars with a view to improving their knowledge and usefulness as workers. The general public had not begun to take an interest in the motor-car as a thing that might become a personal possession.
>
> On Saturday a great feature of the Show was the evidence that it afforded of the remarkable expansion of the motoring community. The majority of the visitors were what is known as middle-class men and their wives, and they were spending their Saturday half-holiday seeing the cars as a preliminary to buying one.
>
> The possession of a motor-car has been brought within the reach of this large class by an easy payment system – £25 down and the rest in monthly instalments – and the provision in large centres of population of garages in which to keep it. So that it would be wrong to assume that the buying of motor-cars is still confined to the high and the wealthy from the fact that such cars at the show as have been sold bear tickets with the name of this lady of society or that film actress. Having regard to the character of the crowd on Saturday it might have been a better advertisement of a car to have it labelled 'Purchased by – , dairyman, Upper Tooting'.

But at the show were a man and a woman with unimpeachable family pedigrees and motor oil in their veins, such that would have passed muster even with *The Times'* motor correspondent. It was at the show on 8 October that Mildred met Victor, a solvent aristocrat who had obvious attractions for the footloose Catholic woman – that he was a Protestant was but a minor irritant. Lawrence, Mildred's father, had been described as 'an expert with the camera and other scientific contrivances that make for amusement';[48] in Victor, she had found a man who echoed her father's photographic and engineering skills.

In 1925, *No No Nanette* was playing at the Playhouse in London. Perhaps more appositely, George Bernard Shaw's *St Joan* had had a very successful run at the New Theatre, and transferred to the Regent, where Sybil Thorndike played the lead. The public was developing a growing appetite for strong female characters. Mildred's future was beginning to take shape.

6

VICTOR: FAMILY AND FAME

Victor Austin Bruce was the second youngest son of Henry Campbell Bruce, the 2nd Baron Aberdare. Henry had had five sons and four daughters by Constance Beckett, whom he had married in the society church of St George's, Hanover Square, in 1880. The 1st Baron Henry Austin Bruce had been called to the Bar in Lincoln's Inn in 1837, but was a listless barrister and soon plagued by illness. At the age of 30 he retired to south Wales to manage the family estate he had inherited at Dyffryn. This produced a steady income from mineral royalties, which grew in the 1850s as the demand for steam coal increased. With a solid financial base, Henry became a Justice of the Peace and Deputy Lieutenant of Glamorgan. Soon, another role as stipendiary magistrate gave him not only an income but an insight into the social problems of south Wales. He gave up that role to become Liberal MP for Merthyr in 1852.

Henry Austin Bruce's first wife, Annabella Beadon, had died only a year after giving him his heir (Victor's father). In August 1854 he married Nora Creina Blanche Napier, the younger daughter of Sir William Napier, the chronicler of the Peninsular War (Bruce later edited his biography). He ascended the ladder of local government and commerce, and became under-secretary in the Home Office in 1862, under Sir George Grey. He retained a keen interest in educational reform and he was known as 'Commander in Chief of the Welsh Educational Army' for being adept at squeezing funds from the government for Welsh colleges.[49] He was defeated in the 1868 general election, but found a new seat in Renfrewshire and was promoted to Home Secretary, a post he held until 1873. He attempted radical reform of the licensing system and a compromise solution led to bars' opening hours becoming regulated.

In a high-level reshuffle, Gladstone elevated Bruce to the peerage in 1874. The Liberals lost office soon after, due in some part, according to some observers, to Bruce's Licensing Bill. From the Lords, he continued to lead an active public life, and was president of the Royal Geographical Society and a major force in improving education in south Wales. He was well-liked as an unassuming and loyal politician with a genuine care for his people.

Victor's father went to university in Berlin, and thence into the Welsh Regiment in the British Army, ending as lieutenant colonel of the 3rd Battalion. As was the habit in the Victorian landowning classes, he followed his father's lead in becoming a Justice of the Peace and Deputy Lieutenant of Glamorgan. He also followed his father's educational interests and later became president of the University College of South Wales.

Victor was born two years later than Mildred, in 1897. He too endured a peripatetic education. At 10, he spent two years at Twyford prep school, but then went to a variety of very small private schools in Norfolk. As the clouds of war began to gather, at the age of 17 he went to Wye Agricultural College with a view to learning about estate management, although the call to arms soon interrupted his studies.

Like Mildred, he had some strong role models close at hand. Victor's uncle, Brigadier General Charles Granville Bruce MVO CB, was one such. He was the youngest son (of many) of Victor's grandfather. He spent much of his career in Queen Victoria's army in the Himalayas with the Gurkha Rifles, based in Abbottabad. He conducted many expeditions over the mountain ranges and into Waziristan, becoming one of the foremost mountaineers of his generation. In 1906, when on leave in England, he planned an expedition to the Mount Everest area, even considering an ascent. The project was vetoed by the Secretary of State for India. In 1914, he did, however, get to Kathmandu.

Fighting in the Miranzai Expedition in 1891, the Waziristan Campaign between 1894 and 1895, and the Tirah Campaign in 1897–98, he was mentioned in dispatches several times. In the First World War, after Egypt, Charles was severely wounded with his beloved Gurkhas at Gallipoli. But, after recuperation in England, he was back in India by 1916 as brigadier general. He fought there and also in the Third Afghan War of 1919. Being invalided out of the army in 1920 did not prevent him leading expeditions to Everest in 1922 and 1924, as well as leaping up the Swiss Alps whenever he had the chance (becoming president of the Alpine Club). It is easy to imagine Victor hero-worshipping his all-action uncle.

Victor's eldest brother, Henry, was another striking and dynamic kinsman. Sixteen years older than Victor, the Hon. Henry Lyndhurst Bruce was born on 25 May 1881; his lights were extinguished on a French battlefield when the First World War was less than six months old.

Ironically, given Mildred's parents, Henry was smitten by watching the most famous of the infamous Gibson Girls on stage. Before 1884, only ten British peers had married actresses in the previous century, but that year the marriage of the future Marquis of Aylesbury to Dolly Tester started a new trend. This caused the press to wonder quite why the nation's aristocrats succumbed to stars of the stage. The *Penny Illustrated*, in an article entitled 'Why Peers Marry Actresses', said:

> Setting aside all considerations of family pride, the Hon. Henry Lyndhurst Bruce, son and heir of Lord Aberdare, whose engagement to Miss Camille Clifford, the Gibson Girl, has just been announced, has determined to throw up his profession as a soldier, and to go into business in order to be able to provide suitably for his future wife. [Henry was intending to purchase a motor car business.]

Unsurprisingly, the match did not meet with parental approval – for Lord Aberdare was denying his son's engagement at the same time as Camille was happily confirming it!

By the outbreak of the First World War, Henry was in good company. The Dukes of Leinster and Newcastle, along with fifteen other aristocrats, had married actresses – and of course there were countless affairs between these two disparate social groups. Henry was luckier than young Dudley Tweedmouth, who fell wholeheartedly for a Gaiety Girl and foolishly promised to marry her. His parents, Lord and Lady Tweedmouth, were aghast, set some private detectives after him and then banished him to the USA until he came to his senses.[50] Which was all rather puritanical, since Lord Tweedmouth was descended merely from a Scottish fish merchant.

Henry's thirty-three-year life was brief, but full of action. Less than a year after the Brooklands track had opened, on 4 July 1908, he was driving in his first motor race. In those days, the embryonic sport had adopted many of the customs of horse racing. The drivers were therefore identified by the colours of their jackets and hats. In his 48.6hp De Dietrich, Henry raced that day garbed in a mauve coat with a yellow cap.

His racing career was undistinguished, until the May Handicap in 1910 when he won his heat. At the 5 October meeting he had a thoroughly satisfying day, coming third in the 76mph handicap, second in the White & Pope Handicap, and second in the 100mph handicap. Thirteen-year-old Victor would have been desperate to slip away from school to watch his elder brother's glories. Henry's attendance at Brooklands thereafter was desultory, but he participated in three handicap races on 1 June 1914, with a 3-litre Vauxhall, less than two months before the nation mobilised for war.

Enlisting quickly, Henry rose to become a captain with the 3rd Battalion Scots Guards. By December 1914, the generals were just becoming accustomed to the notion that there would be no quick victories, that cavalry charges were obsolete, and that trenches would be a permanent feature of the battlescape.

Henry was killed on 14 December. The battle, ordered by General Sir John French, and witnessed by many of the General Staff including the Prince of Wales, was also watched by Major Billy Congreve (who won a Victoria Cross shortly before his own death eighteen months later):

> It was a regular Valley of Death. The losses were, of course, very heavy. They were very, very gallant. Some almost reached the German trenches, where they were killed. One or two even got into the trenches where they were killed or captured. A few lay in little depressions in the mud till darkness and then crawled back. Those who got there could send no communication to the supports etc in the rear. Several men tried to get back but were all shot. They lost 7 out of 9 officers and 250 men.

Three days later, his 29-year-old wife, Camille, received the telegram she would have been dreading, conveying the news of her husband's death, 'Lord Kitchener expresses his sympathy.' (Kitchener was to do a lot of expressing before himself being drowned when HMS *Hampshire* sank at Scapa Flow in 1916.) Camille was left to bring up their 5-year-old daughter alone.

A brother officer, Captain Flint, wrote to Camille in April 1915. He reported that Henry had been buried near a captured German trench near Petit Bois. The Royal Scots may have captured the trench for a while, but due to unwise strategic planning by Sir John French and his staff, the battle was an abject failure. Like a few before, and many after, the life of Lieutenant the Hon. Henry Lyndhurst Bruce was cast away needlessly. As the ground was fought over again and again, Bruce's grave was pulverised into the Flanders mud.

Another of Victor's older brothers, Clarence Napier Bruce, was a cricketer and champion of Britain at both racquets and tennis. Qualifying as a barrister in 1911, he joined the Life Guards at the outbreak of war and survived it, ending his army career as a captain. He then had a distinguished career in public service and was made a GBE in 1954.

Of Victor's sisters, Constance Pamela Bruce, the youngest and known by the family as 'Pansy', went on to have an eventful family. She married Edward Kenelm Digby (a baron). One of their daughters, the Hon. Pamela

Digby, had a succession of marriages that propelled her into the global stratosphere. Her first target, in 1939, was Randolph Churchill, Winston's son. They divorced shortly after the end of the Second World War. In 1960, she married Leland Hayward, a Broadway producer. As soon as he died in 1971, she married Averill Harriman (the subject of one of her many affairs during her first marriage). Other ticks in her little black book included a Rothschild and a Niarchos. She became a luminary in the Democratic Party and was appointed US Ambassador to France by Bill Clinton.

Victor was aged 17 years and four months when he enlisted on 15 August 1914 – less than three weeks after the First World War had erupted. The attesting officer for his enlistment (done at the family home at Dyffryn, Mountain Ash) was none other than another brother, John Hamilton Bruce, who, along with Clarence, was one of the brainier siblings. Victor joined the 5th Battalion, East Kent Regiment ('The Buffs'), possibly because he had been at Wye, in Kent. But by Christmas he became ill. He was discharged in July 1915 with back trouble and managed to do two more terms at Wye, and also ran a 'Kinema' for troops through that summer.

In the autumn, he moved to the engineering department at Cardiff College to do munitions work, and showed more films to the soldiers. In autumn 1916, he developed his engineering knowledge further with a short course at the Technical Institute, Loughborough, and in 1917 had some training in the Aero Shop at King's College, London. This enabled him to work for five months at Gwynne's Aviation Works on rotary aero engines.

Victor did not have a very robust physique – despite being a shade under 6ft tall, he only had a 34½in chest – and in August 1917 he had another shot at military service, applying to join the Royal Flying Corps, but failed the medical. Instead, he enlisted in the Army Service Corps (ASC) as a private and driver in Grove Park, south-east London. However, his time with the ASC was brief – by Christmas, he was admitted with a recurrence of his spinal problems to the army's main orthopaedic hospital, the Royal Herbert at Woolwich (designed by Florence Nightingale's nephew, no less). He was discharged as 'no longer physically fit for war service' at Woolwich Dockyard on 27 February 1918, when the war was still at full tilt. Two months later he met one Dr Low.

Archibald Low was an engineer of great talent. Even before the First World War he had foreseen television and made early trials. In the war, he had been recruited by the Royal Flying Corps to develop a remotely controlled aircraft that could be used as a guided missile. He was thought so innovative by the Germans that they had twice tried to assassinate him. A serial inventor and speed addict, he had visited Brooklands several times before the war, and it is there that he probably first encountered the clan Bruce. After the war, he set up the Low Engineering Company Ltd with Victor's brother, Clarence. It was probably an introduction to Low in April 1918 that caused Victor to make the final switch in his chequered military career. He was commissioned in the Royal Marines in October 1918 to work with Low at an Admiralty Experimental Laboratory in Feltham on various inventions. This lasted until May 1919, when he was finally demobbed.

Like hundreds of thousands of former servicemen, Victor now faced the challenge of forging a peacetime career. The life of a motor-racing professional enjoyed by his brother, Henry, had impressed him, and Victor had developed a lot of mechanical and engineering expertise during his military service. The sporting carmaker, AC Cars, had had some success with higher quality small cars before the war, so young Bruce presented himself at their factory in Thames Ditton as soon as it reopened after the conflict. He was hired as a works competition and test driver in 1920. William Boddy, the esteemed former editor of *Motor Sport*, assumed this was a salaried position, but it seems the relationship was not quite that close, as Victor personally owned many of the AC cars in which he was later to achieve fame.

Victor started competition driving immediately. In 1920, he competed in two 'trials' – long-distance events on public roads, designed to test a car's mechanical reliability and ability to cope with varied road conditions, including steep hills. He was less successful in two hill climbs, but came third in his first race at Brooklands, the MMC Championship race. In May 1921, he swapped to Aston Martin for one meeting, persuading Lionel Martin to lend him the prototype side-valve machine (described by Boddy as 'a most primitive looking car'), and won his two races. He borrowed the machine again in the October 200-mile race. Sadly, after tyre trouble, the big end went twelve laps from the finish. Henry Segrave, who was later to influence Mildred, won in his Talbot-Darracq at 88mph.

In 1922 Victor had some success in more trials, and then the following year S.F. Edge, the owner of AC, thought it would generate good publicity if one of his cars could ascend the 1 in 4 narrow high street (with steps) at Clovelly in Devon. Victor and passenger were lifted out of their seats as the car banged up each step. Edge's next brainwave was to send his cars up Snowdon on a 4½-mile, 1 in 6 track, but the path became too narrow in parts, and the drivers had to divert on to the tracks of the mountain railway. Victor earned his salary that year. Victor had kept in touch with 'Prof' A.M. Low, and in 1922 they co-designed from scratch a motorcycle, complete with a four-cylinder engine.

In 1924, there was a big six-day trial for smaller cars, organised by the RAC. Bruce won his class and a gold medal. He tied for second place in the speed test around the Brooklands track.

After a wartime respite, the Monte Carlo Rally had resumed in 1924, and the following year Victor became the first ever British entrant in the event – the British press yawned. Starting from Glasgow in an AC, he reached the principality in sixty-five hours, won one of the hill climb sections, and came third in the 'comfort competition'! He also won the 2-litre class in a special event on a 50-mile circuit near the Mont des Mules. Handicapped by only carrying two passengers, overall he came a respectable twelfth out of thirty-two starters, despite a holed radiator; in those days the scoring system was complicated and extra points could be gained from arriving at Monte Carlo from a long distance away.[51]

Later in May 1925, Victor was introduced to the delights of the Montlhéry circuit, south of Paris. He supervised Thomas Gillett (S.F. Edge's friend and fellow director at AC Cars), who went for the twenty-four-hour record in a 2-litre AC, managing 1,949 miles and 83mph. The record lasted until September, when it was broken by Woolf Barnato. Victor realised he had discovered his métier, with the bonus of earning some money while having great fun. It was also to lead him to a wife …

7

MONTE AND MARRIAGE

For somewhat obscure reasons, from their first meeting Victor called Mildred 'Jane'. Their relationship developed rapidly, and only a month later they were celebrating her birthday together. He seems to have made a great effort from the start. On 19 December, for example, Victor took Mildred and her young son to the circus in Chelsea Gardens.[52]

Victor did not delay long in proposing, although Mildred's response was somewhat lacking in romance, 'You're entered in the Monte Carlo Rally, aren't you?'

He nodded.

'No Englishman has ever won it – I hope you do.'

Preparation for the Monte took precedence in their lives, and even impending matrimony was not allowed to become a distraction. In any event, his choice of an unmarried mother, and a Catholic to boot, dispatched any notion of it being a large family affair.

For the 1926 Monte, Victor bought a completely standard 2/3 seater 2-litre AC Six Sport.[53] Despite costing him £450 (more than the price of the average home), it lacked a heater. Given that much of the route was snow and icebound, his garb of tweed jacket, plus fours, soft cap and overcoat seems rather practical. After having secured officiating help from the Royal Scottish Automobile Club, he set off from John O'Groats, the furthest point in mainland Britain from Monaco, with his co-driver, the photographer William J. Brudenell. They battled through a fog-laden Rhone Valley and covered the 1,529 miles to the principality – against the next best result of 920 miles – in sixty-nine hours.

Only twenty-four of the forty-five starters made it to Monte Carlo to start the tests of the rally proper. Some competitors who thought they would enjoy an easy journey (with lots of points) from Tunis were thwarted by severe snowstorms in Spain's Sierra Nevada. Despite the Col de Baume being covered in heavy snow, Victor again won the Mont des Mules hill climb. The regularity drive on the Col de Braus was particularly treacherous, as even in fine weather the sinuous road wound up the mountainside in short straights. The previous day it had snowed heavily, making conditions even more testing.

Victor went on to win the event outright by eight points; M. Bussienne came second in a Sizaire-Frères – he had started only from Brest but had carried a small army of passengers. Still dressed in plus fours and checked socks, with trophy in hand outside his Monaco hotel supposedly celebrating victory, Victor looked more strained and fatigued than relaxed and happy. Becoming the first Briton to win the event understandably made Bruce something of a hero in British motoring circles, and the national press awoke from their slumber.

The 25,000-franc prize was put to good effect: on 16 February he married Mildred at the British Consulate at Menton, just up the coast.[54] Why did she take the plunge?

'Because he was a hero,' she later admitted.[55] He had also fulfilled one of her dreams by taking her around Brooklands soon after their first meeting. But let us be pragmatic. Although Mildred was of 'good stock', she lacked the funds for the lifestyle to which she aspired. By now aged 30, she could hardly expect her father, worried about finances as he always seemed to be, to continue to support her. And there was her son, Tony – although his real father, Easter, was still in touch and providing a degree of financial support, Tony would benefit from a male role model close at hand. It is easy to see why Mildred wanted marriage, and why she was attracted to Victor (and his title).

It is more difficult, however, to judge why Victor took the plunge. His new wife was almost two years older than him, with no dowry and a son who was almost 6. But by all accounts, Victor was both a gentle man and a gentleman. Mildred had good looks and undoubted charm, and they shared a passion for speed and adventure.

As for the formalities, it came naturally to Mildred to paint over the darker parts of her past. She described herself to the consul in Menton as 'Mildred Mary Easter' – a widow. Not only had she never married Easter, but Stephen Easter was then still very much alive. Naughty!

The Menton wedding, on 16 February 1926, was a very low-key affair by the standards of most of the Bruce family. With the family being unhappy with Victor's choice of partner, it was best for all concerned that the union had taken place a long way from London.

All of Victor's siblings had already married and their ceremonies comprise an interesting collection, with three of them being very low-key and three of them great occasions in London society. Margaret Cecilia Bruce, Victor's eldest sister, married Orlando Bridgeman (4th Earl of Bradford) in Chelsea on 21 July 1904 – given he was a relatively top-drawer aristocrat, this was also a strangely quiet affair. Henry Lyndhurst Bruce, his eldest brother, married Camille Antoinette Clifford ('the Gibson Girl') in October 1906. Because of the disapproval of Henry's parents, this took place at the Hanover Square Register Office.

Victor's sister, Eva Isobel Marian Bruce, married Captain the Hon. Algernon Henry Strutt at St Margaret's, Westminster, on 26 April 1911. The service was performed by the Archdeacon of Monmouth, and it was an enormous society wedding.

Clarence Napier Bruce married Margaret Bethune Black on 12 December 1912, at St Margaret's, Westminster. This was a grand occasion, full of titled folk. It was the senior marriage that day in the 'Court Circular'.

Constance Pamela Alice Bruce ('Pansy'), the sibling to whom Victor was closest, married Major the Hon. Edward Kenelm Digby (11th Baron Digby of Geashill) on 1 July 1919 at the Guards' Chapel, Wellington Barracks, in London. This was another huge society event, the guest list having a leavening of very senior staff officers from the army.

John Hamilton Bruce married Cynthia Juliet Duff in May 1923. This was another that passed below society's radar.

After marriage, what was Mildred to do? It is difficult to imagine Mildred rendering any service at all to her home. In December 1924, Violet Bonham Carter dismissed upper-class married women as 'drones', who enjoy spending much more cash than their domestic activities would warrant.[56] Marie Corelli, the English novelist, wrote:

> Now or never, women must understand in earnest the task of civilising man. And they must set about it the right way. Not by soft yielding to every caprice of a creature that has still so much more of the monkey than the man in him, but by a gentle yet firm rectitude and purity that shall effectually restrain his simian impulses.

It is perhaps worth noting that Corelli lived with a woman, not a man. It is also difficult to conceive of Mildred treating Victor like a monkey. And 'gentle' and 'purity' are not the first attributes that spring to mind when one thinks of Mildred. We know from her behaviour in later years that Mildred more closely espoused the views of the Victorian feminist, journalist and educator, Florence Fenwick Miller, who in 1922 challenged the prevailing wisdom – endorsed by the Church – that women should blindly follow the blithe instructions of their husbands.[57]

Victor carried on with the con brio tempo of his racing career, winning the London to Holyhead Trial, and entering two race meetings at Brooklands in the spring. Under his tutelage, Mildred entered her first races – at Skegness, of all places – coming third in one race, and first in her class in a handicap.

In the autumn, Victor won a gold medal at the Brooklands High Speed Reliability Trial, but this was no more than a modest way of warming the tyres ahead of the Bruces' plans for the New Year. By their Esher fireside, they hatched a plan to add a 9,000-mile tour of southern Europe and north Africa as a footnote to their entry for the Monte in January.

The first step was to assemble some maps, so once again they made their way to the Touring Department of the Automobile Association. Mildred outlined their plans, and the clerk responded, 'Excuse me, but do you contemplate taking your car through Italy?'

'Yes, why not? And into Sicily, and into Africa! And heaps of other places!'

'Why not?' he repeated in astonishment. 'Why the roads are quite impracticable in southern Italy, and as for Sicily they are completely dangerous.'[58]

The advice was ignored.

After much badgering, the couple again secured the support of the AC factory for the Monte Carlo Rally, this time borrowing a works car, with Mildred entered as driver. S.F. Edge, who had by now bought the company, 'was confident enough in my driving. Well you see he loved a lady driver because he felt sure that it would be good publicity for a lady driver to go through the Monte Carlo Rally. Naturally he wanted publicity for the AC car, and he got it.'[59] (Years earlier, when a director of the Napier Car Company, Edge had, in effect, created Britain's first female racing driver. The pretty Dorothy Levitt had caught his eye as a secretary at his firm in 1902; he taught her to drive and installed her as the works racing driver. She excelled and garnered a lot of welcome publicity for the company until she was dropped in 1910.)[60]

Keen as ever to secure maximum press coverage, Mildred had recruited Bobby Beare, the motoring editor of the *Daily Sketch*, as an extra crew member. Together with Victor as co-driver and Pitt, the engineer, they assembled at the dour hotel at John O'Groats, as Victor had the year before. During the day and a half that they had to wait until their allotted departure time, Mildred developed a raging temperature. However, once they were flagged off after an early breakfast, this soon relented.

It was just before dawn, and with a cold mist rolling in from the sea the Mediterranean must have seemed very distant. The freezing fog had swathed the Scottish tarmac in a coating of ice – on the very first bend Mildred found the AC's wheels skidding. With the weather slowing progress, the team fell into a Spartan regime – a quick bite at Blair Atholl and a 'very acceptable' high tea at a small inn on the far side of the Grampians.

They were therefore looking forward to dinner at the Royal Scottish Automobile Club in Glasgow, but with their soup came an unwelcome telegram, 'Thick fog 50 miles around Carlisle. Mist on Yorkshire moors. Heavy snow falling towards London. Frozen roads very dangerous.' At this, 'interest in dinner fled. With one accord, we rose from the table.'[61]

Mildred hogged the steering wheel, later claiming that this was a unanimous team decision following Beare's advice that this would maximise the media coverage. They were the first British team to arrive at Folkestone (via control points at Doncaster and Leicester Square). With her habitual scant regard for bureaucracy:

Pushing my way onto the boat without passport, ticket or credentials, [I] made for the first cabin I saw – incidentally not the one I booked – and tried hard to sleep. But the boat would wobble, and all thoughts of sleep went west. If I had really gone off to sleep on the boat, I should probably have awakened in a peevish mood, and perhaps not carried through so well.[62]

Some of her competitors had pushed the event's rules to the maximum. A vast Weymann-bodied Laffly coach started out from Stockholm.[63] It was a converted truck chassis that could carry eight people and was fitted with three beds, four armchairs, a table and a bench seat.

The weather remained icy in northern France. 'Darling you really must let me take the wheel now, or you'll only be unfit to take the car past the finish,' implored Victor, but she determined to remain at the helm until Paris, where she snatched a couple of hours sleep in a hotel while the menfolk serviced the car. 'It was only by driving very fast that I was able to keep awake.'

Another weapon she deployed to keep her mind stimulated was to see how much fear she could provoke in her front seat passenger. While Victor was dozing in the back, Beare was at her side as they motored through southern France. With the Alpes Maritimes looming in the distance, Mildred regaled Beare with the extreme hazards they would shortly face when they encountered the vertiginous hairpins in the Massif de l'Esterel to the west of Cannes. By the time they reached the Massif it was dark and Mildred had begun hallucinating. Nonetheless, they safely negotiated the mountains and made the Casino at Monaco perfectly on schedule – after more than seventy hours at the wheel.

The route again went over the icy Col de Baume, and some competitor thought he would benefit by pre-placing flags along the section at three-minute intervals.[64] The organisers thought it an equally good wheeze to rearrange them at random distances. On a snowy Col de Braus, Mildred was unnerved to see a woman ahead frantically flagging down the AC. Since there was no way she could halt in such a distance, Mildred careened past. It was not until several hundred yards up the mountain that the English crew saw the reason for the lady's distress: five cars were in disarray across the road, with just a low wall before the mountain fell away below. Again, with too much momentum to stop, Mildred had just enough room to thread the AC between the carnage.

Sadly, her accuracy was lacking in the regularity test, then a timed climb up the Mont des Mules and a *concours d'élégance* completed the rally. Mildred was placed sixth overall and became the first ever winner of the *Coupe des Dames* (the Ladies' Prize). Equally satisfying, at the prize banquet at the Hotel de Paris, Mildred was seated next to the president of the International Sporting Club of Monaco. Edge, the AC boss, cabled his delight.

Beare had a couple of days before he had to return to England, so the victorious Bruces treated him to a tour of their favourite beauty spots on the coast. Before he left he urged Mildred to continue to do all the driving, as this would resonate more with the *Sketch*'s readership:

> After carefully thrashing the whole question out with my husband we came to the conclusion that no harm and some good might result from my endeavouring to drive all the way. But he made me promise to give in the very moment I felt the task was too big.[65]

So, this time with W.H. Johnson (the motoring editor of *Country Life*) replacing Beare, the quartet set off down Italy. Their first night stop was at

Genoa, but as they headed southwards the AA man's words were ringing in their ears. At times Mildred was restricted to only 3mph. For this speed freak it was a form of cruel torture; it was always easier to concentrate for hours on end if moving at high speed.

Arriving at Florence, the bridges over the Arno reminded Mildred of the medieval London Bridge. That night, she weighed herself on public scales in the Piazza del Duomo. Always slight of frame, she was dismayed to find she had lost half a stone since leaving London. As the roads remained tricky and ancient glories of the Roman Empire hove into view, the atmosphere in the AC became a little fractious. Johnson was the expedition's default photographer and could not resist urging the driver to stop so he could take yet another snap. Mildred's vice was baths: 'Like the others, unfortunately, I was seldom able to indulge it.' The others' 'sordid minds could not rise above letters, coffee and photos,' she acidly noted.

Naples failed to impress, 'Of all the poverty-stricken, dirty and squalid places, Naples must surely hold the record.'[66] But there was some welcome news in that city – the Bruces had arranged to stop at city post offices to collect mail and telegrams. Waiting for them at Naples was good news from Beare, 'Editor appoints you Special Correspondent of the *Daily Sketch*. Send news of tour, but keep eyes open for events of general interest also. Wire acceptance.' There was no hesitation, the offer met two crucial demands – funds and potential celebrity.

Soon the team were to discover that the AA man had been right about the state of Italian roads – 'The roads of Italy are undoubtedly bad at their best; at their worst they are as awful as the scenery is exquisite.'[67] Progress was slow. As predicted, they encountered a broken bridge – local engineers requiring some encouragement from Victor's wallet to effect a quick repair. The Bruces were unimpressed with the work ethic of the Italians they encountered:

> There appeared to be no work done in this town [Lagonegro]. All the inhabitants were lounging about in the sun. Quite contented they seemed; though no doubt this accounts for the poverty and neglect that is rife in Southern Italy, as we noticed this happy idleness wherever we went.[68]

Roads deteriorated further, such that, by the time they neared Pompeii the roadway was a sea of mud with the bizarre spectacle of a dead horse in their path, its head buried in the ground. They spared the time for some tourism 'with vagrant [*sic*] recollections of Lytton's "Last days of Pompeii" in my mind, it was not difficult to find myself back in the days of 2,000 years ago, in spite of the suggestion, conveyed by the turnstile, that one was visiting the zoo'.

Benito Mussolini had risen to power only a year or so earlier, but he made a favourable impression on the intrepid Englishwoman:

> I was interested and amazed to learn that there is a Society for the Prevention of Cruelty to Animals in existence in Italy. We happened to meet the organiser on board, and gathered that lack of funds was the reason why the effect of the society's efforts was not more apparent. Much of the money that is available comes from England, apparently; but I was given to understand that Signor Mussolini is a great lover of animals, and has done much to further the work of the organisation.[69]

They crossed to Sicily via the Messina ferry, and were comprehensively swindled by quayside 'staff'. Sicilian roads were as wild as those they had encountered on the mainland. The AC and crew boarded another boat at Palermo, bound for Tunis. The crossing was sufficiently uncomfortable that the normally indefatigable Mildred succumbed to sea sickness.

An expensive customs scam was their welcome to Africa, but they enjoyed both the scenery and the welcome from the locals. Carthage attracted Johnson and his camera like a moth to a flame, but he had to resort to public transport after Mildred refused to drive him there – she was more interested in shopping in the *souks*. The Bruces then had a romantic night in the former sultan's palace in Fez.

At Algiers, Johnson departed for England with innumerable rolls of film to be developed, and the remaining crew hatched a madcap scheme for a day trip into the Sahara – a mere 300 miles each way – to a village called Lahouat. Not long after their early morning departure, the absence of road signs caused the AC crew to lose their bearings. Once they had rejoined the road, on the last vapours of petrol they struggled into Djelfa, 60 miles short of their destination, just before nightfall. Vigorous sign language miraculously produced a can of petrol, so after a dinner with lashings of tea, Mildred determined to try for their destination – they reached the Saharan town an hour before midnight.

The following morning the arrival of the exotic British team stimulated the locals into some entrepreneurship, and Mildred was soon astride a camel. 'Can it jump?' she foolishly enquired. The attraction of camel riding evaporated after only two minutes.

Eventually, the state of the roads put paid to the back axle of the AC just outside Tangier. They waited a few days while Mr Edge dispatched his chief engineer with a spare. The Bruces made it across to Spain, but while trying to enter Portugal they had the sort of border/customs problem that would have had even Mildred praying for the immediate creation of the EU, had her patriotic tendencies conceived of such a body.

'What's the matter?' asked an ever-impatient Mildred of Victor, 'Aren't our papers in order?' They had left the Spanish border post but were denied entry into Portugal because the RAC had erroneously requested their visa for '*Pologne*' (Poland). The rallyists tried to return to Spain but the officials who had seen them through the frontier were now enjoying their siesta. The Bruces suffered a prolonged bout of bureaucratic ping-pong, but were eventually rescued by a passing Englishman who knew the chief customs officer. The Bruces never made it into Portugal.

At Edge's suggestion, the return to England was interrupted for a visit to the Montlhéry track, their task being to motor the well-worn AC for 1,000 miles. This was achieved with little drama and, at the end, Mildred 'pulled in for the last time, to find a knot of friends waiting for me, with a lovely bouquet of carnations as a little "prize for a good girl"'.

After a celebratory lunch (with medal awarded) in Paris, the threesome headed at last for England. Having enjoyed the freedom of European roads, good or bad, and recovered her thirst for speed at Montlhéry, she was not completely homesick, 'The final run up to London the next day, during which it was necessary to keep strictly within the English speed limit, was wearisome in the extreme.'[70]

Once back in England, the Bruces were feted by both AC and the public at a celebratory lunch at London's Hotel Cecil (where Mildred's mother had stayed before her marriage). In his speech, S.F. Edge, very content with the publicity that they had created (aided immeasurably by Beare), announced that he was donating the trusty car to Mildred.

In May 1927, Victor decided to enter the Six Hour Race at Brooklands – the 'longest race yet held on the British mainland'. The twenty-nine starters had to run to their cars Le Mans style and erect the hoods on their largely unmodified cars, before doing ten laps hood up and then taking them down again. Very British.

By now, Mildred's motorcycling brother, Louis, had emigrated to South Africa, and, like both his parents, he had lapsed into a life of booze. Aunt Maude had nursed plenty of wounded soldiers in the Great War, and so in 1926 she took a break from her theological studies to catch a liner to Cape Town to give her 35-year-old nephew some pastoral care. While he was glad to renew contact with England, she sadly failed to wean him from the bottle.[71] His sister's considerable motoring success had been achieved with borrowed cars and sponsorship obtained on a hand-to-mouth basis. Mildred wanted more – she aspired to a life of luxury and financial independence.

8

NO HOUSEWIFE THIS: MONTLHÉRY AND BREAKING MOTORING RECORDS

Any keen observer of the times cannot have failed to notice that we are on the threshold of a great feminine awakening. Apathy and levity are giving place to a wholesome and intelligent interest in the affairs of life, and above all in the home. There should be no drudgery in the house ... the house-proud woman in these days of servant shortage does not always know the best way to lessen her own burdens ... The time spent on housework can be enormously reduced in every home without any loss of comfort, and often with a great increase in wellbeing and its air of personal care and attention.

From the first issue of *Good Housekeeping* magazine, published in London in March 1924.

The thirties were the decade of women's magazines, with *Woman's Own* founded in 1932, *Women's Illustrated* four years later, *Woman* in 1937, and *Housewife* at the end of the decade. The latter noted, 'Happy and lucky is the man whose wife is house proud.' Even leading clerics were focused on encouraging women to remain shackled to the home. William Inge, dean of St Paul's Cathedral from 1911, considered it to be a matter of national importance that young girls were increasingly unwilling to enter domestic service after the First World War.[72]

Somehow it is difficult to conceive that Mildred bothered herself too much with housework. In 1927, with Victor's help, she began racing at Brooklands in earnest, and on 2 July at a speed of 88mph won a handicap race against seven rivals. A week later, husband and wife, with Bobby Beare again playing gooseberry, set off from London to try to make the Arctic Circle. They were unaccustomed to the pleasures of driving through northern Europe in summer rather than the usual bitter January weather, and so enjoyed that part of the trip. Mildred relates that King Christian of Denmark had heard of their foray and wished to give them an official reception in Copenhagen. He sent a letter to the post office in Hamburg, where they were due to call. But Victor wanted to press on, so they never stopped there and therefore missed the letter. They also misinterpreted the frantic waving at various garages en route, the owners having been asked to pass on the message. It was not until they arrived at their hotel in Copenhagen that the British Embassy could inform them of the royal summons.

The Bruces had their royal audience, and then attended a ball in their honour that night, in the company of Prince Harald and Princess Helene. They arrived in Stockholm two days later. Even before they had reached the snow, Mildred had already collected plenty of material for yarns to spin on her return.

After they crossed the Arctic Circle, road maps became somewhat rudimentary. Their greatest danger turned out not to be navigational error but running into a forest fire caused by the lightning from a summer storm that ignited a pine forest. They joined fleeing elk and reindeer to shelter by a lake until the fire had burned itself out.

The Bruces drove their AC as far north as Petsamo in Finland, and 'when we ran out of road we planted the Union Jack'.[73] During this epic journey, they drove 6,000 miles, averaging 210 miles each day. Mildred related this in the first of her books, the snappily titled *Nine Thousand Miles in Eight Weeks: Being an Account of an Epic Journey by Motor Car through Eleven Countries and Two Continents* (published by Heath Cranston, July 1927) – a rather loose and hyperbolic grip of arithmetic was characteristic of Mildred.

Their return route took them through Sundsvall in Sweden where the Swedish Automobile Club gave them every assistance, including maps. Having been advised that local major roads were always kept clear of snow through the winter, they decided that they would start the next year's Monte from there.

Driving at whatever speed they wished – or could manage – had clearly gone to Mildred's head. Soon after their return to England she was forced to return to a place she knew well from her youth – the magistrates' court, this time at Bow Street, hard by Covent Garden. She had taken unkindly to the request of a police officer to stop where he wanted on Shrewsbury Avenue in London's West End. He had to ask her three times to reverse her car into Neal Street. Their conversation became more ill-tempered.

When she told the court she had not seen the PC's signal, 'He answered somewhat aggressively that she should not be in charge of a car! She asked him to speak a little more politely, and it was then that he said "he would summons her".'[74] Mildred exercised her charm – the JP was Sir Chartres Biron, who proclaimed, 'It is a very trifling matter if this lady has driven to the North Pole [sic] and back. She must pay 10s.' Had she been over-egging her driving exploits?[75]

Later in 1927, Edge, the AC boss, suggested that the Bruces pursue the ultimate proof of endurance – 1,000 miles around the Montlhéry race-track near Paris. This circuit had been created only three years earlier by Alexandre Lamblin, who wished to stimulate his nation's car industry. A French industrialist making radiators for cars and aircraft, he also owned a magazine, *L'Aéro-Sport*. He was conscious that, while Great Britain had already built the very successful Brooklands, which had opened in 1908, and the USA had Indianapolis, France lacked a circuit to sustain the competitive edge of its motor manufacturers. Montlhéry was very accessible from Paris, being only 20km to the south, yet had a major advantage over Brooklands – it was surrounded by woodland, not Nimby neighbours, hostile to night-time (and indeed daytime) noise. So Montlhéry became a haven for record-breakers from across Europe.

Like Brooklands, the 2.5km elongated oval featured concave, banked turns. The degree of banking was designed to hold a 1,000kg car travelling at 220kph (137mph). Given that the circuit record for many years was 235kph, drivers of the fastest cars were at the limit of adhesion and common sense, risking flying off the top of the banking. The Bruces met their target of a 60mph average for the 1,000 miles, and returned to Thames Ditton to an understandably vigorous welcome from the factory staff. Among the most treasured letters of praise Mildred received was one from her hero, Malcolm Campbell.

In the autumn, she heard that Chrysler in the US had broken the record for driving 10,000 miles, and that Sunbeam was planning to better it in Britain in spring 1928. The Bruces wanted to deny Sunbeam its chance at glory. Back to the AC works, where she interrogated the chief engineer, Mr Smith. 'Will my Montlhéry model go 15,000 miles?'

'Certainly,' he replied. 'It will always go, even if you have to push it.'

'Please don't try to be funny. I mean will it run 15,000 miles?'

'Yes. I see no reason why it should not.'

'Well how fast can it be driven for 15,000 miles?'

'That is rather hard to say; probably about 75 miles an hour.'

'That settles it, I am going to wipe out all Miss Cordery's records. And I'm going to drive myself.'

'But my dear young lady, you cannot drive 15,000 miles.'

'No, but Victor and I can.'[76]

Having won Edge's support, together they plotted how to achieve the audacious feat of 15,000 miles in ten days. Again, Montlhéry was to be the venue, and a December date was chosen to economise on timekeepers' fees, even though there was a high risk the track would be icebound. The Bruces needed sponsorship, and the depth of their need was such that they secured money from the manufacturers of Horlicks, even though Victor detested the drink. Colonel Sempill, of whom more anon, sent a telegram wishing Mildred 'greatest success hoping you will capture all the records'.

The AC's wheels began to roll on Friday, 9 December. Primitive hurricane lamps had been placed all around the circuit but these soon became shrouded in an evening fog – yet Mildred, who was the first driver, still managed an average of 80mph.[77] The Bruces initially planned to do nine three-hour shifts, thereby allowing themselves at least one period of proper sleep each day. Pitstops were a mere three minutes. Mildred went back to the nearby chateau where they were staying to try to snatch a couple of hours of slumber. By 1 a.m. she was back at the wheel in the crucible of endeavour that was Montlhéry.

After four days (!) the fog dissipated, but the temperature fell and the task proved even more arduous than they had anticipated. The couple had decided that a short three hours of sleep was insufficient, so they extended their driving stints to six hours. Apart from a precautionary change of a magneto, mechanical problems were thankfully largely absent.

The temperature fell further and, despite being clad like First World War fighter pilots, in order to prevent frostbite they had to cut shifts to one hour apiece. Mildred did indeed suffer mild frostbite on two fingers, despite the ministrations of a Parisian doctor (himself a racing driver), who had come down to the track to see if he could offer help. He counselled the mechanics to massage warm engine oil into the Bruces' numbed hands! The extreme cold meant that the car accumulated ice – however, this helped to seal a leaking radiator on the third day.

Their AC carried on magnificently at speeds of up to 90mph, 'purring like a great cat, it was a fantastic engine'.[78] The stamina of this indefatigable couple was helped by them both being non-smokers and teetotal. At night, with little lighting, the monotony of driving round an essentially oval track seemed worse and they both had the sensation while driving of feeling like the only human on the planet:

It was a weird and uncanny feeling, to be all alone at the wheel, forever, it seems plunging into the darkness, with only the glimmer of red lights dotted around the track as a reminder that there are some other human beings near at hand. Many a time during one of my long night stretches at the wheel my nerves became so taut that I felt I must scream, if only for relief.[79]

Even though, unsurprisingly, they both found the experience very tedious, they were doing well – their average speed was 79mph – but on the seventh night, patches of black ice began to appear around the steeply banked circuit. Even the pits became treacherous for the mechanics trying to refuel the car. They too were numb with cold and fatigue, and it took them a little while to realise that they had not heard the thrumming AC for several minutes. Two mechanics dashed off down the track on foot, and eventually found the AC upside down on the muddy infield. A tired Victor had hit one of Montlhéry's notorious bumps, there was a coating of snow, and the AC had spun like a top off the circuit. He remained underneath it; the steering column was depressed by three inches, but had not broken. This alone saved Victor from being crushed to death. The windscreen was shattered.

'Tom, is that you?' Victor asked anxiously.

'Yes sir, are you hurt?'

The mechanics lifted the AC off its shaken driver. In shock, Victor returned to the chateau to wake the sleeping Mildred. Oily and dishevelled, he had clearly survived, but had the car? 'The engine's fine,' he assured her as nonchalantly as he could manage, but he needed her help – immediately. Under the record-breaking rules, only the drivers could move the car on the track. So, while the mechanics had been allowed to lift the machine off Victor, it was he and Mildred who then had to push the AC back to the pits where the mechanics could set to work on repairing the windscreen and steering. It took them two precious hours to push the car back to the mechanics' care.

By the time the AC was back in action at 10 the following morning their effective average speed had fallen to 65mph, so they set to with renewed determination. The smashed windscreen had to be replaced by a much less effective tin deflector, adding to the drivers' hardship. Their chief mechanic then succumbed to pneumonia. J.A. Joyce had a trying flight from the AC factory (where he was the works driver) to do some driving shifts to relieve a little of the Bruces' workload. But he had never driven at Montlhéry before, let alone through a snowy and icy winter night, and so first he had to put in a few laps in a saloon car. Once in the AC he managed to average 86mph.

Two hours from the end of their ordeal the sleet turned to snow. The final shift fell to Mildred. By the time they achieved the 15,000 miles, at the end of nine days, four hours and thirty-three minutes (at an average speed of 68mph), a large crowd had gathered to cheer their success in beating the previous record by two days. They had also broken innumerable other records from 4,000 miles upwards. Muffled like an Arctic explorer, Mildred drew to a halt and, dwarfed by the two enormous bouquets thrust into her hands, she was carried aloft to the pits on the shoulders of their mechanics.

It was teatime on the Sunday, but the Bruces dragged themselves to the chateau craving only sleep. But at 2 the following morning the exhausted couple were awoken by smoke. Mildred tried to tie the bed sheets together for an escape by the window. When this proved fruitless, Victor ventured outside the room and found the cause of the fire. One of the equally exhausted mechanics had fallen asleep in bed with a lighted cigarette. Victor plunged him into a bath and extinguished the smouldering mattress. The Bruces then belatedly clawed back their sleep deficit.

Returning via Paris, the Bruces were feted by the French Automobile Club, with a dinner hosted by its president, the Comte Robert de Vogué. Castrol Motor Oil and British Petroleum proudly trumpeted the Bruces' achievement in the press. On the afternoon of 22 December, London celebrations were again held at the Hotel Cecil.

Victor later drily wrote, 'Long distance record-breaking is a matter of organisation – and determination. But determination is almost automatically maintained if organisation has been given proper attention, and if the right spirit is animating the attempt.'[80] There was the occasional curmudgeonly comment. The *New Statesman* considered the drive:

> At once an exceedingly wonderful and an exceedingly stupid performance, and as such deserves examination ... Publicity men are always trying to devise 'stunts', and occasionally receive enormous fees for the mere germ of an idea. Hence pleasant, sensible people like the Bruces are condemned to waste nearly a fortnight of their earthly term in giving imitation of caged mice.[81]

Strangely, Mildred chose to keep the article rather than lob it into the wastepaper bin.

Cheques from happy motor industry suppliers dropped pleasingly through the Esher letterbox: £240 from Dunlop, £50 from BP, £20 from Herbert Terry (springs), and so on. In the aftermath of the publicity of their record, Selwyn Edge of AC became rather acid, believing that the Bruces were putting self-promotion several steps ahead of promoting his cars:

I quite agree that when we have done praising the pluck and enterprise of the Bruces, much may be said for the helpers on duty day and night for 10 days, while the truly amazing Acedes AC six cylinder normal Sports car continued to run around the Montlhéry track at some 85 mph. It is just wonderful.[82]

For the 1928 Monte, Mildred entered an Arrol-Aster, this time starting from Stockholm. She was influenced in choosing a car from this Dumfries company because it had made the bodywork for Malcolm Campbell's *Bluebird*. The firm had only been founded a year earlier but was to go into receivership in 1929. Sammy Davis, sports editor of *The Autocar*, summed up the challenge of the Monte that year:

> When you have succeeded in arriving at Monte Carlo and have checked in on time, had the party's passports looked over to see that the faces have not altered en-route, and been subjected to a scrutiny of the seals placed on engine, chassis and body when you started, as well as a measurement by template of the prescribed dimensions of the seats in the body, it would be human to conclude that the serious part of the job is finished. Not so; there is the test of regularity to be undergone.
>
> On paper it sounds an easy task – to pass through three control points pretty well dead on time. All the way the car is either climbing or descending steep gradients, varying a rough guess from 1 in 12 to 1 in 6.5; to get some idea of the corners, think of the sharpest hairpin bend you have ever negotiated, make it a little sharper, give it a gradient of 1 in 8, then lift it 2000 feet high on the side of a mountain, and on the sheer side of it place a wall about eighteen inches high, usually with a broken gap just about where you would go through if anything went wrong with the brakes. Then repeat that hairpin every 150 yards for about five miles at a time.[83]

Mildred came a creditable fifth overall, and by October she had secured a contract with Arrol-Aster to supply and maintain a car for further events. By the end of 1928 the Bruces were plotting an expedition to the Black Sea, the Boulogne Rally and several more mundane events. Her fame had secured her a very favourable deal from British National Newspapers (for a paper yet to be launched) – 1,000 guineas per year, together with 500 guineas 'expenses'.

Sir Charles 'Cheers' Wakefield (the owner of Castrol) hosted a large lunch at the Savoy on 28 November, in honour of RAF Squadron Leader Bert Hinkler, who had recently become the first solo aviator to reach Australia. The guest list included luminaries from Wakefield's orbits – motorsport and aviation. Air Vice Marshal Sir William Sefton Brancker KCB AFC, the paterfamilias of British Civil Aviation, was one of the speakers; Mildred's hero Malcolm Campbell was there, and so, too, were the Hon. Victor and Mrs Bruce. It was probably at this event that she met the man who was to exercise a considerable influence on her activities two years on – Colonel the Master of Sempill.

It was only a week later that Sefton Brancker had a jolly dinner with some chums at Rules Restaurant, in Maiden Lane in London. From an old Dorset family, but with a German grandmother, he had enjoyed a distinguished career with the Royal Artillery in India and on the Western Front. A true aviation visionary (the first person to fly as a passenger in India), he had transferred into the RFC and rose through its ranks as it evolved into the RAF. He was 'an irrepressible man whose bouncing walk betrayed his eagerness, he gave the impression that conscious charm was more in his line than unassuming tact'.[84] He had shown his modest level of tact by being a perennial thorn in the side of Lloyd George, who failed to share Brancker's vision of Britain being an aviation superpower. So, Lloyd George did what any sensible politician would do – he brought him into the fold and made him Director of Civil Aviation in 1922. Brancker had been invited to the dinner in 1928 as the figurehead for the formation of a City Guild for the burgeoning aviation industry – his original idea was to call it the Company of Airmen but it ended up as the Guild of Air Pilots and Air Navigators. By the time the port had arrived that evening there was little doubt that he would be its first Master. The diners were well looked after as the restaurant's owner, Tom Bell, was another former RFC pilot in the First World War.

Mildred was now looking to enjoy speed thrills in another environment – the water. In *Nine Lives*, Mildred attributes her inspiration to start racing powerboats to driving past the Welsh Harp Reservoir in north-west London and noting the little craft speeding around buoys. In later life, she had a habit of expunging the influence of her ex-husband but, more prosaically for her image, her interest in power boats is likely to have been influenced by Victor. He, you will remember, had begun to extend his engineering skills into the realm of marine craft with his work with the Admiralty at the tail end of the First World War. Moreover, his new business colleague, J.S. Holroyd, had begun speedboat racing himself. Mildred, in turn, started to learn powerboat racing in a modest way at that same Welsh Harp. Her first craft was a tiny speedboat with a crude early outboard motor hung from the stern – it was called *Mosquito*. 'Racing over the water in a paper-thin hull scarcely large enough to hold you, with a little 250cc outboard engine clamped to the transom, is the most thrilling pastime of the day.'[85] Weekends were now spent learning the art of cornering as fast as possible. Weekdays were for recovering her hearing.

Having done some club racing at the Welsh Harp, Mildred then took a fancy to establishing a record for crossing the Channel. Under the auspices of the Royal Cinque Ports Yacht Club, she departed Dover on 8 September at 1.45 p.m. in *Mosquito*, with 'the sea calm as a mill pond', and arrived at Calais at 2.10 p.m. Steering problems meant she did not return to Dover until 4 p.m. A week later, she went for a faster return journey time and, although the sea became choppier during her return, she managed to record 107 minutes for her fleeting visit to France. The Bruces' coffers were helped by a bonus paid to them by Shell for using and advertising its fuel on this venture.

Later that month she offered a trophy for anyone who could beat her record in a speedboat with an outboard motor. Victor later wrote (in a letter to *The Times*) that his wife had had to wait for three and a half months for favourable weather and sea conditions. In 1929, one Commander Lightoller attempted to win the trophy but was more than a little thwarted when his steering wheel came off in his hands halfway across on his outbound journey.

Preparation for the 1929 Monte Carlo event was cast into chaos when Mildred's AC was damaged in a car park only a few days before she was due to start. So, she resorted again to an Arrol-Aster, this time starting from Riga. However, it soon started snowing unremittingly[86] and by the time they were 6 miles from the Polish border it had deteriorated into a blizzard – the Bruces slid into a ditch. It was 3 miles to the nearest habitation and by the time they found the small hut the Bruces were nearing hypothermia. The following morning, with the help of hut's owner and two dray horses, the car was pulled out of the ditch and taken to the nearest town. They made Berlin, and gained permission from the Monaco Club to restart but, while driving down France, the car caught fire at Avignon due to a short circuit and their rally was finished.[87]

In 1929, the Bruces terminated their relationship with Arrol-Aster, believing that the car supplied by the Scottish firm was not up to their requirements. The company folded only months later. The AC car company also collapsed, so in March they offered their publicity-generating skills to Sir William Morris, founder of the mighty MG Car Company. His fellow director, Cecil Kimber, was delegated to break Morris' prescience to the Bruces:

He is averse to this form of advertising … regarding the possibility of your making the proposed Russian trip in a Morris car, his feeling in the matter is that at the present time, Russia is not sufficiently civilised in a commercial sense to make this worthwhile from the Morris standpoint … Sir William feels that Russia as a nation are [*sic*] still capable of repudiating any business undertakings into which they might enter, and he therefore considers that a project of this nature had better be left over for a few more years.[88]

Mildred had secured sponsorship from the KLG Spark Plug Company, but only to the tune of £25 per year. A few months later,[89] Mildred joined the Alvis works team, but on an unpaid basis. However, she had long been niggled by the fact that Thomas Gillett in his AC retained the world record for single-handed driving over twenty-four hours. She realised that it was unlikely that an AC could be tuned further to improve on Gillett's distance. Moreover, Edge was by now in poor health, and the finances of his business little better.

With favoured marques falling by the wayside, the Bruces switched to the Bradford firm of Jowett. But possibly Mildred's normally robust constitution was wobbling a little, and having secured the use of a Jowett to make an ascent of the mountain railway on Snowdon, she wrote to postpone this in May, claiming doctors had told her to rest ahead her next exploit.[90]

Mildred had become friendly with some of the Bentley drivers; she knew the capabilities of their machines, so she approached 'W.O.' Bentley, the owner of the firm, to borrow a machine for Montlhéry. Having done her sums, she told him it needed to be capable of averaging more than 100mph. He only had a (still mighty) 4.5-litre car available, already allocated to the dapper Sir Tim Birkin (who always raced with a blue and white spotted kerchief around his neck).[91]

Wolf Barnato provided the money behind the Bentley team. Disconcertingly known as 'Babe', although he was a heavyweight boxer, he expressed his concern, 'It's going to Le Mans – don't you do any damage.'[92] (Earl Howe was due to drive it in the twenty-four-hour race in late June.) The trio spent a few minutes discussing how the car's set up should be changed, and she left elated with W.O.'s benediction. Even better, he volunteered to arrange transport to France for the car, and to supply an engineer and two mechanics to fettle it.

Despite Bentley's munificence, Mildred well knew she would still be incurring substantial costs, so she called on the chairman of Dunlop, one Sir George Beharrell. By this time, he was also chairman of the SMMT (Society of Motor Manufacturers & Traders), the trade body for the whole of the motor industry, so a good man to have on one's side. After hearing her plans, Beharrell told her she could not hope to do it without a co-driver. That was hardly the idea, so she left the meeting empty-handed, yet believing that she would obtain some funds from Dunlop once she broke the record.

Never one to tarry to prune her roses, only a week after the Bentley meeting she left a flu-ridden Victor at home and set off for France. In her Paris hotel, she dashed off a quick note to her mother telling her of her plans:

> Dear Mama, I'm over in Paris just about to make an attempt on the twenty-four hour record. I hope to drive the whole time myself and cover about two thousand miles in the twenty-four hours. If you buy Friday and Saturday's *Daily Sketch*, you'll be able to read all about it.

One assumes that Jennie had long ago given up expecting her only daughter to confine herself to safer pursuits such as flower arranging ...

After a somewhat exciting taxi ride from Paris (the Frenchman trying to prove he was the match for any British woman driver), she arrived at Montlhéry on 5 June 1929, with a promise to W.O. to have the car back in his hands three days later.

Clearly, driving a much heavier car unaided for twenty-four hours was a stiffer challenge than her already arduous previous records at Montlhéry in an AC. A succession of storms lasted two days before the team considered the track was dry enough to start the attempt. During the morning, Mildred conferred with Wallace ('Wally') Hassen, the Bentley engineer, planning the pit stop schedule – breaks of no more than three minutes every three hours, when fuel would be replenished and tyres and water checked.

The early morning drizzle had changed into proper rain before the intended start at noon – everyone could see that the track surface was slippery. Wally counselled a postponement but, mindful of the car's Le Mans deadline, Mildred told her team they were going ahead. The mechanics had to add three cushions to the driver's seat to enable the diminutive Mildred to see over the coaming of the beast and work its pedals. This petite English rose made an arresting sight in the racing behemoth. She was, of course, wearing her traditional garb of blouse, skirt and a twin row of pearls underneath her driving coat. 'I was a girl among five brothers, and I always tried to remain feminine,' she later said.[93]

After a few test laps she drew in, checked that the team of timekeepers was in place, had a final conference with Hassen and the two mechanics (Jack Sopp and Wally Saunders), and set off at noon into pouring rain. In this faster car, she was much nearer the top of the track's banking – only 1ft away. She could not afford to lose concentration for an instant. She later recalled, 'The principal things which one fears, in contemplating such a record attempt in advance, are sleepiness, the monotony, and a breakdown of one's physical strength.'[94]

Mildred settled into a steady rhythm of lapping at 107mph. Later analysis of the time sheets showed that, for hours on end, her lap times varied by no more than a fifth of a second – the mark of a truly expert driver. What became almost 'unendurable' after a few hours was a result of the state of the track. Montlhéry retained a rough section with an unavoidable bump – the one that had pitched Victor over on their last record attempt. With the stiffer suspension of the Bentley, this not only jarred the car's frame but also hers. It made it painful to breathe. Yet, even by the middle of the night she was averaging 105mph – easily enough for her to gain the record (which stood at just over 72mph for the twenty-four hours).

It was at night-time when the feeling of loneliness was most acute and her mind started to wander, 'I often compared the car and myself with some poor little lonely asteroid following its preordained orbit in illimitable space, with never a hope of non-disastrous contact with other occupants of the firmament.'[95] However, on her sixteenth hour, just before dawn when the human body is naturally its most somnolent, she dozed and nudged the barriers. The change in engine note woke her with a start. She headed into the pits for some water and for the car to be checked. After she had hopped out of the Bentley, she grabbed a bottle of mineral water on the pit wall, and took a swallow. She gagged – the bottle had been filled with petrol rather than water. One of her mechanics, seeing her distress, slapped her hard on the back and she regurgitated most of it, but it was fifteen minutes before the doctor considered her fit enough to resume her driving. The taste of petrol lingered for weeks thereafter.

This delay threatened her schedule, so she cancelled her last pit stop and drove for six hours at a stretch. The end could not come quickly enough. By the time the second noon came round, Mildred had driven 2,164 miles, averaging 89.57mph – she had improved on the previous record by more than 23 per cent. Banging into the circuit's bump every lap for twenty-four hours left a painful souvenir – 'it was almost a week before I could walk comfortably again'.[96]

This was an amazing achievement that garnered immediate widespread plaudits. Again, Malcolm Campbell was effusive in his praise. Earl Howe had found time to slip away from his job as Junior Lord of the Treasury to come down and watch the day's proceedings (and to take his steed to Le Mans). Impressed by what he had witnessed, he invited her to lunch in Paris. After the meal, he told Mildred he was proposing her for honorary life membership of the British Racing Drivers' Club (BRDC), of which he was president). This was a most serious accolade since the BRDC was, and remains, the preserve of the best in British motor racing. Rather uncharitably, Mildred dozed off as Howe was trying to impart this good news.

Returning to the embrace of the *patronne* of Chateau Montlhéry, Madame Patrice, she retired to her room after a snack, sleeping for two full days. By the time she awoke, the status of women back home had improved further. On 8 June 1929, Ramsay MacDonald appointed Margaret Bondfield as Minister of Labour – the first woman to join the British Cabinet.

On Mildred's return to Britain she went to see Beharrell again.[97] He was full of bonhomie, and asked her to take an envelope from his secretary on her way out. When she opened it later, a cheque for £1,000 dropped out – Mildred's hunch had been correct. The Dunlop cheque did not bounce.

There was a celebratory dinner in London and the audience was astonished when W.O. Bentley was so moved that he broke his lifelong habit of not making speeches.

Later in the month Woolf Barnato invited her to accompany him in the Bentley on a parade lap before the Le Mans race. This was an invitation impossible to refuse and she stayed to watch the race itself. Although 'her' Bentley sadly retired after just seven laps, Barnato and Tim Birkin won the event in another machine, and Bentley made a clean sweep of the top four positions.

Seeking to exploit his engineering skills and contacts, on 15 August 1929 Victor incorporated the business of Bruce & Holroyd Ltd as 'general, marine and aeronautical engineers, and experimenters in and exhibitors of aeroplanes, flying machines, motor boats, aeronautics, and aerial navigation'. J.S. Holroyd was a marine engineer who lived at Farnham, Surrey, near the Bruces' Esher home.

Kaye Don, Brooklands racer and speedboat driver who went on to gain the world water speed record in 1931, beat Mildred's Channel time, taking the record down to ninety minutes. Mildred did not find it in her heart to award him her trophy, claiming he had a larger boat, but it spurred her into borrowing a similar boat (a freshly varnished Chris-Craft with a 200hp engine), and on 19 August she attempted to improve her cross-Channel powerboat record.[98] She brought the return journey time down to seventy-three and a half minutes.[99] Afterwards, she dropped a comment to a journalist that was Mildred at her headline-creating best, 'In future when I want to cross the Channel I shall use my speedboat in place of the Channel steamers, which are push carts by comparison.'

Then she thought she might replicate her twenty-four-hour land record on the water. The 'Blue Riband' was then held by Cunard's liner, RMS *Berengaria* (its flagship before the original RMS *Queen Mary* entered service in 1936). In a David versus Goliath challenge, Mildred borrowed two

23ft powerboats from Hubert Scott-Paine. (She had been introduced to this entrepreneur and marine racer by her racing acquaintance, Sir Henry O'Neal de Hane Segrave.) Scott-Paine's British Power Boat Company had built the *Miss England* for Segrave's attempt on the outright water speed record. He had also founded Supermarine Aviation, which of course went on to build the Spitfire.

She took Scott-Paine's boats to the Solent, where the sea conditions could be expected to be more benign than those in the Atlantic endured by the *Berengaria*. Having decided on a 3½-mile oval course, she set off from Hythe Pier at 6.20 p.m. on Thursday evening. This proved inopportune timing, given the number of liners sailing out of Southampton Docks towards her. She carried on through the night, but in the darkness came to a sudden halt with a dead engine. As she drifted helpless, a liner steamed towards her, and in the end only missed her by yards. Her support crew arrived to tow her back. She had assumed the attempt was over, but Scott-Paine encouraged her into the reserve boat to start another twenty-four-hour stint. The weather was perfect, and she achieved 694 miles in her night and day – scraping past the *Berengaria*'s record by 4 miles.

In November, the peripatetic Brancker went north to visit one of the most important projects in British civil aviation – the construction of the R101 airship. Brigadier General the Right Honourable Lord Thomson of Cardington, as newly appointed Secretary of State for Air in 1924, had initiated the airship programme, whereby the R101 would be built by the state and the R100 by a private consortium. They were intended to provide a new and faster than sea form of travel to India, and strengthen links with that part of the Empire. This would be underlined by Thomson going on a return trip to India and returning to London in time for the Imperial Conference on 20 October 1930, where the delegates were to discuss air power.

As 1930 approached, the Bruces' motoring outlook had become more complicated. They were in a quandary – the AC car company was still in receivership. So, for the 1930 Monte Carlo Rally Mildred started from Sundsvall in Sweden in a purple, cream and silver Hillman Straight Eight. (Later she liked to claim that Billy Rootes, chairman of the Hillman Company, had employed her as a professional driver.)

The departure point, halfway up Sweden's east coast, gave them a run of more than 2,100 miles, which had to be accomplished in ninety-three hours. It was not long after their night-time departure from Sundsvall that Mildred skidded on an icy hill and the Hillman bounded over rocks into the forest. Repaired overnight, more ice and fog attended the Hillman's run to Paris via the ferry at Helsingborg, and thence to Hamburg. There were more than 100 entrants for the 1930 Monte, but Mildred was the first Briton and first woman to arrive at Monaco. She finished the rally twenty-first out of eighty-seven cars.

The Bruces were back in the UK for the Easter meeting at Brooklands, one of the most important in its calendar. At 8.00 on the Friday morning, a maroon was fired from the far banking and fifty-nine drivers sprinted to their cars to start the Double-Twelve meeting – so called because the local neighbours prevented night racing and hence a twenty-four-hour race was impossible. So, two twelve-hour races were held over one weekend. The betting was intense. The Bentleys were favourites and soon confirmed the punters' faith, lapping consistently at more than 90mph, horns blaring on the banking as they sought to encourage the smaller, slower cars to descend to a more righteous and lowly path on the turns. After three hours, the Bruces were doing well, in their 'unobtrusive' green car (a Silver Eagle Alvis), at an average of over 80mph, and only 17 miles behind the leading Bentley.

The public watched Mildred cornering very skilfully in her Alvis, but she then had to slow due to valve trouble. It started raining just after midday and a hail shower made life even more uncomfortable for the exposed drivers. After seven hours, the troop of Bentleys demoted the Bruces to fifth.

A Riley overturned trying to avoid a slower car, and the driver slithered from the upturned vehicle unhurt, but at four minutes to seven on the Friday evening, in an instant, a greater disaster unfolded. Six cars of varying speeds were coming down the finishing straight in a gaggle. The leading Talbot, driven by Colonel Rabagliati, suddenly braked and swerved. A similar machine, driven by Hebeler, caught its tail, ripping off its front axle and causing it to somersault. Rabagliati's machine went over the kerb and through iron railings, killing its mechanic (Edward Ellery) and a spectator (F.R. Hurworth, who had come all the way from Ashford to meet his maker). Hebeler escaped with a small cut to his face and his mechanic was somehow unhurt. The colonel was seriously injured, and there were eleven other casualties. The third car in the Talbot team retired in sympathy.

The race continued for another three-quarters of an hour to end an exhausting and distressing day. Race organisers rightly judged that ending the race prematurely would have caused a stampede for the exit that would have prevented the ambulances from taking the injured to hospital.[100]

Saturday dawned dry and warm. Thirty-eight cars had survived to start again. At 100mph on the Railway Straight a wheel hub fractured on Earl Howe's Bugatti. It slithered to a halt and Howe sprinted back to the pits for a bucket of tools and spares. He rebuilt his car at the side of the track and recovered to go on to win his class. HRH Prince George arrived in the afternoon and toured the pits of the Bentley Boys.

Just before 4 in the afternoon the heavens opened again and conditions became very treacherous, but the weather relented an hour or so before the end of the race at 8 p.m. Victor and Mildred ended thirteenth out of thirty finishers in their Alvis, the race being won by the iconic Woolf Barnato and Clement in their Bentley.

However, Mildred preferred rallying and record-breaking to motor racing, for one simple reason – the major racing clubs were set against ladies competing in the same races as men. Mildred wanted to pit her skills directly against men so only the arenas of rallying and record-breaking would suffice. In May Mildred was back on the water off Hampshire. She shared a 24ft 'hydrocar' with Mr W. Brooke, the designer of its 100hp engine. Together they created a new British record of 174 miles in six hours – 28mph. But, there was never the same intensity of emotion in her writing about deeds on the water. It was simply a means to break more records and to extend her celebrity.

Mildred had now done powerboat racing, female motor-racing drivers had become more commonplace and so Mildred needed to raise her sights to the skies.

WOMAN ON A MISSION: FAIRY TALE AND FACT

The peculiar genius of our race has always manifested itself in strange new enterprises where the individual stood uninspired save by the spirit of adventure.

Oswald Mosley, former wartime pilot and recently elected MP, in a speech on the Aerial Navigation Bill in 1919.

The charming story of how Mildred fell into becoming a pilot and flying around the world is portrayed by her as happenstance. In her two books covering the subject, *Nine Lives* and *The Bluebird's Flight*, she tells the tale:

> Arriving in London about 12 o'clock, and, having an hour to spare with nothing to do before lunch, I parked the car and walked down Burlington Gardens towards Regent Street. As I strolled along, I noticed in a shop window a little aeroplane called 'Bluebird' with a ticket on it bearing the words 'Ready to go anywhere'. It was painted a pretty blue and silver and seemed so neat.

She walked past and entered a 'frock shop' to try something on, but decided it did not suit her. With forty-five minutes still to spare, she returned to the showroom and noticed that the aircraft was now festooned with a 'Honeymoon Model' sign. Its price was £550, with an extra £5 for chrome handles.

'Could one fly around the world in this?' she asked the 'charming' salesman.

'Oh, madam ... easily,' he replied with an assurance that belied his ignorance.

In her books, she described how Victor was late home for dinner that night. This gave her time beforehand to take out her *Times Atlas* and study it. She began to plot a route around the world and included New Albany in Indiana, the birthplace of her mother, who had left there forty-two years earlier. Two days later, she went to visit her mother to explain her plans. After some initial hesitation and heartache, Jennie, long separated from her husband, blessed the project and reached into her desk to give her daughter a Stars & Stripes flag to drop on her old house. Two days after that, Mildred returned to the salesroom and bought the Bluebird.

Now the owner of an aircraft but not yet with the skills to fly it, she visited the Air Ministry breezily to discuss her plans for a round-the-world flight. Then, as now, the main issues were twofold – circumventing diplomatic and bureaucratic hurdles, and finding the least unfavourable weather. While it may not have been explained to her in quite these terms by the men from the Ministry, she would have to fly through the Intertropical Convergence Zone (ITCZ) – the nasty confluence of airstreams from the northern and southern hemispheres. (The Ministry was to go on and provide a sheaf of sixty-nine pages of weather briefing.) A departure from the UK in winter was clearly not a good idea, but on the other hand, no pilot would want to fly through the monsoon season in Asia, when the problems of the ITCZ are at their most severe. The ideal date was therefore suggested as the beginning of October – only eleven weeks hence.

The roving aristocrat bought a bundle of maps at Stamford's (or the AA – the two books differ), and when Victor saw them spread over the dining table, he said, 'That's settled it; now you will jolly well have to go!' It was three weeks before she found time to arrange any flying lessons. She sent the Bluebird back to Brough (the headquarters in East Yorkshire of its manufacturer, Blackburn Aircraft) to have an additional fuel tank fitted in the spare seat in the cockpit. Mildred writes that two days later she followed suit, asking the chief instructor for flying lessons. Due to their workload with providing training for the RAF, he said he could not oblige for a fortnight. '"That's no good," I said [with characteristic melodrama]. "I shall be flying around the world in a fortnight".' He deferred to his boss, 'A daft lass has arrived and says she wants to learn to fly because she's flying around the world in a fortnight.' (The boss was Norman Blackburn, one of the brothers who founded the firm). How could he refuse? 'I'm only against you breaking your neck,' he went on.

'That day I had my first lesson in flying, and at the end of the week I went solo.'

It made a great yarn, but does not ring true. Did Mildred really buy her Bluebird and learn to fly on a whim?

Let us take a few steps back. The vast tract of grass on the infield of Brooklands made an ideal landing ground for aircraft. From the birth of aviation, the symbiosis between cars and aircraft was complete: many aficionados liked the technology, speed and danger of both. The first public flying demonstration at Brooklands took place in autumn 1909, shortly after it opened – Ethel Locke King, the wife of the Brooklands' owner, was a passenger of Louis Paulhan in his Henri Farman biplane. By 1911 the aeroplanes were attracting more people than the racing cars.

Even when Mildred was still in her teens, for the *haute monde* it was almost as imperative to take at least one flight with a dashing aviator as to have their portrait painted by a luminary. Moreover, Mildred's novella, *The Peregrinations of Penelope*, had been published earlier in 1930. A compendium of her short stories, which had been previously published in the *Daily Sketch*, it is a barely disguised account of her life thus far. It starts with the heroine learning to drive, 'If I don't rush it, I'll have to change speed, and as I'm sure to foozle the gears, we shall probably run backwards down the hill!'. Penelope is then given a motorboat as a twenty-first birthday present. The final saga is that she learns to fly, obtains her licence a week later and, enjoying the fashions of flying suits, is lucky enough to be given a new aircraft (the fictional *Flutterby*) by her father. The notion of learning to fly had obviously been implanted in Mildred's mind for months, if not years.[101]

As we have seen, her teenage years were spent at Shoreham with young army officers taking to the skies above her. Several kinsmen to whom she was close had been keen pilots from almost the birth of the sport. Mildred had flown as a passenger twice, probably with those cousins. In November 1928, Sir Charles Wakefield (the magnate behind Castrol Oils) hosted a dinner at the Savoy in London for Bert Hinkler, the Australian who, earlier in the year, had become the first pilot to fly solo from England to Australia. Mildred was one of the guests, surrounded by the glitterati of the aviation world.[102] She had already met one of Great Britain's leading pilots of small aircraft, Colonel Sempill.

Not only had she witnessed much flying during the many weekends she had spent at Brooklands, but many of her fellow racing drivers were also pilots. Indeed in 1929, cousin Henry Petre was fervently advocating the practicality and low cost of private flying. Since he had bought his Moth, he claimed never to have used a car for a journey of more than 30 miles:

One weekend in July I was asked to go and stay with some friends in Gloucestershire, 100 miles by road from London (in the motoring days

I have often done the trip by car, and the best time I have ever done it in is four hours). Now on the Saturday in question I left the RAF Club in Piccadilly at 5 p.m., had tea at Stag Lane [aerodrome], filled up my aeroplane with petrol, had a strong head wind against me all the way, and yet landed in a field near my friend's house at 7.15 p.m. That surely speaks for itself.[103]

Although Mildred was no doubt a faster driver than her cousin, it would have been music to her ears.

Civil aviation had doubled in size in Great Britain in 1929. The home of the Motor Show, Olympia, had hosted an International Aeronautical Exhibition that July. The monocled, but far from monocular, Sefton Brancker had received an unsigned letter at the beginning of the year, soliciting his help. Typically, he went to great lengths to find its author. It was a 22-year-old secretary in an advertising agency. The Director of Civil Aviation never refused a meeting to those who requested one. After seeing her, he put the girl in touch with Lord Wakefield of Castrol Oils, who funded her aircraft.

By May 1930 Great Britain was gripped by the flight to Australia of Yorkshire secretary and copywriter, Amy Johnson. She reached Darwin on 24 May after twenty days of adventure, and the newspapers went wild. Her parents' house in Hull was deluged with fan mail. Songs were written about her. The prime minister, Ramsay MacDonald, sent a telegram of congratulations; the king cabled, 'The Queen and I are thankful and delighted to know of Miss Johnson's safe arrival in Australia and heartily congratulate her upon her wonderful and courageous achievement. George RI'. Amy was awarded a CBE in the Birthday Honours of 3 June.

Mildred took to heart the thoughts of one of her mentors, the pre-eminent racing driver and record-breaker, Sir Henry Segrave. After breaking the World Land-Speed Record in 1929, the patrician had confided to her that he thought 'the development of speed lay above ground rather than on it'.[104] According to Victor, Amy's flight to Australia had demonstrated that:

Neither the danger nor difficulty of long distance flying was sufficient to debar women from participation in it. Up to that time my wife had a definite premonition, or so she called it, that disaster would attend her entry into the ranks of airmen, or airwomen.

It is clear that Victor realised her thoughts had been skyward for some time.

Finally, there is Victor himself. Among his other engineering training, he had worked on aero engines in the First World War. He had also included aeronautical engineering in the ambit of the firm he had jointly created in

1929. The feats of aviation pioneers would have been a frequent topic at the Bruces' dinner table in Esher.

And what were Mildred's career options in 1930? In terms of her career behind the wheel, she had competed in the Monte Carlo Rally again in January, finishing twenty-first out of eighty-seven finishers. On the weekend of 19 May she competed in the JCC Double-Twelve Race at Brooklands with Victor in an Alvis Silver Eagle, coming third in the class. She must have been thinking there were few endurance records left to seek, and as for racing – it had lost its initial allure, and anyway Brooklands was edging towards the margins of European motorsport. Further, directly influencing her likely income, Bentley – her racing car of choice – had just closed down its racing activities.

That £550 price of the Bluebird (without chrome handles!) represented 2.8 times the average annual income in the UK that year. While Mildred was pondering buying an aircraft in the summer of 1930, unemployment had risen in the first year of the new Labour Government by 64 per cent, standing at 1.9 million. By December it had swelled to 2.5 million.

The Brooklands Aero Club had been founded by the Brooklands Automobile Racing Club (BARC) a month earlier, and held its inaugural air display on Saturday, 17 May. The club's objective was 'to provide cheap flying for qualified pilots' – a Gipsy Moth was on offer for £2 per hour. HRH Prince George (later the Duke of Kent) was made an honorary member. At this display, John Tranum, a Dane, parachuted from a Bluebird piloted by Norman Blackburn. He landed on his appointed spot in the middle of the aerodrome – a better performance than a previous display when he had managed to land in the infamous Brooklands sewage farm (as immortalised in the film *Those Magnificent Men in their Flying Machines*, which showed a fictionalised account of early Brooklands flying activities). Mildred had participated in the Double-Twelve Race which started at Brooklands only two days later, so this may have been the first time she saw a Bluebird aircraft.

So, there was a certain inevitability if Mildred wanted to continue her path to fame and fortune – she *had* to learn to fly and carry out some daring flights. Amy Johnson landed in Darwin, on Sunday, 25 May and at teatime that day Mildred picked up the telephone and placed a call to Byfleet 436, the Brooklands School of Flying.[105] On Monday, she hopped into her AC for the short drive to her first flying lesson. Afterwards, with the elation of having made a small step towards joining the aerial sisterhood, she drove down to Esher post office to send a cable to Amy in Sydney, 'Heartiest congratulations on your marvellous endurance and skill.'

Moreover, there is conclusive proof that another aspect of the Bluebird-in-a-shop-window story was, to a large degree, fantasy. She had created the notion of a round-the-world flight *before* she passed the showroom. De Havilland – the leading British manufacturer of light aircraft at the time – wrote to the Air Ministry on 10 July, informing it that Mildred was intending a long-distance flight in one of its Puss Moths. Mildred did indeed visit the Air Ministry a week later, and confirmed at that stage that she would use a de Havilland Puss Moth.

When Mildred eventually started her epic flight, she began a new pilot's logbook. She noted, as one is bound to do, her previous flying experience. It is most unusual for a pilot to start a new logbook only forty hours into his or her flying career. The logbook covering her learning period is strangely missing. One cannot therefore verify some of her key assertions about this period in her life.

She was also mistaken about the birthplace of her eventual choice: the manufacture of all Bluebirds had been subcontracted by Blackburn to Saunders-Roe at its factory on the Isle of Wight. Blackburn was primarily a manufacturer of heavy flying boats and torpedo bombers for the Royal Navy and had no other interests in the consumer market. It had therefore delegated the marketing of the Bluebird to Auto Auctions (as its name implies, this was primarily a car dealership). When she did – later – buy a Bluebird, she would indeed have done so via the showroom of Auto Auctions in Burlington Gardens.

Another falsehood is that she learned to fly at the flying training school at Brough. As we have seen, she started her career at the Brooklands School of Flying (BSF), where she had seen so many friends fly. It was, after all, only 5 miles from her house in Esher, rather than the more than 200 miles to the East Riding of Yorkshire.

Financial help for her expedition was a necessity – she visited some motoring contacts in Coventry in a fruitless attempt to obtain sponsorship for her plans. But, with Victor's backing, she started flying in the middle of June and went solo after six lessons over the course of a week (according to her). Her instructors were Captain Duncan Davis AFC, the tall, suave managing director of the school, and George E. Lowdell, a successful air-racing pilot in Bluebirds and chief instructor by 1933.[106]

Mildred gained her licence on 26 July (oddly a Saturday), having coerced the Air Ministry into providing it only one and a half hours after she had submitted the application. A day later, Bluebird G-ABDS was registered in her name. So, she had changed horses sometime in the previous week – well after her planning of the round-the-world project was under way. It was Victor, of course, who in the end had signed a cheque for the aircraft.

The neophyte pilot celebrated her licence immediately, as almost all new pilots do, by carrying her first passenger. On Sunday she took Victor from

Brooklands to Heston (very near the current Heathrow Airport), which was handy for the office of his company, Bruce & Holroyd, at Feltham.

Proud and elated by the time she returned home that evening, Mildred belatedly realised it was time to share her plans with her parents, and only then informed her mother. Lawrence had wed Jennie when she was only 20 and Jennie had not found the transition from actress to matriarch easy: two of her five children had died before their first birthdays, and England was an alien land. Perhaps it is not a surprise that she had taken solace in the bottle. Lawrence, a quiet soul, had separated from Jennie a few years earlier. After their split, Mildred tended to communicate with her mother rather than father. The timing of this letter again contradicts the story at the beginning of this chapter, this time about the nature of any earlier discussions with her mother:

Dear Mamma,
How are you? I have taken up flying and got my wings yesterday. I am leaving for a flight around the world alone on October 1st. Hope to make a fortune ...

One can only surmise the degree to which this latest news from her adventurous and headstrong daughter sent Jennie's tipsy head into more of a spin. It seems that Mildred did not confide in her mother to the extent she would have us believe; the letter confirms that her motive for the flight was financial gain (through celebrity).

Why did she choose to buy a Bluebird? The BSF had originally purchased a Moth, but there was a surge in demand for lessons that summer, and in June (when Mildred had started her instruction) it acquired a Bluebird as well. It had the advantage of side-by-side seating and not only did this make communication with the pupil easier in a windy cockpit, but the instructor could also see what his pupil was (and was not) doing.

With this surge in interest for flying, the school flew 150 pupil hours that month and Mildred did not have enough time before her epic flight to progress to a more advanced type. Tyro (inexperienced) pilots typically feel comfortable building up their experience on types the same as, or very similar to, those in which they learned to fly. Mildred had learned in a Moth and a Bluebird (by the time she departed, her stated experience totalled eight hours on a Moth and thirty-two on a Bluebird).

Additionally, it is clear she was attracted by the space of the Bluebird's cockpit. This gave her room to fit not only a long-range fuel tank, but also a primitive radio and a dictating machine. The Bluebird was almost unique for its time in having this side-by-side arrangement. Most small aircraft of the era, including Amy Johnson's Moth, favoured a tandem layout. The Bluebird's configuration in theory carried a small penalty in terms of lower cruising speed because of the larger frontal area, and therefore higher drag. In practice this was not evident.

Mildred would have been aware that the Bluebird had already established its credentials as a suitable machine for long-distance touring – most notably by the RAF's Squadron Leader Slatter, who had flown a Bluebird back to his native South Africa in February 1929. The Bluebird also was of metal construction and had proved its robustness for operating in hostile environments. The disadvantage of this metal construction was that any damage down route would be less easily repaired by unsophisticated engineers than the Moth's wood and canvas construction.

Brancker was also aware of the Bluebird's genesis and its strengths. The day after he had dined at Rules in 1928, to found the Guild of Air Pilots & Air Navigators, he had travelled up to Hull to encourage aerodrome development. He had visited Blackburn Aircraft's headquarters at Brough and inspected its RAF flying training school, which operated the B2, a machine very similar to the Bluebird. That evening, he dined with the burghers of Grimsby trying to persuade them of the need for a municipal aerodrome.

The vivacious and sociable Brancker, who loved the company of women, took a liking to the equally sociable Jessie (Jessica) Blackburn, the wife of gruff Robert Blackburn, chairman of Blackburn Aircraft. Jessie loved the air and embraced the hospitality required of a chairman's wife. Despite Brancker being regarded as no better dancer than he was a pilot, mixing with his like was no hardship for her and the two became very firm friends.

To build her flying hours, Mildred started providing an extra wifely service – bringing Victor home by air each evening with a short flight back to Brooklands. His office was only 1,000 yards from the Hanworth Aerodrome. When he was notified she had taken off, he would walk over and she would have landed before he arrived. She also tried to cram as much cross-country experience into the few days left before her trip, visiting Bangor, Hull, Shanklin (where she and Victor took part in an 'aerial pageant') and Hamble. There, she met A.V. Roe, the legendary pioneer and founder of the Avro Aircraft Company, and gave joyrides to most of his family. She was determined to fly in 'all weathers'[107] – normally a recipe for a brief life as a tyro pilot. One day, she was forced ever lower by bad weather until she had to land in a field. The long grass concealed a gulley that unfortunately wiped out the aircraft's undercarriage. The episode dented the aircraft, but not its owner's enthusiasm.

She flew the Bluebird up to Coventry to attend a luncheon at Humber Cars and meet some of the Rootes company's overseas representatives. The press reported that she had secured their help to provide Humber cars to be at her disposal at her stopping-off places around the world. More likely, she was trying to procure some sponsorship money.

How keen was Mildred to court publicity? On 23 July – i.e. before she had received her licence – she invited reporters to her home to brief them about her ambitions. Sensibly, she did not commit herself to a specific destination:

> I am keeping details of the project secret. All I can say at present is that I am preparing for a very ambitious flight within the next month or so. I shall be flying alone. In about six weeks' time I hope to leave, but I positively refuse to say where I shall be aiming for.

The headlines therefore referred to a 'mystery flight'.

She was planning to fly to Australia by the route that was becoming well-worn and had been used by Amy Johnson, then north to Japan via Hong Kong and Korea.[108] Here, the aircraft would be shipped across the Pacific and then she would fly across North America, down the eastern seaboard from New York to the Caribbean. Thence to Dakka (*sic*), returning to London via west Africa.

Attitudes to women risking their lives in aerial adventures were still very ambivalent. In 1927 an American starlet, Ruth Elder, had determined she would become the first woman to fly the North Atlantic. She asked her instructor, George Haldeman, to accompany her. Falling oil pressure caused them to ditch alongside a Dutch tanker 360 miles north of the Azores. They made it to Europe in the ship. The *Belfast Irish News* commented afterwards:

> A woman had no business to attempt such a flight. It was perfectly ridiculous to read of this young person's chatter, of her preparations for the event: her vanity bag, Chinese ring, knickerbockers and red and black four-in-hand tie and pastel-shaded band over dark brown hair, and to remember that she was going to risk her life just to gratify her stupid vanity. She is a married woman. Her husband wisely remained at home. If Ruth has any sense she will join him now and keep house for him.

It had become the habit for many pilots, particularly women, to name their steeds. For example, Amy Johnson had flown to Australia in a Moth she had christened *Jason* (an abbreviation of the name of her father's fishery business in Hull). For Mildred, reporters and photographers were unsurprisingly on

hand as she posed with paintbrush, pretending to inscribe the name 'Bluebird'
on her Bluebird's nose. It may be assumed that she was completely lacking in
originality in choosing that name. However, it is more likely that she chose it
in honour of one of her heroes, Malcolm Campbell (knighted the following
year), who used that name for all his racing cars and speedboats. (He, in turn,
had chosen it because he had been deeply impressed by the play *Bluebird*,
by the Belgian poet Maurice Maeterlinck, which he had seen in 1911 at
the Theatre Royal in London's Haymarket. He dashed round to his local
ironmonger and bought up its supplies of blue paint, and promptly renamed
his racing car, which until then had rejoiced in the unsuitable name of *The
Flapper*.) He, in fact, christened a D.H. Moth aircraft that he had bought in
1928 (G-AAAJ) *Bluebird*, but sold it to South Africa the following year, so
when Mildred acquired hers the British skies were devoid of 'Bluebirds'.

On 6 August 1930, Mildred attended a lunch at the Savoy Hotel hosted
by the Hon. Esmond Harmsworth of the *Daily Mail* empire (he later became
the 2nd Viscount Rothermere), who presented Amy Johnson with a cheque
for £10,000 and a gold cup from the Youth of Great Britain. Amy's convoy
to the Savoy had brought the West End to halt. Other guests were from the
top drawer of European flying – A.V. Roe, Sir Sefton Brancker, Sir Philip
Sassoon, Bert Hinkler, Louis Blériot and Winifred Spooner – together with
some very A-list celebrities – Noel Coward, Ivor Novello, Malcolm Sargent,
John Barbirolli, Alfred Hitchcock, Cecil Beaton, Evelyn Waugh and Gordon
Selfridge. Mildred's attendance was due to her motor-racing prowess but,
as a novice pilot, she was thrilled to mingle with the aviation élite. (Gordon
Selfridge, he of the department store, together with his family had become
a great fan of flying. Indeed, his daughter Violette went on a round-the-
world flight with her pilot husband in a Gipsy Moth). Mildred sat between
Selfridge and Sir William Morris, the motor car tycoon. Even the menu
feted the new heroine, including 'Coeur de Romaine Amy Johnson' and 'Délice
de Sole Jason' (after her Moth). The event strengthened Mildred's resolve to
carry out an epic flight.

A week later the Automobile Association was asking the Air Ministry to
obtain the necessary permits for Mildred's voyage, and was still referring to
a route via Australia. The Bluebird's departure date was set for 15 September,
but the inevitable last-minute irritations caused this to be deferred by ten
days. Even with Victor to assist, arranging the complex logistics of the trip
had left precious little time for what some might consider an essential – for
the pilot to learn the black arts of navigation. Having enlisted the help of a
master mariner, Mildred could only squeeze in six short lessons. These were
trying, for both parties. The old salt led her to a blackboard in his office and
drew a series of lines on it, 'Now you see those meridians?'

'Meridians?' replied Mildred, 'What are they?' ('They might have been mountains for all I knew,' she later asserted.)

She would rise at 4.00 a.m. each day to study her books, and two years later she would say, with no hint of irony, after these mental exertions 'my head became a good quarter of an inch larger, and I actually had to change my previously quite comfortable flying helmet for a larger size'.[109] Her father's preference for scientific accuracy had clearly not been inherited.

Press interest mounted in the 'mystery flight', and on 13 August the *Dundee Evening Telegraph* reported that Mildred was 'undecided whether to attempt a round the world flight or to join an expedition to the South Pole'. By 1 September, the *Daily News & Chronicle* reported that Mildred might be planning a flight to the Cape:

'I have not yet made up my mind, but it is quite likely I shall make Capetown [*sic*] my destination. Wherever I go it is my intention to lower the record for a return journey to England. The nearness of the North East monsoon puts Australia out of the question for a return journey.'

This was quite deliberate obfuscation, given her already detailed planning for a round-the-world trip. Having abandoned the notion of including Australia in her route, she advised the Ministry on 28 August that her plan was now to make for China and Japan. She rightly concluded that Australia was a well-trodden path and that she would gain little publicity from going there. More pertinently, it would have set her star directly against that of darling Amy.

While time for navigation lessons was at a premium, she did find time to keep herself in the papers by carrying a few select passengers. One such was Teddy Baldock, an East End boxer who was world bantamweight champion. Meanwhile, telegrams were flying off to overseas embassies and consulates to obtain permission for the Bluebird to land.

On 9 September, a newly promoted 24-year-old flying officer in the RAF arrived at 1 Squadron, whose motto *In Omnibus Princeps* (First in All Things) reinforced that its fighter pilots were the proudest of the proud. For young Eric Edward Noddings flying the Siskin at RAF Tangmere, life could not be sweeter. His flight path was later to cross that of Mildred's.

The Bluebird G-ABDS was flown down by a Blackburn employee from Brough to her stepping-off point at Heston (the original London Airport) on 13 September. Victor wrote, 'My wife took advantage of the opportunity to obtain experience in other machines by flying me down in a Segrave Meteor, in which we averaged 150 miles per hour. This after only a few weeks of flying!' Blackburn had taken over the manufacture of the Meteor,

named after its designer, her friend Sir Henry de Hane Segrave. He had been
a First World War RFC fighter pilot before he became distracted by motor
and speedboat racing. Sadly, Sir Henry had been unable to see his creation
fly – he had died only three months earlier, when his *Miss England II* crashed
during an attempt on the world water speed record in Lake Windermere.
His prophesy to Mildred had come to pass in the saddest way. The Meteor
(G-AAXP) was a twin-engine aircraft, a lot more complicated than the
aircraft Mildred had previously flown. There is no record of her having been
instructed on the type, and the flight was not later entered into her logbook.

Her Bluebird was fitted with a special automatic wireless set, designed to
send out one of five pre-set signals every fifteen or thirty minutes, allowing
Mildred to confirm that she was still safe – or to alert rescuers. The succinct
options were 'forced sea', 'forced land', 'trouble', 'normal landing' and 'in
flight', each prefaced with the aircraft's call-sign. As *Flight* magazine noted,
'No mechanical knowledge of wireless is necessary, as the message is sent
out by clockwork motor.' Mildred had not had time to learn the intricacies
of radio communication.

Mildred had to make another quick visit to the Blackburn factory and
returned on 22 September from Brough to Heston. Packing for a great
expedition was always going to be fraught. An Englishwoman abroad had
certain standards to maintain. Even an Englishman had to be prepared for
all exigencies: Alan Cobham, on his record-breaking flight to the Cape,
related his equipment:

> We carried in a special compartment beneath the cabin, an extra pro-
> peller, a number of small spare parts, complete photographic supplies; a
> gun, rifle, and revolver, in case we had to land in an uninhabited part of
> Africa; and, of course, emergency cooking utensils and rations. Another
> small compartment back of my cockpit was filled with sun-helmets, light
> tropical clothing, and the inevitable evening clothes without which no
> self-respecting Englishman will venture even into tropical Africa.[110]

To carry this panoply of luxuries in her Bluebird was impossible, and with
radio, extra fuel tank, her dictating machine and plenty of spare parts,
including a propeller, the poor machine was carrying a very full weight.[111]
It all added up to 2,080lb, yet the aircraft had only been certificated for
1,950lb.[112] Something had to go – the Dictaphone or the parachute. Victor,
knowing Mildred as only a husband can, advised her to ditch the parachute
'since she would not have been happy had she not been able to talk'. By
necessity, she packed light – 'a sun helmet, two light cotton frocks, one
evening dress, and the clothes I stood up in!'[113]

Amy Johnson had suffered the same agonies of what to take and what to discard. Amy wrote to her mother four days before she was due to depart with rather more girlish enthusiasm than Mildred was displaying by now:

> You won't forget the dressing gown will you? If it doesn't come, I shall be rather in the soup as after Saturday morning I can't purchase one. Maybe Daddy will bring it with him. Are you sure it's convenient to lend it to me? Has Daddy told you I'm taking a parachute … I had it fitted specially yesterday and had some photos taken in it this morning. My machine is progressing well … [114]

Mildred's defining adventure beckoned – without a parachute.

10

DEPARTING ENGLAND: DOING HER BIT

Do you know the story I brought back from Basra – a story sweeter than dates?

Sa'Di, *Bustan*, 1257.

So, after a sleepless night, the diminutive adventurer rose very early and was too nervous to eat any breakfast. Victor drove Mildred and her son to Heston through the misty dawn of 25 September. With goodness knows what emotions, Tony helped her strap in to the Bluebird. In a rare moment of emotional candour, she related that 'a terrible loneliness came upon me'. Airily, and with the foresight of the *Titanic's* navigator, she told her family, 'I hope to be back by Christmas.' But Mildred was feeling far from confident – as she took off from Heston shortly after 7 in the morning, the waving of the bystanders reminded her of a funeral. The heavily laden Bluebird climbed but slowly.

She dropped a message on to Heston's grass, which she implausibly claimed to have scribbled in the last few minutes, but its length, lyricism and thoughts indicate much work beforehand – not to mention the possible help of a public relations specialist at her elbow. It swings wildly from intimations of mortality to moments of naive over-confidence:

Sitting in this cramped cockpit and scribbling my last notes before setting out on the greatest venture of my life, I am conscious of a great peace.

Away in front, fingers of mist wreathe the trees making them appear ghost-like, and there is a subdued mutter of talk from the mechanics who are putting the finishing touches to the Bluebird. For weeks past I have lived in a whirl. Plans, maps, distances – figures that danced like motes in a sunbeam. Oh! The advice I have received. Words, arguments, pouring over me like a cascade! Discussions of weight, loads, petrol capacity and a hundred and one details!

Bluebird carries 80 gallons of petrol, sufficient for a 'hop' of a little more than 1000 miles. Will that prove enough if I meet with headwinds over Burmese jungles? As it is I have had to jettison 10 precious gallons in order to carry the latest wireless device. There it is within a foot of my hand. A switch when turned to the right sends out automatically my code number followed by 'OK'. I shall hear nothing, but all the while my husband and my friends will have news of my progress. If trouble comes away ahead in that greyness I shall reverse that switch, and then the message becomes an SOS. The thought gives me a twinge, the sort of sudden spasm that comes when a boxer steps over the ropes to face his opponent. No good thinking of that now! How the minutes crawl!

I thought I had got inured to adventure, but I haven't. There was the time when I drove a 4½ litre Bentley on an ice-covered track for 24 hours, covering more than 2,000 miles at 90 mph. A sticky business that!

On another occasion my husband and myself spent 10 days and nights at the wheel – he being my relief [*sic*] driver. Then that ghastly moment when we rocked, skidded, half-straightened, and then turned over. Sliding upside down on a sheet of ice, and in a smother of snow! Death at your elbow! Somehow one never thinks of death as something concrete. Usually because at the critical moment there is not time. The worst part of it is waiting for the gong. Like going over the top when enemy machine gunners have you taped to an inch! So much easier when you are racing forward, doing something.

Will there be a crash on this greatest of ventures – somewhere in the jungle or plains where my poor little SOS cannot help!

At Montlhéry I had the roaring drone of my engine in my ears day and night, just as I shall have it now. Someone said 'fifteen days to Japan' – that's humanly possible, but I'll get as near to it as I can. With luck it will be the first solo flight to Japan, but if I do as well as Amy Johnson I will be proud. With only six weeks flying behind me it's a bit of a risk. Then there is the whole hour of flying time absorbed by the weight of the wireless gadget; but the machine is ready to the last split pin, and I believe my luck will hold.

It is the adventure that matters, not the details. Almost certainly the worst part of the trip will be the 660 miles between Shanghai and Hiroshima, 500 miles of that clean out of sight of land. Just enough juice to do the trick so long as there are no strong headwinds.

The first part should be easy enough – nowadays almost a highway to the clouds. Across Europe to Constantinople, over the Taurus Mountains of Asia Minor, then Baghdad and on to Karachi. Forward over the plains of India to Calcutta. The meteorologists have told me that I shall meet the tail end of the monsoon. Even so, I do not think there should be much trouble. The second half is by far the worse – from Calcutta to Rangoon, then Hong Kong, Shanghai and over the China Sea.

Bluebird is loaded down till her cruising speed is only between 85 and 90 miles per hour and in some parts of Burmah [*sic*] we shall have to feel our way between the passes if the clouds are low. It is not pleasant to think of a forced landing a hundred miles from anywhere – but I do not feel it will come to that.

Behind me my 'iron rations' have been packed tightly in little tins. So little of it, and yet enough if all goes well! Biscuits, chocolate, a flask of brandy – anyway I shall not have time to eat much.

It will be like watching the map of the world unroll between my feet, flying into the rising sun. Each morning the start will be made at dawn, and I am praying that there will be no mishaps such as a broken propeller or a smashed undercarriage to delay me. There are many fields for women to conquer yet. This is one of them. I am out to do my bit in this age of record-breaking and record-making.

A mechanic is shouting something. Contact? Yes, contact. The engine splutters into life, roars up full 'revs', and then ticks over like a giant watch. Beautiful. Four minutes to go, and then …

In spite of a leather helmet and coat I am cold. Nerves! This time tomorrow I shall be up to the Golden Horn. This time next week, either far on the way to successor – well, it is no use thinking of failure. Now that the last moment has come somehow I do not feel in the least anxious. It will be the greatest fun in the world.

After Japan flying across America to New York and then maybe down to the West Indies. Hullo! Time's up. They are signalling to me. Cheerio England! All clear … [115]

It must have been a blessed relief to leave the days of frenetic planning behind, but a touch of guilt about leaving Victor and Tony; apprehensive about the danger, both known and unknown, yet at the same time relishing the adventure to come, the scale of the task now weighed heavily.

Victor 'stood on the ground watching the little machine growing tinier in the distance until it finally disappeared, I cheered'.[116] Rarely effusive, he was so overcome with emotion that it was eight hours before he was to speak again.

At Heston the weather was reasonable, but by the time she was flying over Croydon half an hour later, the clouds had lowered. Her mood was sombre, but 'by the time the English Channel hove in sight I had cheered up a little'. Her previous cross-country experience had, of course, been limited to trips within the UK, and murky weather would still weaken her resolve. There was only so much she could plan and even she realised that the Bluebird's journey would depend a lot on the vagaries of the weather. So, on her Croydon customs form she airily gave her destination as 'Nurnberg, Vienna or Buda Pesth [*sic*]'.

While heading generally in the direction of the Austro-Hungarian Empire, her very simple radio fused over the Channel – a small problem, but one that made her worry what would break next. Laden with all her fuel and equipment, the Bluebird could cruise at only 75mph, so any headwinds made progress difficult. Fortunately, the wind was ushering her onwards for this first leg of her epic. Flying over Brussels, she adopted her primary navigation technique – IFR, as in 'I Follow Roads [or Rivers, or Railways]'.

In this case, it was 'I Follow the Rhine'. After Frankfurt, the Rhenish rain and low cloud caused tremors of fear in the inexperienced pilot. Mildred turned back for Frankfurt, where she waited for the poor weather to clear. By the time she made a landing at Munich (instead of Vienna, her original ambition), it was almost dusk. Six hours and ten minutes' flight in an open-cockpit biplane, exposed to the elements, requires no little stamina, and her petite frame had yet to adjust to the rhythms of long days.

In exultation at completing this first day satisfactorily, she phoned Victor – with a bad line, and sceptical of her expertise, he thought she was calling from somewhere in Kent! Besieged by journalists for the first time on the trip, she revealed some of the tension caused by her inexperience and mechanical problems:

> I was given a weather report which turned out to be incorrect. I had to fly over some hills in which I became hopelessly lost. When I found my bearings again, I was alarmed to detect a smell of petrol, and on landing I found that the front petrol tank had sprung a leak, and that petrol was leaking within half an inch of the exhaust pipe. My misadventure in the hills, which at one time began to look rather serious, delayed me by an hour and a half. I was flying in heavy rain, and for some twenty miles I couldn't see anything.[117]

If the problems were as Mildred described, she had already had her first brush with death, since she could easily have been incinerated in moments. The fuel tank was repaired by Imperial Airways staff overnight.

Much to her irritation, the press were inevitably matching Mildred's progress with Amy Johnson's achievements – Amy had made Vienna on her first day, but her technical problem had been noxious petrol vapour every time she pumped the tanks. Less than an hour after Mildred left Munich the clouds lowered again and she was flying in heavy rain – for a pilot with ostensibly so little experience, she was coping very well. Now fixed, the radio was used to send a 'flying in trouble' message to Victor and her followers. Very rattled by these misty conditions, she managed to find the River Danube, which led her, bumped around by mountain turbulence, to Vienna.

On 27 September it was a case of Viennese pastries for breakfast, Hungarian goulash for lunch in Budapest, and then a 'lonely dinner' in Belgrade. Her next target was Constantinople, or 'Stamboul', as she called it. Revelling in having escaped the clammy and cold northern European weather, the hazards of her navigation and low-flying techniques were brought into sharp relief when, following a railway line up the Dragoman Pass in Bulgaria, she almost flew into a tunnel. For the next hour she circled, trying to persuade *Bluebird* to clear the pass. It was just before nightfall when the aircraft touched Turkish soil at Istanbul's aerodrome in the suburb of San Stefano.

Bureaucracy – the bane of the lone flyer – reared its ugly head for the first time, and delayed her obtaining an exit visa at Istanbul. The Turks would not allow any further landings in their country, 'All our aerodromes are secret!'. In her dream world, Mildred had been oblivious to political sensitivities along her route and, for Turkey, political stability was still just an aspiration.

An unfortunate oil leak meant she had to return to Istanbul. By now she had negotiated to land at Angora (Ankara) but, failing to spot the airfield, she instead latched on to a sports field – unluckily full of sportsman. Undeterred by such trifles, Mildred soon dispersed them by dropping a smoke bomb in their midst! (These inoffensive weapons were carried to drop before an off-airfield landing so as to show the wind direction.) Once she had landed, a rather brusque military escort took her to the local governor, whom she charmed into providing some hospitality by claiming she had flown all this way just to see him.

The governor alerted staff at her next halt, Eski-shehr, thereby ensuring a five-star welcome there from its commandant. Eski-shehr was 120 miles south-east of Istanbul, yet required almost ten hours in the air. Her flights must have been very circuitous, as in these last two flights she took seventeen hours to fly a direct route of only 600 miles. Perhaps the Bluebird had a tendency to fly in circles …

Mildred had a very, very close shave on the next leg en route to Aleppo (still in Amy's footsteps). The governor had warned her to turn back if there was any bad weather rather than try to overfly the Taurus Mountains, which rise to nearly 10,000ft. She carried on into much turbulence, claiming later, with her usual British understatement, that the wind was blowing with 'hurricane force'. Flying at only 500ft above the ground and while trying to clean oil from her windscreen the Bluebird entered a spin. She finally recovered only 20ft (in her melodramatic judgement) above the ground. Somewhat rattled, she landed in open country on a great plateau at Konia before her fuel ran out. A two-and-a-half-hour hitchhike on a peasant's wagon saw her in Konia looking for fuel. The town had been the scene ninety-eight years earlier of the Ottoman Empire's defeat by Egyptian invaders. But now it was a political hotspot – the local high priest, the *Chelebi*, had been wielding too much power for the liking of Mustafa Kamal, Turkey's autocratic leader.[118]

Mildred was again warmly welcomed by Konia's governor, with whom she conversed in French. He presented a craggy old fellow, '*Voici l'homme le plus agé du monde*', and then a Turkish Air Force general awarded her a decoration. She spent the night at his mother's house while the Bluebird enjoyed an armed guard out in the desert.

With more petrol aboard, Mildred again had fuel problems on her next leg: gauges were crude in those days, but her planning had been hopelessly optimistic. Her maps for central Turkey were devoid of useful detail, and 60 miles short of Aleppo she landed in the Syrian Desert. In her quest for fuel she had no option but to hop up on a horse behind the tribal chief, who demanded her water supplies. An Armenian trader extorted some money – and then more – and eventually almost £5 secured only four rusty tins of petrol. The chief became even more difficult and she was rescued by some military horsemen who restored Mildred's faith in humanity once back at their outpost.

It was 2 October when Mildred flew from Konia to Aleppo. The day before, after R101 had had an incomplete and less than convincing trial, Air Vice Marshal Sir William Sefton Brancker KCB, Director of Civil Aviation, dug into his reserves of courage and took his doubts about the safety of the airship to his superior, Lord Thomson. The Labour minister 'was usually polite, even courteous in manner. But he was not always pleasant.' He presented Brancker with a gut-wrenching ultimatum, 'If he was afraid to go in the airship, plenty of men would be glad to take his place.'

Brancker dictated a letter to his secretary for Mildred (it is not clear when this message was intended to be transmitted, since Brancker would have been expected to be out of communications for several days):

Hearty congratulations on a very fine flight. You must have had a most interesting journey. Your enterprise will be a fine example to other people in this country to do likewise.

   If we can persuade the sportsmen and sportswomen of Great Britain to travel to every country in the world in their own aircraft, we shall be establishing goodwill everywhere and proving the high standard of British aeroplanes and engines to everybody. Tomorrow I am off to India on the R101.

   The very best of luck to you.[119]

It was Brancker who needed the very best of luck. By the middle of August 1930, the R100 had made a successful Atlantic crossing, but the R101 was being bodged (not too harsh a word in the circumstances) in an effort to produce a half efficient machine and had made only a handful of small flights around the UK – in good weather conditions. However, political considerations were coming to the fore. Thomson's airship programme had cost £2.5 million with little tangible benefit so far. Thomson had to reach his conference in India, so the big flight had to go ahead. Brancker tried to lighten his mood by taking his mistress, Auriol, and some friends to see the hugely popular *Bitter Sweet* at the theatre once again. Afterwards, he introduced his party to the cast backstage – Brancker's connections with the stage were as strong as with airmen.

   Friday, 3 October saw Mildred trying to sort out her machine and her onward route. In London, Brancker took Auriol and Sir Alan & Lady Cobham out to dinner. Afterwards he confided in Auriol that he 'hardly expected to come out of the ship alive'.

   On Saturday Brancker slipped into his London office to clear his in-tray. The aerodrome officer at Lympne, Lieutenant Commander S. Deacon RN retd, called in to see him and was worried by the change in the great man. He had never seen him less than self-assured. Brancker dropped his monocle, now 'he was fidgety; he fingered the ornaments upon the mantelpiece. His manner was noticeably different.' Deacon, like Brancker, had flown with the Royal Flying Corps in the First World War and could recognise the signs of inner turmoil.[120]

   At least Brancker had not given himself any spare time to dwell on his forebodings. Another of his protégés was Winifred Spooner, an air racer and rising star who had just returned from representing Great Britain in an international rally in Germany. Brancker had taken to her, and also taken to using her as an aerial chauffeur. After seeing Deacon, Brancker was flown by Spooner up to Norwich for lunch with its aero club. Afterwards, the duo flew to RAF Henlow, as no aircraft were permitted within 3 miles of Cardington while the R101 was hanging like a hooked whale from its mast.[121]

Meanwhile, in the Middle East, Mildred was hoping to make Baghdad. On the flight down, the lake at Habbaniya was difficult to miss. It marked the beginning of the zone of British influence. A string of safe havens were stretched out to her right – basic aerodromes set up to protect the oil lines in Iraq. Following the Tigris to Baghdad, even the overweight *Bluebird* managed to overtake the black *guffas* (melon boats) down the river. Mildred missed the capital first time around, due to a dust storm, but landed to a great reception at the RAF base, where a long drink of iced lemonade revitalised her to do a short hop over the city to the civil aerodrome.

At her hotel that night there was no time to slip into the warm waters of the Tigris for a quick dip. She hurried to dinner and encountered journalists who obviously wanted her story. With customary veracity, they reported that Mildred had been abducted by a sheik – causing some alarm for Victor back home when he read his morning papers!

Mildred had unwittingly now joined the 'Third Route' – Imperial Airways' link to India, which had opened only a year or two earlier. Philip Sassoon, the Aviation Minister, believed that Baghdad would inevitably become a successful tourist destination once the country had proper hotel accommodation; the wealth of its archaeology would draw as many visitors as Egypt.

For the next few thousand miles Mildred was calling at outposts of an Empire struggling to retain its ascendancy. She could not have embarked on her journey ten years later, for all the countries were at war. Another twenty years, and these countries in her Esher atlas were no longer pink. Her voyage was sweetly timed.

Major Oliver Villiers, a friend of Brancker on his staff at the Ministry of Civil Aviation, had collected Brancker's baggage and picked him up at Henlow for the drive to Cardington. Turning to his friend, Brancker made a poignant request, 'I want you to do something specially for me. Amy Johnson is in a nursing home – get her a big bunch of roses and give them to her with my love.' Since Villiers grew roses in his own garden, which the general had seen on more than one occasion, Villiers suggested that he should pick some of his own. 'Splendid!' replied Sir Sefton. 'And don't forget to give her my love.'[122]

The R101 had been granted a certificate of airworthiness despite the fact that its test flights had been very limited and had revealed problematic handling. The airship struggled to carry a worthwhile payload, and everything possible had been done to reduce the weight of its equipment.

Yet Thomson turned up at Cardington on Saturday afternoon with luggage weighing more than 1,200lb, including such imperatives as a dress
sword and a Persian carpet weighing 129lb (to be rolled out at the state
dinners his ego was to attend). There were ten passengers apart from
Thomson and Brancker, almost all senior figures in the RAF, the airship
world and civil aviation.

In fine rain and the simpering light of countless headlights from sightseers'
cars parked around the perimeter, R101 lifted sedately from Cardington at
6.36 p.m. It made its way over London and the Channel, by which time the
weather had deteriorated and the craft was fighting heavy rain and strong
south-westerly winds. Just after a crew shift change at 2 on Sunday morning, the craft entered a dive from which it failed to recover. Forty-eight of
the fifty-four souls on board – including Brancker and Thomson – were
incinerated.

Shortly after 6 a.m., Ramsay MacDonald was woken by a telephone call
telling him of news of the crash. His diary records:

> The R101 was wrecked and Thomson was not amongst the living! As
> though by the pressing of a button, confusion & gloom & sorrow came
> upon the world – was the world. So, when I bade him goodbye on Friday
> & looked down at him descending the stairs at No. 10, that was the last
> glimpse of my friend, gallant, gay & loyal. No one was like him & there
> will be none ... Why did I allow him to go? He was so dead certain there
> would be no mishap ... This is indeed a great national calamity, & today,
> I distracted in the midst of it, grieve.

Amy Johnson echoed the loss of Brancker felt by many aviators:

> I think he took a certain pride in me, as he doubtless felt – what was
> perfectly true – that it was his faith in me which led to the achievement
> of my ambitions. The more I saw of him the more I admired him for his
> terrific store of energy, his keen interest and enthusiasm for aviation, and
> amazing foresight ... I never knew anyone with such a remarkable power
> of swift action.[123]

Jessie Blackburn heard the news of her friend's death at Beauvais while driving
back to Yorkshire. The airship's wrecked and charred carcass was later recovered
from Picardy. Ironically, 5 tons of the scrap metal was later sold to Britain's
arch rival in this endeavour – Germany's Zeppelin Company. But that Sunday,
ignorant of the catastrophe that had killed her mentor, and undaunted by the

trying conditions she had experienced the day before, Mildred departed from Baghdad to Bushire, the offshore island port 500 miles away.

Soon she saw the magnificent arch of Tagh-e-Kasra at Ctesiphon, the old Parthian capital. With Babylon and then Ur off her starboard wing, she was searching less for remains of ancient temples than for the Euphrates River that would guide her way until it entered a marshy plain around the al-Hammar Lakes. The Gipsy continued its metronomic beat but the horizon became more difficult to discern. Mildred now had a nagging remembrance: it was from this swampland that a Marsh Arab had fired at Sir Alan Cobham's seaplane on his famous flight to Australia, four years earlier. Like Mildred, he too was prone to hugging the ground and he was flying at only 50ft when the single shot severed a fuel pipe. This severely wounded his mechanic, Elliott, whose white engineer's suit soon turned crimson – nonetheless, he stoutly handed Cobham a report from his cabin saying he was 'bleeding a pot of blood'. Elliott died in a hospital in the bustling port of al-Basrah (Basra) at 11.15 p.m. the following night.

Mildred alighted at lunchtime at RAF Shaibah, only 13 miles from Basrah where, only a year earlier, Sassoon had noted, 'Sinbad's city is a charming Arab Venice.' Sassoon's comments were to seem comically lyrical in the context of twenty-first-century developments.[124] Looking forward to some female company at dinner and with the temperature above 120°F in the shade, the officers of 84 Squadron were keen for her to stay overnight. Had she known what Kingsford-Smith had endured after his beers in the Officers' Mess at Shaibah only three months earlier – he had commented on the size and appetite of the bed bugs – Mildred would have been even more eager to press on.[125]

She followed the Shatt-al-Arab, with its desolate marshland of thickets of *qasab* reeds, the occasional *mudhif* house made of the self-same reeds, with dense flocks of storks rising at the noise of the Bluebird. Turning the corner of the Persian Gulf over the surf at Bandar Dilan, the coastline shepherded her, still with a bad oil leak, towards the white stone buildings of Bushire. She landed in the pungent town at 3 p.m. – it had been an exhausting day with eight hours' flying. Bushire was another staging post in Imperial Airways' route to the east. The airline's mechanics greeted her and attended to the Gipsy's oil leak; their considered advice was to wait for new crank-shaft seals to be sent out from England.

Bushire had been chosen by the Persian ruler in 1734 to become the country's principal port and naval station. Its importance was cemented twenty-five years later when the British East India Company was turfed out of Bandar Abbas by the French and relocated to Bushire. The British resident here had exercised British control over the whole of the Persian

Gulf region since 1822 but, latterly, Reza Shah had begun to extend his influence over the northern part of this territory: the political temperature was increasing.

Chatting to the current resident, her host Lieutenant Colonel H.R.P. Dickson, she asked, in her naivety, whether it was always a full moon there since it had been a full moon when she had left England. He explained that with her eastwards navigation, she was merely keeping up with it.

Had she done more than a hurried repair to her ailing engine, the following day might have been less eventful. As it was, her haste was almost to destroy the Bluebird and its pilot ...

PLENTY OF SWEAT

On 12 October, *Bluebird* was just a silver spot on the ground at Jask when Charles Kingsford-Smith, the Australian hero clad only in singlet and shorts due to the baking humidity, sped past 4,000ft above her. He was on a flight from Persia to Karachi, trying to break the record to Australia. 'Smithy' had heard of Mildred's flight and her forced landing, but later discovered she no longer needed assistance and so flew on.

He knew all about being marooned in dire straits. Two years earlier, on a flight to England from his native Australia (to research new aircraft), the crew had become lost in bad weather, ran out of fuel and force landed on a mudflat in Western Australia. Surviving on little more than mud snails, hemmed in by crocodiles and attacked by flies, the three aviators were rapidly losing strength when they were finally discovered after a fortnight. It was another four days before they could liberate *Southern Cross* from the hellhole. The sorry episode had an even sorrier epilogue: two aviators who had been searching for Smithy and crew had starved to death when they had force landed in the wilderness.

Back in England, Victor and the Air Ministry were batting off objections from the Chinese Government, which had learned that the Bluebird was carrying a radio (her original authorisation did not cover such equipment). Mildred would have been unaware, and probably dismissive, of such bureaucratic nonsense. During her enforced wait at Jask, the petite Mildred borrowed freshly laundered dresses from Murray's 14-year-old daughter. The arrival of the weekly airmail flight at Jask was always a huge event for the community, the Imperial Airways DH.66 Hercules soon mobbed by berobed locals. Its English crew and passengers brought Mildred into welcome contact with home.

The Imperial Airways flight arrival on 15 October carried the vital spares, and Wilson, the Imperial Airways engineer who had already sweated long and hard over the Bluebird, set to work to install them. Three days later, all was set for the test flight, and a two-hour flight up to the cooler heights of 8,000ft proved the worth of Wilson's work.

Then, another pioneering aviator arrived on the scene – a tired and dusty Oscar Garden. He had left England a few days earlier, bound for Australia (his family having already emigrated to New Zealand). Mildred was ready to leave the following morning, so persuaded him to stay the night and then fly in loose formation until their routes diverged. The 27-year-old Scotsman was another Brooklands pilot, and had chosen a similar route to Amy Johnson's and flew a Moth like hers. His aim on this journey was an attempt on the record to Australia, and to complete suffi-cient flying hours to gain his commercial licence. Oscar had picked up the Moth for £450 from the Aviation Department of Selfridges on London's Oxford Street. It had had one (careless) owner – Gordon Selfridge Jnr, son of the store's owner, who had crashed the poor machine into a tree.[126] Selfridge Senior, a keen espouser of light aviation, was chronicling Oscar's adventures in his house magazine.

On Saturday, 25 October back in England, the Imperial Conference on Aviation, given the R101 disaster, had proceeded in an understand-ably strained atmosphere. That day, the delegates visited Croydon Airport. The movie cameras were on the apron when Prime Minister Ramsay MacDonald arrived there from Chequers in a Fairey IIIF – a fairly crude publicity stunt. (He flew off again immediately after lunch.) Underneath his flying suit he wore a pair of plus fours 'cut with Gaelic economy'.[127] Delegates could have a brief flight in an Imperial Airways Argosy before it trundled off at 12.30 for its daily flight to Paris. The VIPs enjoyed lunch in the warmth of the Aerodrome Hotel, before venturing outside in a 'raw, cold and a very rough wind' to witness a flying display by nine of 43 Squadron's Siskin fighters. Their party trick was to fly tied together (in flights of three) before breaking the cords in a 'Prince of Wales Feathers' burst. Among the many civil and military aircraft the delegates could inspect was G-AAVG, a sister of Mildred's Bluebird.[128] The Siskins returned to their base at Tangmere in Sussex while the delegates returned to the nearest coal fire.

Mildred could at last continue her journey. The next leg would have been almost a holiday for her. Not only did she have companionship, with Oscar's Moth off her wingtip, but the navigation was easy. All the duo had to do was fly down the coast for 580 miles, keeping the mountains to their left.

Flying in to Karachi would have been a vivid olfactory experience for her.[129] As she neared Karachi's airfield, she noticed the sad reminder of the folly of the R101 project – an enormous shed built to house the airship that never arrived. She stayed in the city for two nights, with some friends rather than at the RAF base. The extra night was at the request of the local de Havilland man, who wanted to inspect her engine.

Heading off over the Indian continent, Mildred flew over the Sind Desert in the Punjab, with Jodhpur her destination. After the Sind, her route covered a region where British rule was in the process of changing the landscape and some large irrigation schemes based on the Indus River were being created. These turned the eastern fringes of the desert into 'endless vistas of wheat, cotton fields, trees and tropical vegetation of the plains'.[130] But Oscar and Mildred saw little of this as they had flown into a sandstorm, having to fly for an hour on instruments with no visual references – again, a challenge for one with such limited flying experience as Mildred. Once that stress had passed, the Moth and the Bluebird attracted the attention of hostile vultures, who objected to the invasion of their airspace by these alien and noisy creatures. But the two relieved British pilots eventually landed safely at Jodhpur to be greeted by Colonel Wyndham, the British resident; Mildred, who had long ago developed a taste for the best in motor cars, enjoyed the ride back to his palace in his Rolls-Royce.

The following day, they set off for Allahabad, and Mildred's logbook records her flying for an astonishing nine hours directly there. In fact, they stopped off at Delhi.[131] The 290-mile leg took them an aching five hours, but at last the Jumna (Yamuna) River guided them into the city. As Mildred was using rivers as her primary navigation aid here, she was unwittingly following Cobham's route – he had, of necessity, to follow rivers since he could only land on water.

At this stage in her journey, Mildred made an observation that was clearly Edwardian in tone:

What struck me as the most remarkable sensation of my flight was the changing colour of man. Each time I landed, peoples' faces were darker. Soon they would be almost black. I thought how interesting it was going to be to see them gradually turning yellow as I journeyed Northwards to China and Japan.

Mildred did not tarry at Delhi. Leaving Oscar, who was having some mechanical trouble, behind she departed the same day for Allahabad. The landscape was desolate and tedious – sand and scrub, interspersed by the odd rock and river, perhaps a small village. Even Mildred could not have any difficulty locating her destination, since Allahabad was at the confluence of the Jumna and the Ganges. Here, a strong British garrison based in the Qila Fort guarded the Jumna from its northern bank. Completed in 1583 during the reign of Akbar, the Moghul emperor, it had remained in Moghul hands despite the plundering of the city of Allahabad by the Mahrattas in the eighteenth century. The fort and the city were acquired by the East India Company in 1767.

The moustachioed Captain James Willie Pendlebury MC, together with wife and two excited small sons, escorted her from Bamrauli Airfield to the garrison. Just three months earlier, he and his colleagues had been kept busy fighting an insurrection – this posting was no sinecure. He revived her with a drink on the Officers' Mess veranda overlooking the Jumna. The soldiers were accustomed to revictualling tired British aviators, as Cobham had spent a night with them in 1926, Amy Johnson had graced the Officers' Mess on her flight down to Australia only five months earlier, and Kingsford-Smith and his crew on 3 July.

There was a temple underneath the fort, and Cobham had noted that the sands in the shadow of the fort's walls were a sacred spot of the Hindu, and a favoured site for religious ceremonies (there is an annual *Magh Mela* festival there). 'My bedroom window looked out on to a small balcony which overhung the gaunt fortress walls washed by the waters of the Jumna beneath. The walls of the fort were anything from ten to twenty feet thick.'[132] It was on leaving here that Cobham had met the full force of the monsoon.

Over dinner, Mildred sketched out to Pendlebury her plans for the rest of her round-the-world journey. A man of war and action who, in the Second World War, was to add a DSO to his Military Cross, he was aghast that she did not possess a personal firearm, so he gave her his automatic pistol. Unfortunately, he did not have time to give her much instruction in how to use it – Mildred was to regret this.

Leaving the hospitable soldiers after breakfast, she resumed the path of India's holy river via Benares all the way to its delta at Calcutta, not landing there until 4 p.m. – a day of almost seven hours' flying. Here Mildred had accepted an invitation to stay with some friends from Scotland. They quickly brought her up to speed on the local political scene: there had been plenty of unrest and 'the inhabitants in the squalid part of town had been particularly troublesome'.[133]

Although she had been very weight conscious (for the Bluebird) back in England, she was gaining confidence in the machine's performance. The naivety that had attended her preparations in England had been dispatched – she was now more aware of the perils of her flight and was facing more prolonged stretches over the water. At Calcutta's Dum Dum Airfield, she bumped into Chabot and Pickthorne, two airmen who had already given up on the London–Sydney Air Race when they encountered the birdlike Kingsford-Smith at Karachi, and so when they offered to sell her their 'little rubber boat', a deal was soon struck.[134] She would have had the benefit of rudimentary weather forecasts before setting off from the various RAF bases in the Middle Eastern section of her route, but now she was about to depart from Calcutta with very little idea of the hand the weather gods were about to play as she ventured further east.

Oscar Garden had now caught up with Mildred, so when she departed at dawn on 30 October for the very long flight to Rangoon, the little Moth was again at her wingtip. She was grateful for his company, as the landscape of the Ganges Delta became more and more inhospitable. 'Miles and miles of swamp with never a human habitation', changing to the lush tropical growth of the Sundarbans – the delta of the Ganges and Brahmaputra Rivers that would swallow any stricken aircraft. After turning the corner at Chittagong and Cox's Bazaar, the terrain changed from paddy fields and swamp with occasional 'little native huts high up on poles', to mountains. The duo hugged the coastline.

On a later trip in October 1935, Kingsford-Smith was in more of a hurry and flew directly over the Bay of Bengal from Allahabad – he was never seen again. Once they were flying down the Burmese coast, Mildred and her shadow would have noticed that the jungle-covered mountains of the Arakan Yoma range extended almost to the sea. There were few places where a successful forced landing could be made in the event of any mechanical trouble. Two Australian flyers, Matthews and Hook, had also recently come to grief in the jungle here – Hook was eaten to death by leeches.

Mildred and Oscar landed successfully at Akyab (now Sittwe) after nearly eight hours' flying, to be welcomed with warm coffee. Cobham had encountered severe monsoon weather with blue-black rain clouds on this leg, but Mildred and Oscar had a more benign time. Within minutes they were on their way to Rangoon. It was to be one of her longest days – covering 700–800 miles. By the time they arrived at the Burmese capital, they had flown for nearly twelve hours. In an open-cockpit aircraft, with little in-flight refreshment and the need for constant vigilance, this was turning into a feat of endurance to surpass her efforts at Montlhéry.[135]

Looking demure in a pleated skirt, the self-assured Mildred said her goodbyes to Oscar (who was more sensibly wearing a sola topee). He was heading south-eastwards for Australia with his record hopes abandoned, while her destination for the day was Bangkok.

The U-shaped coastline would have been a natural guide, but with typical preference for risk she decided to save time by heading straight across the Gulf of Martaban to Moulmein. Cobham waxes lyrical over the landscape here:

> We arrived over Moulmein just after a severe rainstorm. There was a break in the clouds and the sun was shining, giving us a beautiful vision of the many pagodas and the oriental splendours of the temples standing out clearly as the sun shone on the glistening wetness of their golden roofs. Out of the monsoon period the waters are so clear that from an altitude one can look right through the ocean to its bed in fathoms of water and it is difficult to tell exactly where the surface of the water begins.[136]

Leaving this vista behind, Mildred urged the Bluebird to 7,000ft, or so, to clear the heavily wooded granite and limestone hills of the Dawna Range. There was solid cloud above her, so she had to dodge the clouds in narrow valleys – not an activity to be recommended for pilots wanting to live long enough to see their grandchildren.

The Menam (now Chao Phraya) River was her guide to Siam's capital. The riverbank temples with their distinctive architecture became more numerous as the Menam wound directly to Bangkok's airfield at Don Muang. Here, the British influence was less than that to which she had become accustomed. At that time, Siam was the only country in south-east Asia that was not under the control of a colonial power and Mildred was discomfited to find no English speakers.

Through interpreters, the Siamese officials tried to prevent her onward progress. They pointed out the dangers of flying east over 1,400 miles of largely uninhabited jungle, and with scant weather forecasts. However, once the Siamese realised her intransigence, they became more helpful.

Dinner in the Officers' Mess was in the presence of the largest and most brazen mosquitoes she had ever seen, and the lack of English-speaking assistance brought on an attack of melancholy, which was not helped when Mildred awoke the following morning to a heavy black sky. She had known, even when back at her Esher home poring over her AA maps, that the next 2,000 miles would be among the toughest on the route. She was leaving behind the relatively well-trodden path to Australia.

Yet, Mildred had determined that a good record to aim for was to be the first person to fly from Britain to Japan, and so it was here that she truly began to pioneer. This was proving to be Mildred's very twentieth-century version of a Grand Tour. (British aristocrats had a long record of touring the globe to assimilate foreign cultures. Towards the end of the nineteenth century this had reached almost epidemic proportions.) While liner and train were the favoured modes, some rich adventurers were not slow to embrace opportunities presented by new technologies, and in 1883, Sir Claude Champion de Crespigny crossed the North Sea by balloon. However, few parts of the globe – from Jamaica (the Duke of St Albans) to Alaska (Lady Grey Egerton) – escaped wealthy inquisitive Britons, and Mildred was pursuing the tradition.

The airport manager had counselled that she aim initially for Korat, suggesting there might be some fuel there. It was humid, there was a ground mist and visibility was poor. She took off at dawn from Don Muang with sweat trickling down under her leather flying helmet, more apprehensive than she had been at any stage in the flight. Initially she could follow a railway towards Korat, but as the sun warmed the jungle, the railway disappeared into the mist. 'I shall have to trust my compass now,' she confided to her Dictaphone. Some trust, as Korat was barely more than an outstation by a clearing in the jungle. It was imperative to fly an accurate heading, navigating by dead reckoning over an endless panorama of dense jungle that was only occasionally interspersed with a crocodile-infested river. Soon rain made the task even more difficult.

All the while Mildred was causing ripples in diplomatic circles. The Siamese Government was not beholden to any other nation. On 18 November its Minister for Foreign Affairs felt compelled to write to the British Ambassador in Bangkok. He noted Mildred's passage across his nation: Don Muang, Korat, Nagor Panom (*sic*). More importantly, it had been noticed that Mildred was carrying a radio, which contravened the permit she had been given. 'In order to avoid future misunderstanding, I shall be much obliged if Your Excellency would be good enough to impress upon British airmen who will pass over this country the necessity of complying with the law in this respect.'

Mildred flew on, untroubled by the ructions she was causing, fully focused on staying alive and reaching Japan.[137] Why had she determined on Japan as her objective? Aside from the prize of the first solo journey there from England, another reason lay in a Svengali figure in the background. Mildred first met fellow Catholic, Colonel the Master of Sempill (William Forbes-Sempill) in 1928, if not before. Their paths subsequently crossed many times – for example, he too had attended the lunch for Amy in August before Mildred's departure. Following a distinguished career in the Royal Navy and Royal Flying Corps in the First World War, when he was awarded the Air Force Cross, he had embarked on a series of consultancy activities to fund his expensive lifestyle. Naval aviation was his specialism, and Blackburn Aircraft one of his targets. He became involved in Blackburn's help to the Greeks in setting up their own naval aviation. Indeed, he may even have encouraged Mildred to buy the Bluebird. The trouble was that Sempill's scruples had gone walkabout.

Like the Greeks, the Japanese were looking to match the progress achieved by Britain in naval aviation, and their strategic ambition had already alighted on Malaya. From the early 1920s, the Japanese had been looking to recruit spies in London – it was top of the in-tray for their naval attaché in the capital, Captain Teijiro Toyoda. First in the net was 'Rutland of Jutland' – Squadron Leader Frederick Rutland, a First World War RNAS pilot who had distinguished himself in the Battle of Jutland. He had a unique knowledge of aircraft carriers, for which the Japanese were glad to pay him £3 million (in modern money).

Sempill had been on an official British mission to help the formation of the Imperial Japanese Naval Air Service,[138] but when this finished and the British Government told him to cease any contact with the Japanese, Sempill re-offered his services. From 1926, if not earlier, he was in the pay of the Japanese as a spy. British counter-intelligence had been watching Sempill from at least 1922, and their interest heightened as Japanese money flowed into his bank account. Letters and telephone calls from his office and home to Toyoda and his embassy in London were commonplace, and the security services were tapping his phone and intercepting his mail. Sempill continued to receive money from the Japanese Government and the Mitsubishi Corporation (which it owned), even after the start of the Second World War.

At the very least, Sempill would have been inordinately proud and pleased that Mildred had chosen to fly to Tokyo. More likely, he had orchestrated the destination and the welcome she was to receive – the fatigued Englishwoman was now an unwitting accomplice in the hands of a man plotting against her own beloved motherland.

12

ONWARDS TO JAPAN

Trouble in the air is very rare. It is hitting the ground that causes it.

Amelia Earhart (1897–1937), American pilot.

On 19 November, alongside a piece noting the fourth marriage of Edina, Countess of Errol, the front page of the *Daily Express* carried, 'Englishwoman's Air Triumph – Mrs Bruce near end of 11,000 mile lone flight'.

After four hours or so (according to her) on her steady north-easterly heading, she noticed a patch of jungle that was a shade darker, flew towards it, observed a clearing surrounded by some houses on stilts, and decided it must be Korat. She landed and was quickly refuelled by the Siamese soldiers. Her navigation had been pinpoint accurate at the time it was most crucial.

Hanoi was her next major port of call. According to her plans made in England, she intended to fly to Vinh, en route to the capital. After only half an hour on the ground, she again pointed the Bluebird north-east and settled down to more hours of flying over endless jungle. 'This jungle is getting on my nerves, no sight of anything or any human being.'

Her instructor only weeks earlier in England had counselled her, 'Keep high, going low can be dangerous.' But with typical spirit (or stubbornness) Mildred was choosy about what advice to adopt:

I used to be almost at ground level – by flying low about a hundred feet, I got the sense of speed. The boredom of going up high was more than I could stand, and I used to see things ... people going along the road, that sort of thing.[139]

The jungle denied her such simple stimulants. Although, at one point over some scrub, a herd of elephants took fright at the Bluebird's low-level droning.

Doubts about her real position mounted but she carried on until she met an unmistakeable feature – the Mekong River. Beyond its eastern bank, the jagged peaks of the Annamite Mountains were masked by 'heavy black clouds'. After three and a half hours' flying she saw darkening skies ahead, but realised she did not have enough fuel to return to Korat. While following the river northwards, Mildred became engulfed in the monsoon rainstorm. It was as if she had been enveloped in a black sack, and one that jolted the Bluebird with impunity. Escape from the storm's clutches was vital and, remembering her instructor's advice and eyeing her compass, she performed a 180 degree turn as steadily as she could. 'The rain is beating the aircraft down and I can't see.' Conscious that her fuel was by now low, very low, she realised she had to land soon.

Just before she thought she would have to alight (and probably crash) on the river bank – the least bad option – she noticed a nearby clearing and put the Bluebird down there. It was bumpy ground, and some bamboo stumps tore the fabric on the underside of one wing. She had been navigating with a now soggy basic map: it was 60 miles to the inch, and carried the minimum detail of the terrain in a ribbon only 20 miles each side of her intended course. Mildred had therefore been unaware of other danger or salvation in the region. A larger scale map hastily retrieved from Bluebird's locker showed that she was only half an hour or so from the reasonably sized town of Lakhon, still on the Siamese side of the river, which here formed the border with Laos.

It was 3 p.m. so she had plenty of time to get there, but the clearing in which she had landed was much too small for her comfort. She paced it out at 180 yards and the Bluebird needed 150 yards to take off. A further difficulty was that the clearing was surrounded by tall trees. So, to lighten the aircraft she jettisoned all but her essentials. Having chocked the Bluebird's wheels she swung the propeller, but its Gipsy engine refused to sing. In the heat and humidity of the monsoon, a damp Mildred resignedly took out her toolkit to change the spark plugs and clean the magnetos. The ripped wing fabric, however, would have to wait.

Her toil was rewarded when the engine fired up, but the sun was now very low on the horizon. She bumped slowly over the rough ground right to the edge of the clearing and swung *Bluebird* into the wind. It would be fruitless to try and pull the aircraft into the air too early, so Mildred left it to accelerate on the ground until the correct take-off speed was reached. However, the trees grew larger over her small

windscreen and she heaved the Bluebird into the air as late as she dared.
There was a crashing noise as the aircraft brushed the tops of the tree
canopy, but it staggered aloft. For now she was unconcerned whether the
undercarriage was broken, or if *Bluebird* had lost more feathers from her
wings. All that mattered was that she had managed to extricate herself
from that remote clearing.

Mildred flew up the Mekong to Lakhon by moonlight, and landed in the
largest field she could discern.[140] Once dismounted, she discovered that this
happened to be alongside the governor's house, a somewhat austere building
by Siamese standards, at the side of the Mekong River:

> On arriving I was very interested to see how English everything was.
> The interior of the house was a perfect example of an old Elizabethan
> dwelling. The Governor was particularly proud of his garden, and I was
> highly amused to see that even the banana trees were surrounded with
> white palings to create the atmosphere of an English park. The entrance
> to his drive was also typically English, with a five-barred gate, and at the
> side an old-fashioned English stile. Round the porch was a great arch of
> foliage with a mass of orchids.[141]

This time the Siamese official, the governor, spoke perfect English.
Moreover, despite the late hour he gave her tea – again in the English
style. Whatever weather she had endured that day, he told her she was
lucky she had not been there a day earlier when the remnants of a
Chinese typhoon had swept through the town. However, the hardest
part of the journey to Hanoi had yet to come and the governor underlined the challenge of the Annamite Mountains. She reported him as
saying, 'The peaks are twenty-five thousand feet high, and at this time of
year we have only one day in twenty-nine that's not raining. You will do
better to take Bluebird to pieces and send it to China by canoe. It will
arrive there in three months.'[142] (Either the peaks have shrunk in the
intervening seventy years, the governor was exaggerating, or Mildred
was using her customary dramatic licence. In the twenty-first century,
the peaks are measured at 9,000ft or so – still dangerous enough.) The
governor went on to relate to her that two French airmen had recently
died trying to make the same journey.[143]

She was escorted to a nearby house to stay until the weather improved.
Unfortunately, with no windows her room was too prison-like for her.
Indeed, her ill humour was not helped by the occasions when clanking
chains marked the passage of a column of Chinese prisoners making their
way to work past her cell.

One evening, she dined with the governor under the palms on his lawn. The French commissaire had boated over from Takhek on the Laotian side of the river, so after the meal Mildred picked up an accordion and startled the guests with a rendition of the 'Marseillaise'. A day later, she fell into a fever, with a temperature of 104 degrees. Quinine sorted out that issue in time for her to join the governor on a tiger shoot, although Mildred took her camera rather than a gun. The men looked pleased as they posed alongside the diminutive Englishwoman over the slaughtered animal.

She described crossing the Mekong by canoe on the Sunday to go to Mass in Takhek, with lovely shop houses and French architecture, but this was possibly another fiction. The priest there was very concerned about her impending journey. When she answered that it would take four hours to fly to Hanoi, he gave her a St Christopher medal and said that when he heard her fly over he would pray for her for the full four hours. The governor donated half a month's supply of petrol from his car to give her enough fuel for her next leg.

Receiving a telegram the following day informing her that the weather was clear east of the mountain range, she took off from Lakhon, buttressed by religious support. Although she had never done it before (and had not been trained to do so), she climbed through a solid overcast cloudbank to 11,000ft. She expected to reach the Indo-Chinese coast – and clear air – after two hours.

With no oxygen, at this height her stamina was sorely tested, and the engulfing 'sea of clouds' was interminable. After four hours' flying, with just an hour left until both her fuel and daylight expired, and completely lost, fatigue magnified her anxiety. She confided somewhat dramatically to her dictating machine, 'I'm lost above the cloud. This may be my end. I've done the best I can, and if I come through it will only be by the grace of God. Goodbye.'

Mindful that the clouds may be hiding more mountains ('cumulo-granite' in pilots' pessimistic parlance), she had little choice but to descend. The moisture of the cloud magnified her nervous beads of sweat. When, and if, she broke out of the cloud she hoped and expected to see the sea, because she thought she ought to have passed the coast two hours before.

The altimeter read less than 1,000ft by the time she eventually broke out of the cloud to see 'miles upon miles of swamp. But then the miracle happened. Sparkling beneath me in the rays of the setting sun I saw a railway.'[144] Five minutes later, a large town hove into view and she soon identified the aerodrome. The nervous strain dissipated after she had landed. As she left the Bluebird's cockpit she asked the aerodrome staff in a Livingstonesque moment, 'Is this Hanoi?'

'*Mais oui*'. Her track had taken her directly to her destination, instead of her intended place of meeting the coastline much further south. The wind had shifted since she had received that forecast many hours earlier. 'I was simply dazed and I couldn't possibly believe I had reached Hanoi.' If she had strayed a few times from the strictures of her Catholic upbringing, the flight brought her closer to God. She always looked back at that day's journey as a miracle 'wrought in answer to the prayers of the priest at Lakhon, and the St Christopher medal'.

Mildred had arrived in what a contemporary British Pathé newsreel called 'far off French Indo-China, where streets are dusty and the ladies dusky'. By now weather-beaten and dirty, but certainly not dusky, Mildred was well looked after by Colonel Prémoral (the chief of the French Indo-China Air Force in Hanoi) and his wife, who hosted a function that evening in her honour.

During her two-day stay she rested and shopped for jade and embroidery ('at ridiculously cheap prices'). Mildred clearly felt more at home with this strongly Franco-Asian culture than the more exotic Siamese environment where she could not speak the language. Despite having stared danger in the face several times on this trip, Mildred took fright at what she regarded as a perilous and chaotic mix of cars, rickshaws and motorbikes on Hanoi's streets.

Madame Prémoral had persuaded her guest to stay more than one night. Later, Mildred realised the wisdom of this notion – it allowed her to recuperate a little from the fever and from some taxing flying. She planned to depart for Hong Kong at noon, after the morning fog had lifted.

Being, by now, well off the beaten track for transglobal pilots had two consequences. First, she had attracted a great deal of interest from the public at the city's aerodrome. For the first time on the trip many wanted to sign their names on the Bluebird's wings. Second, while she was making her last-minute preparations for departure, her host from the previous night, General Borzcki, stepped forward, planted a kiss on both her increasingly ruddy cheeks, and, having received a telegram from the governor ordering him to do so, pinned a magnificent gold and enamel medal on her flying coat. This was in recognition of Mildred being the first Briton and first woman to land in Laos. The medal was the 'Order of the Million Elephants and White Umbrella'. Gaining this esoteric award allowed her to own the former, and have the latter held over her head if she attended a feast.

Borzcki had also arranged for a military band to send her off with her ostensibly favourite accordion tune – the 'Marseillaise'. In a final display of friendly French military power, Borzcki had also ordered a squadron of air force aircraft to accompany her as far as the Gulf of Tonkin. For a woman who always thrived on attention, she must have been giddy with pleasure by this time.

Elated, once airborne she flew into headwinds so strong that her ground speed was more than halved to barely more than 30mph. As she plodded on at this funereal pace, thinking that her million elephants would almost have been able to keep up, Mildred realised this meant giving up any notion of making Hong Kong. She diverted to Fort Bayard (now known as Zhanjiang in Guangdong Province), only halfway to Hong Kong. After a little game of hide and seek, she found the small field that was the fort's aerodrome. Again, her bread had fallen jam side up.

Mildred was invited to the residency, and promptly fell asleep on a sofa. On waking she was invited to a Chinese wedding, encountering that sort of Asian cuisine (the dishes were 'mysterious') where it is best not to ask about the ingredients. However, her sense of adventure, augmented by hunger, meant she ate most of what was offered.

Escaping any gastrointestinal after-effects, on 9 November she enjoyed a relaxing flight up the coast to Hong Kong. At the time, this was an aviator's paradise:

> Flying round Hong Kong was indeed a delight. The scenery was marvellous, the air exceptionally calm, and visibility good. To our intense joy, we need no longer worry about low flying; we could do exactly as we pleased, and with nobody to report it. Practically all day and every day there was one plane or another skimming over the peak, diving down Happy Valley, shooting up the ships in the harbour, or roaring over the Repulse Bay Hotel on the other side of the island. [145]

On landing, and not having 'shot up' any ships, Mildred was swept up by the governor's equerry, and taken in style in the governor's launch to his house. Sir William Peal and his wife had only taken up the posting some five months earlier. Mildred was bewitched by the beauty of the colony, but less enamoured of the fog the following morning, so she was taken to the Happy Valley racecourse to ride a pony. The lust for speed was undimmed and at full gallop 'the blessed animal's knees gave way for some unknown reason'. It tumbled over, and Mildred suffered a badly grazed arm as both horse and rider cannoned into the rails. Back at the governor's house, she received an anti-tetanus jab and then a telegram from Victor and young Tony wishing her happy birthday – in her focus on reaching Japan, she had quite overlooked that she had reached the age of 35.

While Mildred's right brain wanted to participate a little more fully in the colony's social whirl, her left signalled that she faced another very testing part of her trip – the crossing of the South China Sea. So, only two days after arrival, she was on her way again, this time to Amoy, a small coastal town halfway to Shanghai.

A member of the Hong Kong Flying Club flew alongside her for the first 50 miles, before waving goodbye. It was now 11 November, Armistice Day, so at 11 a.m. she turned off her engine to have the normal respectful two-minute silence. Unfortunately, Mildred had to abort her serene glide after thirty seconds as the ground was rapidly approaching![146] While this episode might have been one of Mildred's little whimsies, it does capture the spirit of the times. It might seem hard to believe ninety years later, but on many airliners in the 1920s at 11 a.m. on Remembrance Day, all the passengers – and as many crew as could be spared – stood together in the cabin to hold a two-minute silence.

A few miles down the route she claimed to have had a grandstand view of a Norwegian liner being captured by pirates. Later, again beset by monsoon-driven 60mph headwinds and plenty of turbulence, she struggled to achieve even 40mph over the ground. As the hours passed, her anxiety about running out of fuel increased, but she eventually found the aerodrome at Amoy (now Xiamen) despite its being marked on the wrong island on her map. With only a 250-yard run, and with a hill at one end making it only possible to land in one direction, it was as well that a fatigued Mildred pulled off a tricky landing in the stiff crosswind.

She stayed with the local manager of the Asiatic Petroleum Company. Admiral Lin, 'very handsome and almost European in appearance', was the town's senior military figure. At her audience with him the following morning, he imparted some bad news over coffee. Her next intended fuel stop was Foochow (now Fuzhou), China's main tea port, only 140 miles up the coast. Unfortunately it was enmeshed in the Chinese Civil War.[147] She cabled the officer commanding its garrison, requesting permission to land. 'Sorry impossible for you to land. Too busy with the war,' was the unsurprisingly testy military response.

Out came the Mildred charm, and with some coercion from the admiral, the commanding officer relented, telling his men to exchange their rifles for shovels to remove the bunkers on his private golf course 20 miles away so she could land there. Unfortunately, this provided less than 150 yards of runway, which she decided was inadequate. So, disregarding all that bunker-relocating effort, Mildred decided to fly straight over, leaving another 370 miles to Shanghai.

However, first at Amoy there was a dinner invitation to accept with the captain aboard HMS *Cornflower* in the harbour. Mildred faced another long day, so needed to take off before dawn. Like some Georgian demirep, she was taken by sedan chair from ship to aerodrome. After an hour's flight she passed Foochow, and rather frivolously dropped a smoke bomb onto the warring crowds below. She noticed the golf course, which had been ripped apart in her honour 'havoc having been wrought amongst the bunkers'. The curses of the sweaty soldiers did not reach her noisy cockpit as she cruised past.

Mildred endured an exhausting eight-hour flight (which she later described as 'very frightening'), in a sky with almost no visibility, leaden with industrial pollution and lashed by the remnants of a monsoon.[148] A crowd of several hundred were waiting at Shanghai to greet her landing, and the three days there were spent as a guest of the British consul, Mr Blunt.

Mildred's adventure was indeed turning into an aerial equivalent of the Grand Tour. While Amy, Amelia and Lindbergh had been driven by a relentless need to establish or break records, Mildred's only time imperative had been to avoid the monsoon season. Her early mishaps had rendered that impossible, so she grasped the opportunity to enjoy her exotic surroundings. Discovering her inner small boy, she rejoiced in a display in her honour by the International Fire Brigade of Shanghai, particularly since it involved her speeding in the commander's car leading twelve engines through town, alarms blaring.

Once again, she was entertained by the Royal Navy, this time in the Officers' Mess aboard HMS *Bridgewater* – a modest 1,000-ton sloop seconded to the so-called 'China Station'. The RAF did its bit by tending to the oil metering plugs in her still worrisome engine, and swung her compass, as navigation had to be as accurate as possible in the sea crossing to come.

There was such a significant British military presence in the city not only to protect Britain's trading interests, but because the political situation had been volatile for the previous five years, occasionally spilling over into hostility towards foreigners. The British Government stepped up pressure on Mildred to abandon her flight at this stage, arguing that she had insufficient fuel to cross the Yellow Sea. Dismissing these concerns, she said she would only go if the weather were favourable.

Five days after arrival at Shanghai, she rose at 3 a.m. for her momentous journey to Korea. Jesuit priests, the unusual custodians of the Ziccawei Observatory on the hill above the town, delivered her weather forecast over breakfast. It concluded, 'Weather at sea Fine. Best Wishes, Father Glazie'.

Her mood cannot have been lightened by a postcard she received before her departure from the UK from a fortune teller prophesying that it would be here in the Yellow Sea where she would meet her death. This was to be her longest sea crossing so far – 790 miles in her logbook, albeit 520 miles on twenty-first-century maps!

The Scots record-breaker, Jim Mollison, had become chronically dependent on alcohol, not least for long over-water flights. Kingsford-Smith, the Australian serial seducer, slipped on to the same downward path after he started to have panic attacks over the sea. In one such episode, while trying to break the record from Australia to Great Britain, he lapsed into half consciousness, stalled and entered a spin, recovering only a few hundred feet above the water. Overcome by nausea, he started to vomit over the side of the cockpit. He only regained his composure after swigging some brandy following his landing at Dum Dum. Thereafter, brandy, or *sal volatile* (which was near pure alcohol disguised as medicine), was his almost constant companion in the cockpit. As a teetotaller, Mildred had no such prop – there was no question of her resorting to a bottle of anything more stimulating than Ovaltine. With years of training behind a steering wheel, Mildred was inured to the need to concentrate fiercely for hours on end under conditions that could swing in an instant from boredom to terror.

The Bluebird left Shanghai in the half-light, just before 6 in the morning, its pilot glancing at the packed harbour behind, where she 'saluted' HMS *Bridgewater*. She found flying over the sea less stressful than over some of the more remote mountainous jungle she had recently encountered. However, like any pilot, once over water, she listened more intently for variations in the tone of her engine. There was a small leak in the exhaust pipe, just by the manifold, to unnerve her. It would have sapped the engine's power by a horse or two, but was not a reason to return.

In a cold cockpit, after three and a half hours' flying, boredom was suffused with overpowering loneliness. After six hours' flying, and not having seen any shipping since she had left harbour, Mildred became worried that she had yet to sight land – it was quite possible she could have drifted southwards and missed the southern tip of Korea entirely. A few minutes later, as she was craning her head in a more desperate attempt to find land that was not there, her goggles blew off – another little stab to her self-confidence. Like many airmen before her, the possibility of a watery grave beckoned.

After a further tense hour, she sighted the tiny Ross Island, dead on track – her navigation had been faultless. It was only 90 miles from the mainland. 'That was quite the worst part of my journey flying over the cold dark sea, and I am very glad it is over.' Luckily, she now had a 60mph tailwind to urge her along.

Once at Mokpo, she could have followed the western coast for a relatively easy path to Seoul, but instead she incomprehensibly followed a railway through narrow passes. When the track forked, she made a bad choice. The line drew her towards high mountains, so she beat a retreat. Eventually, after almost nine hours at the Bluebird's controls, she landed at Seoul Airfield to be greeted by some charming children bearing flowers. She had become the first pilot to make a direct crossing of the Yellow Sea from Shanghai to Korea. Mildred claimed it was the longest sea crossing since Lindbergh's famous flight over the Atlantic.[149]

Her flock of well-wishers had accumulated steadily through the trip. The RAF crew who had attended to the Bluebird in Shanghai remained very solicitous. Its commanding officer wrote to Mildred at the end of November when his team knew she had successfully crossed the Yellow Sea, 'The anxiety of sitting and waiting for news of you while you were crossing was pretty awful. When we heard that you were safely across we felt more glad than I could tell you.'

At Seoul, Mildred was looked after by Oswald White, the consulate general. He had been in post for four years, in what was a quiet backwater of Britain's interests in Asia. White handed over a mound of congratulatory telegrams. Later, over dinner, he gave Mildred the benefit of his knowledge of Japan from his previous postings in Osaka and Nagasaki.

Unfortunately, an unexpected hurdle prevented a swift departure, when she learned that no one was allowed to overfly the Emperor of Japan, who had inconveniently decided to stay somewhere on her route. So, it was not until three days later – when he was back in his palace – that she could set off for Japan. It was another long stretch in the cockpit, almost eight hours flying that day, and most of the time she was chilled to the marrow. Osaka Airfield was waterlogged, with the Bluebird almost, but not quite, burying its nose in the swamp.

Over the following days, Mildred was very taken with the Japanese way of living and the design of their houses. Mrs Kishimoto, the wife of her host, presented her with a beautiful silk kimono. An enormous banquet was held for her, although a moment arrived when she wondered whether her travails in crossing the globe had been worthwhile – she was presented with the honour of eating the eye of a massive fish. Mildred averted the danger by cunningly gifting it back to her hostess.

Feeling now on the home run, she elatedly sent a telegram to her allies at Blackburn Aircraft, 'Congratulations to directors and staff on the wonderful performance of the Bluebird England to Japan – Bruce'. No message was sent to de Havilland, the manufacturers of her incontinent engine.

At 11 in the morning two days later, in perfect weather for a change, she flew towards Tokyo's aerodrome at Tachikawa. An escort of fourteen aircraft (two of which were piloted by pigtailed Japanese ladies) rose into the skies for her near Mount Fuji – the beauty of its snow-covered peak leaving a lasting impression.

After a bumpy landing at 1.50 p.m., she was thronged by a crowd of thousands – more than any other aviator had witnessed there. Sempill had clearly whispered into the ears of his Japanese friends. 'Epochal Flight Ends in Wild Cheers' was the *Japan Times* headline. Hundreds of Japanese schoolgirls enthusiastically waved British and Japanese flags and Mildred disappeared under a welter of posies and bouquets thrust from all sides, not least by Miss Koizumo, the little daughter of the Minister of Communications. Mildred retained a sweet composure as she was ushered towards a hangar for an official reception and a belated light lunch.

She was welcomed by one of Japan's pioneer aviators, Miss Boku, and 74-year-old General Nagaoka, the country's 'Father of Aviation' and president of the Japanese Aviation Society, who had a moustache that was reputedly the widest in the land – at 20in it certainly made Louis Blériot's example look stunted. Struggling to his feet, he toasted her in champagne, leading cries of 'Banzai!' The many Britons present cheered her wildly. In all the acclaim, Mildred had no time to eat. When Nagaoka kissed her on both cheeks the tickling was insufferable. Admiral Funakoshi, head of the Mitsubishi Aircraft Company, was also there. He had formerly been the Japanese naval attaché in London, and therefore the master of Sempill, the puppet.[150]

Followed by a phalanx of reporters, the party drove in a cavalcade from the aerodrome to the Imperial Hotel in the city. Her first need was food, her second, some sleep, but the reporters had not yet been able to gain access to her, so she had to succumb to some interviews before any rest. At 7.30 in the evening she had to attend the local radio station to make a broadcast. Afterwards, among the pile of telegrams of congratulations she could read two that really mattered: 'Congratulations on wonderful sea crossing and Japanese landing, Love Victor', and 'Delighted your success Henry Petre', from her veteran pilot cousin. Victor – mistakenly – believed that her arrival in Japan was the end of all risk and trouble.

Another night, another banquet, this time with the Rising Sun Petroleum Company – diners sitting cross-legged on the floor, the Anglo-Saxons uncomfortably so. A few hours later, she was rocked in her bed at the Imperial by an earthquake (in which she believed several hundred people lost their lives). Despite her bill at the Imperial (which was regarded as earthquake-proof) being settled by Mr Kishimoto, she moved to the British Embassy, where the ambassador hosted yet another dinner for her. The envoys of all the countries she had overflown were invited. She enjoyed making a speech about her experiences – at least as much as they enjoyed hearing it. The British Women's Association of Tokyo and Yokohama also held a reception in her honour, 'which was attended by members of the British community in large numbers', the embassy noted approvingly.

In reaching Japan from Europe, Mildred had become a true aviation pioneer. There is no doubt that by now she was enjoying her place in the limelight. The British Embassy was somewhat in awe of her keen commercial eye, and her stamina in putting up with so many newspaper interviews, 'She conveyed a real impression of British courage and British sportsmanship to the hundreds in Japan who met her, and the millions who were reached by the variegated tales of her adventures.'[151]

But, while she was living it up, civil servants back in Britain were feeling less well disposed to her. Mildred's casual attitude to bureaucracy had meant that she had provided neither the Koreans, nor the Japanese with her carnet – the customs form to allow the temporary admission of the Bluebird and its contents to their countries. Telegrams were flying between the capitals.

Despite acclaim in the press and at banquets, she polarised opinions in Tokyo. Some Japanese aviation naysayers believed her flight had proved nothing, 'other people say she is a publicity seeker; that she aspires to join the ranks of the lady-endorsers of advertised merchandise'. One can picture why they might think that. On balance, the conclusion was that she appeared to be 'a normal, fine, courageous young modern who prefers making her cross-country tours in the most modern of conveyances and is only politely interested in the medals and publicity she is receiving'.[152]

However, her allure to men of all ages was still flaming like a meteor. A young man from Tokyo had written:

> Oh I cannot too much admire you of your successful flight and wonderful valor shown during the adventurous journey which has quite taken off my heart. Why are you so courageous and what has made you such a lady of decision as you are? I envy you. I longed for searching out your position in a map through the newspapers which informed very often the sorrowful mission of you that tormented me with anxieties. Now you are here in Tokyo safe and sound with great glory. I don't know how to admire you of your wonderful success. If I should, I could only cry at the highest pitch of my voice 'Hurrah! Conqueress of the air, Hurrah! Queen of air!'

Besotted, then … Another poor Japanese schoolboy was reported as being in a quandary about what he could bring Mrs Bruce, so he sent her 2 Yen and asked her to buy anything she wanted. Down the route, she had not deterred welcoming admirers from writing messages on the fabric of her Bluebird. This fan graffiti reached fever pitch in Japan. One enterprising, if idle, chap in Shanghai scrawled to his mother who lived in London, 'Dear Mother, heaps of love. This is my mail for the week.'

But, she also exerted strong appeal to Japanese women, who saw in her an astonishing icon of liberation and ambition. More suppressed by their menfolk than their Anglo-Saxon sisters, Japanese womanhood numbered few pilots.

Her popularity had not gone unnoticed by the British Embassy. With his gimlet eye, T.M. Snow reported back to London, 'In short, despite the exhausting experiences to which she had been subjected during her flight, spared herself no effort to remain in the public eye by unstinted compliance with the many demands made upon her time in Tokyo.'[153]

So, on the surface, harmony reigned in Anglo–Japanese relations. But two events presaged that the two nations would be at war only a decade later. Firstly, the Japanese Government had forbidden her chosen route from Korea to Tokyo because of 'military grand manoeuvres'. Secondly, at the surprising suggestion of the British Embassy in Tokyo, the Mitsubishi Company had been eager to overhaul her craft before it was shipped out of Japan. It can be no coincidence that Sempill had been a consultant to Mitsubishi since 1925. One suspects the Japanese corporation was keen to take the rare opportunity to examine British aircraft manufacturing skills. Unfortunately, while its engineers were thorough, they were not quite thorough enough to ensure Mildred's safety. Mildred instructed them to examine only the airframe, as she intended to have the engine replaced on arrival in Vancouver.[154]

13

A STOUT-HEARTED LADY

Mildred delighted in Japanese culture, architecture and what little she could enjoy of the countryside. Once more in an environment where her social skills could be deployed, she rapidly made many new friends. She did, however, develop an aversion to green tea – something of a handicap for a teetotaller.

After its inspection by Mitsubishi, the Bluebird was taken, its wings folded like some pelican, to Yokohama's docks where it was loaded aboard *Empress of Japan*, the splendid new flagship of the Canadian Pacific Line. As the liner eased from her berth on 4 December, Mildred again experienced pangs of loneliness, this time caused by watching many of her new friends, including Miss Boku and the genial general, waving goodbye from the quayside below.

Although her stewardess had welcomed her to her cabin with, 'We never feel the weather very severely on the *Empress of Japan*'; later on her first night on board ship, Mildred's ox-like constitution let her down. At 2 in the morning she was violently ill, although a cure seems to have soon presented itself – in holiday mood, the adventurer claimed she danced through each storm until dawn. There is an old pilots' adage: 'Better to be on the ground wishing you were up there, than in the sky wishing you were down there.' Mildred was not on the ground, but as she swayed through the Pacific storms aboard the *Empress*, she was relieved she was not fighting her way through those storms a couple of thousand feet above the hellish seas.

Loneliness on the week-long crossing was averted by fellow passengers Mr & Mrs Pratt, to whom she had been introduced in Hong Kong. The moth had flown to the lamp. Pratt was chairman of the Standard Oil Company in the USA (his father had been one of the founders of this giant). The couple invited her to dine with them and as she entered the dining saloon for the first time, the band struck up 'Singing in the Rain'. 'For a moment I felt quite homesick, for the last gramophone record my husband had given me had been this one.' The conversation turned to one of their shared passions – horses. Herbert Pratt was later to cause another Standard Oil man to figure large in Mildred's life.

The social whirl of an ocean liner absorbed her, yet most days she paid a visit to *Bluebird* in the hold, to maintain that umbilical connection between woman and machine. Due to the generosity of her admirers in Japan, Mildred could wear a different ballgown each evening. On occasion, while dancing into the small hours, she rued her accordion was not to hand to allow her again to rattle off the 'Marseillaise'.

On the seventh morning out of Japan, the passengers left their cabins for their first glimpse of Canada. A group of large aircraft were circling the liner in greeting – Mr Pratt had arranged for his company's machines to perform an aerial welcome.[155] The passengers' first view of North America – this vista of Vancouver's skyscrapers twinkling on the horizon – made a deep impression.

Bluebird and owner disembarked from the *Empress* a few hours later. Mildred's reputation had preceded her, and on quitting the *Empress* 'the aviatrix' was singled out by the customs staff for VIP treatment. Reporters in Vancouver were soon treated to a new spin on her route:

Originally I had intended to fly right across Canada, but I'm weeks over-due here now, so I'm compelled to take the Southern route. I shall have my plane ready by the first of next week, I will probably be here for four or five days. I shall go south by easy stages, as far as Los Angeles, and then cross the continent by the southern route. [156]

The Bluebird was trucked to the airfield, its wings unfolded and the air-frame soon restored to health, but Mildred decided that the troublesome engine should be overhauled over the weekend.

Public interest had now risen to such a pitch that the night after her arrival 600 people turned up to hear her lecture about her adventures. The following day, there was an informal civic luncheon in her honour at the Hotel Vancouver. The audience had the benefit of Mildred's world view, 'In countries where there is sport there is more progress and less fighting.' Mayor Malkin concluded his response, 'We welcome her as one who can control her spirit.'[157]

Early on Wednesday morning she made the short hop from Vancouver's temporary airfield at Lulu Island across the water to Victoria Island where the governor, coincidentally one Lieutenant Governor R. Randolph Bruce, had invited her to lunch at his mansion. Once over the water, some unusual smells appeared in the cockpit, but Mildred dismissed them as overheating radio valves (unlikely on such a short flight) and went to lunch.

As soon as she elegantly could she left the governor for the 135-mile flight across the Salish Sea and Puget Sound to Seattle. However, in her haste to depart she had omitted to investigate the fumes. This soon proved a frightening mistake, and after take-off smoke filled the Bluebird's cockpit.

Nothing terrifies an aviator more than fire in the air. She had no hesitation in dipping the Bluebird's nose back towards the island. As soon as it had come to a halt on Victoria's grass she discharged the fire extinguisher at the smoking instrument panel. A cracked exhaust, overlooked by the Mitsubishi inspectors, was the cause.[158] It had been perilously near the spare fuel tank in the cockpit.

Fortunately, Canadian shipwrights at Yarrows in the harbour managed to fabricate a new exhaust pipe overnight. Sydney Pickles[159] conjured a very different design to the original, the exhaust pipe now leading upwards over the upper wing. His modification was later to cause Mildred some grief. The members of the Women's Aeronautic Association of Canada, who had earlier stood out in the freezing weather at the airfield to wave a Union Jack for her arrival, took the opportunity to invite her to dinner.

The following day Mildred, clad in her normal cold-weather garb of tweed coat with fur collar and brown stockings, was back at Lansdowne Airfield for her 11.00 a.m. take-off. However, this time she had an escort. Herbert Pratt, concerned about her safety over the mountains, had solicitously arranged for one of his Standard Oil pilots in a Stearman aircraft to accompany her for her flights in the north-west. While in Japan, British residents, upon hearing that she had but the most basic wardrobe, had showered her with gifts of 'frocks, shoes, all kinds of things, so I really had a better wardrobe than if I had planned to take a journey at leisure around the world'.[160] Despite her having dispatched several cases of gifts home, the Stearman proved a useful carrier for the rest of her baggage!

The pilot, a Captain Hans Walter Looff, was 'one of the company's crack pilots, he turned out to be a most charming fellow'. Ten years earlier, with youthful exuberance, he had related his wartime experiences as a 1st Lieutenant in the US Air Service to the magazine of his university (Oregon State):

> I went to Verdun this morning in a car, and brought back my second plane this afternoon. You didn't know that I had two assigned to me and that I'm a flight commander, did you? I felt the same thrill I had when I was elected captain of the old baseball team. My two ships are beauties

and the finest that ever saw the front. My insignia is a black knight with a long plume on a charger prodding the devil in the hinder parts. I have seen so much hell and ruin between Rheims and Verdun that I am sick of the whole business. I want to go home now that the excitement is over.

Ironic that he gained such thrills from fighting his own kin – Hans Looff's parents, Adolph and Johanna, were first-generation immigrants from Germany. There were plenty of Looffs in the German Army and Air Service, and indeed now at final rest in German military cemeteries.

Mildred flew low over the Straits of Georgia, better to admire the island and its pine trees. The snow-covered Mount Baker and Glazier Peak appeared. Then, when Seattle hove into view after an hour or so, a bevy of larger aircraft appeared to escort the Bruce/Looff duo. Seattle Airport provided Mildred with the challenge of landing on her first tarmac runway – it passed uneventfully. In what was to become the pattern for her American odyssey, there was a full civic welcome, headed by the city mayor.

The flight to Portland was more demanding. The scale of the challenge to fly across the American continent was beginning to dawn on this inexperienced pilot. By circumstance and planning, she was now flying across some of the USA's most inhospitable landscape in the depths of winter:

> By now I was really beginning to realise the enormity of the task I had set myself. It's all very well to sit in a cosy armchair with maps spread out on one's knees, and draw straight lines across continents and say: 'That's the way I shall go'. It is another matter to try to carry out that scheme at a time of year when civil aviation has practically closed down.[161]

Although she was fortified by a thermos full of hot Ovaltine, on this flight the air was so chill that Mildred promised herself a new flying coat once at Portland. That evening she was hosted at dinner by the Women's International Association of Aeronautics, based in California. This was the first time she met its founder and vice president, the formidable Mrs Ulysses Grant McQueen of Beverley Hills. Given a perambulator and baby, Mrs McQueen could have passed for Mrs Doubtfire, but this frumpy dynamo was one of Los Angeles' first pilots. She and Mildred immediately established a great rapport, sharing a deep-rooted evangelism for women's aviation.

Leaving the city on 23 December, she was determined to spend Christmas Day in San Francisco. The authorities had given her the Union Jack and the Stars and Stripes to drop on City Hall in nearby Olympia, as Charles Lindbergh had done before her. As she flew at only 50ft over its main square, the crowds had a good view of the silver biplane.

In Portland, the weather report was 'fairish', in her opinion, but her interpretation was over-optimistic. After three hours of extremely difficult navigation over cold and clammy coastal fog, she was fatigued and anxious. The fog lifted just enough to make out Medford's airfield – a dirt strip inside the town's racetrack. Mildred intended just a quick fuel stop, however, during the landing the undercarriage, abused in jungle and desert, finally snapped (possibly the landing was not one of her best). After running a few yards on the strip's coarse gravel surface, the aircraft tipped over, leaving Mildred hanging upside down in her straps, seat belt snagged on her coat, with fuel dripping from an overflow pipe. Seconds seemed like minutes as she struggled out of her harness, then to burn her hands on the hot exhaust, which, after the modification, was now above her head. An old friend, whom she had not seen since they were 13-year-old schoolgirls, had driven over to welcome her and dashed anxiously to the inverted Bluebird. Both main spars in its wings were kinked, and several of the wing ribs broken. Mildred had escaped with merely burns to her hands and a modest with-drawal from her welling account of self-confidence.

Christmas at San Francisco was clearly now but a pipe dream. The old school friend lived many miles distant, but happily Captain Looff's parents lived at Grant's Pass, only 20 miles from Medford's airfield, so he suggested they stay there. That evening, melancholic at the disintegration of her plans, she managed to phone Victor, but the call was far from ideal. It cost £1 per minute, with the operator unhelpfully tolling each passing minute. She asked her husband to wire £200 for repairs. Victor's laconic reply, 'What? More money? It's lucky for you that it is Christmas. I was expecting you to be sending money home by now, not asking for it!' They had a brief discussion about her intended route – she still dreamed of visiting Canada, South America and thence by liner to Africa, returning to England by April. 'Eight minutes!' chimed the Californian hard heart. There was little time for other sweet nothings before her money ran out at £9 4s 8d. Victor later fed an edited version of the conversation to the British press.

The following day, her engineering and project management skills led to a swift decision that the Bluebird would have to be sent by truck back to Seattle, which was fortuitously the home of Boeing Aircraft. 'A very wise move,' said Sydney Pickles in a letter to Robert Blackburn, founder of Blackburn Aircraft, 'as it is one of the finest factories in the States'. Mildred was rather worried about her financial position. According to Pickles, the repairs cost $100 (so she had over-egged the cake to Victor), but she had of course incurred many other repair costs in patching up *Bluebird* on her journey to date.

Mildred in her youth. (Courtesy of Wendy Grimmond)

Mildred sipping tea in the AC used by the Bruces in the 1927 Monte Carlo Rally. (Courtesy of Wendy Grimmond)

Husband and wife sharing horsepower. (Courtesy of Wendy Grimmond)

Mildred in front of Bluebird G-AAIR at Heston, September 1930. (Author's collection)

With her steed. (BAe Heritage)

At Bach Mai Airfield, Hanoi, already having been given the Order of the Million Elephants and White Umbrella. (Courtesy of Caroline Gough-Cooper)

Arriving in Japan. (Courtesy of Caroline Gough-Cooper)

The reception at Tokyo. (Courtesy of Caroline Gough-Cooper)

A tired aviatrix and her aircraft (note the medals). (Courtesy of Caroline Gough-Cooper)

The perils of landing in a very muddy field (probably Baltimore). (Courtesy of Caroline Gough-Cooper)

Holding a mystery baby
on arrival at Croydon.
(Courtesy of Caroline
Gough-Cooper)

Flanked by Amy Johnson
and Winifred Spooner at
Croydon. (Courtesy of
Caroline Gough-Cooper)

Her celebratory dinner
at the Mayfair Hotel.
L–R: Tsuneo Matsudaira,
Mildred, Sempill,
Viscountess Elibank.
(Courtesy of Caroline
Gough-Cooper)

Collecting the Windhover at Gibraltar. (Courtesy of Caroline Gough-Cooper)

Captain of her ship. (Courtesy of Caroline Gough-Cooper)

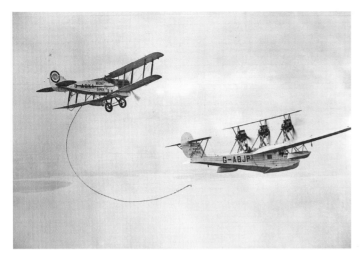

Husband refuelling wife during the endurance attempt. (Courtesy of Caroline Gough-Cooper)

The endurance team. L–R: Pugh, Victor, Mildred, McLeary, anon. (Courtesy of Caroline Gough-Cooper)

Mildred with her adoring public – probably at a rally at Hanworth. (Courtesy of Caroline Gough-Cooper)

The ill-fated Cierva autogyro. (Courtesy of Caroline Gough-Cooper)

The Air Dispatch team: Pugh standing third from left; Daphne Kearly sitting third from left; Mildred fourth from left. (Courtesy of Caroline Gough-Cooper)

Captain Looff was already taking his protection duties seriously – he was keen that the incident did not damage Mildred's growing reputation as a capable aviator. So, on 20 January he wrote a long missive to Blackburn's manager for the Bluebird programme, Squadron Leader Claude Ridley in London, describing how the 'stout-hearted little lady' was in no way to be blamed for the accident. The rough aerodrome surface and crystallisation of the metal in the undercarriage bolts were the cause. 'Further, I have yet to see either pilot or mechanic who was more thoro [*sic*] in the care and upkeep of an aircraft engine.' He omitted to mention that his heart was already beating in unison with that stout one.

Boeing managed to fix the aircraft in less than five days, enabling her to carry out a test flight on New Year's Eve, this time compelled to wear a parachute by the Boeing management. The girls at the Boeing factory who were tasked with restitching the wing fabric had taken Mildred's endeavour to their hearts. They left messages of encouragement on the aircraft, one of the more lyrical being, '*Bluebird, Bluebird*, try and try. You'll be an aeroplane by and by'.

Eschewing party invitations, that New Year's Eve was spent in a Seattle hotel, again feeling homesick. The North American part of her voyage was supposed to be joyous – full of visiting old family haunts and collecting a new circle of admirers. But as 1931 began, she was alone, Looff not having been able to conjure an excuse to be with her. Fatigue set in and she longed for home, 'Oh how I wished the flight was over!'

It was a far from ideal time of year to be trying to cross the next obstacle – the Cascade Mountains. Two days earlier an air mail pilot had disappeared and Looff had reluctantly to join the aerial search party. The air mail pilot was thought to have been brought down by the winter weather. Sleet on a light aircraft swiftly transforms to ice, which can force the machine out of the sky despite the urgings of its engine.

With *Bluebird* back in action, on 5 January Mildred had to retrace her steps alone from Seattle to Medford. The sullen grey sky matched her spirit and gushed an unavoidable snowstorm. At the halfway point, just after midday, Mildred, chilled to the bone, decided to land at Eugene to obtain an updated weather report. According to Mildred, they told her the weather would be 'fair', but only half an hour after she was back in the air, the sky turned grey and stormy again and it became even colder. She began to doubt the wisdom of her decision.

Halfway across a mountain pass – over the most inhospitable terrain – at her cruising height of 6,000ft, the snowstorm worsened; visibility fell to only few hundred yards, but, worst of all, ice started accumulating on the Bluebird's wings and windscreen, which dragged her craft down. Mildred confided her terror to her Dictaphone as the snowstorm worsened. She had to descend almost to the canyon floor before the ice melted.

Scraping in to Medford, she could breathe deeply after an uneventful landing. Mildred's luck had held again – that day, the weather had been sufficiently bad to prevent the arrival of the mail plane. Indeed, the wretched winter weather detained her for another two days, by which time Looff had hastened back from his search mission. He too had encountered severe icing. By now, the American pilot had escalated his escort duties and he was irredeemably in love with the intrepid English rose, 'Dear Little Bluebird', as he addressed her.

Over the Shasta Mountains and into the Sacramento Valley the weather turned warmer and Mildred could remove some of the sweaters and coats she had used to stay alive in her cockpit. San Francisco Bay opened out in front of her. At Mills Field there was a crowd of Japanese proportions and bouquets of roses were thrust into her oil-stained hands. She enjoyed the scale of the welcome, but even better was the journey into town. A police cavalcade with no fewer than thirty outriders speeded her way. 'It was simply lovely to be able to go as fast as one liked in and out of the traffic without a quarrel with some constable on point duty.'

The cops ushered her to the city's flagship hotel, the luxurious Mark Hopkins on Nob Hill, which had only been open for four years. The Bluebird again needed more repairs, this time taking four days, which, given the welcome presence of Hans, was no hardship. She crossed the bay and regaled members of the Rotary Club at Alameda with her adventures so far. Mildred also took the opportunity to visit her mother's old school in Oakland – Mills College's motto was singularly appropriate, *Una destinatio, viae diversae* (one destination, many paths).[162]

Her revised target was to reach New York by the end of the month – Victor was anxious to see his wife again. But he had, of course, yet to learn of her assiduous escort. Sadly, Captain Looff now had to return to more normal duties, both with Standard Oil and his wife, Edna. (He was to father a daughter, Mary, two years later, to add to his 3-year-old son, Hans Junior).

However, Captain Chadderton, manager of Standard Oil's aviation department, deputed another pilot, Walter Case, 'in an even larger machine', to serve as Mildred's baggage train to San Diego. On 11 January they left on the 350-mile flight to Los Angeles. With Case on her wingtip, there was more drama on the way to LA. Over the last three months Mildred had become as attuned to the metronomic beat of her Gipsy engine as a conductor to his orchestra.

When that beat faltered, her pulse quickened. The engine started to lose power and then failed completely over the San Rafael Mountains. She waggled her wings as a distress signal to Case, but fortuitously this dislodged some water in the fuel system and the engine surged back to life. Heading away from the mountains over the sea, 'this part of the flight [down the Santa Barbara Channel] was simply glorious'.

After landing at Los Angeles' United Airport, Mildred's political antennae were quickly re-erected. 'There is not the slightest question it is the finest airport in the world.'[163] With the press having played up Mildred's half-American ancestry, as well as the inevitable mayor and party, the LA welcome also included some of Hollywood's finest. Jackie Coogan, the film star, came and added his signature to the collection on *Bluebird*.

Awaiting her at the hotel was further confirmation of acceptance into the stars' galaxy – a telegram from Mary Pickford, the celebrated film actress, who had wanted to greet her but was detained in New York. In the following days, Mildred strengthened the bond with Hollywood by touring the Warner Brothers Studios.

In LA she was welcomed to the bosom of California's women flyers: Edna May Cooper (an endurance record holder) and the very mannish Bobbie Trout added their signatures to the Bluebird's wings. Then, when she confided to Roy Steckel, the city's chief of police, that she did not know how to use her revolver, he escorted her to a shooting range. Steckel gave her a .38 Colt to try. Mildred was mightily impressed that he could hit the bull's eye with revolvers in each hand.

The hitherto enjoyable visit took a turn for the worse when he said he would shoot the ash from a cigarette in her mouth from a distance of 20ft. Her 'feeble excuse that I am a non-smoker' fell on deaf ears. 'Anyway, by now my habitual love of risk made me suddenly want the experience.' He missed with the first shot. Mildred grabbed a cigarette holder to extend his target further from her face. 'Better luck next time,' the cocky cop drawled. His second shot sent a shower of ash into her right eye. The adrenaline rush was a welcome tonic, 'I left the revolver range feeling a better and bolder woman.' The return drive to the hotel allowed a shaky Mildred to ogle some of the film stars' mansions in Beverly Hills.

Leaving Los Angeles, Mildred's route would ideally have been straight to Texas, but she detoured to San Diego to stay with friends, General and Mrs Terry, whom she had met on the Pacific crossing. Two squadrons of naval aircraft leaped from the San Diego naval base to welcome her. In a fit of exuberance she dived between them and zoomed low over a parade of soldiers on the airfield – twice. A seething Case in the Standard Oil aircraft drew closer and shook his fist at her, beckoning his charge to follow him to a smaller airfield. The squadrons were not her escort – she had just spilt up the display at the base's major military review of the year! On landing, Case could barely contain his embarrassment and his fury. There was clearly no question of her adding another Standard Oil pilot to her tally.

She loved the climate, architecture and landscape of San Diego, 'I could have spent my life there easily,' but her stay was to be less than twenty-four hours. She wrote a quick note to Looff, who was still in her thoughts. That night the Terrys took her to a casino over the border in Mexico, where the band asked if she had a request. In her travel-weary state she asked the Mexican musicians, 'Please play something Hawaiian!'

The following morning she headed for Phoenix: after the Jacinto Mountains near the coast, there were miles of scrubby plain covered in big cacti. If the Cirrus stopped beating … Mildred had time to remember her great-grandparents who had trekked over this inhospitable country, 'I could not help thinking of what they must have gone through, and the perseverance and determination they must have possessed.'[164]

By lunchtime she had made Phoenix, where Beth McQueen of the Women's Aeronautic Association again looked after her. The two plotted how to maximise publicity for the rest of her American odyssey. The Governor of Arizona handed her a letter for the 'King of England' to mark the first time a British woman had arrived in his state by aeroplane. (Scotland, Wales and Ulster could apparently go hang.) After lunch, with *Bluebird* also refuelled, Mildred had only a short 100-mile flight to Tucson.

By 18 January it had been less than a week since they had parted, but that night, having flown from Portland back home to Seattle, a pining Looff penned his first letter to his 'Dear Little Bluebird'. It was going to be difficult for a man with a job as peripatetic as a company pilot to make illicit writing contact with another pilot hopping from city to city. That evening his wife, Edna, had slipped away to her writers' club, leaving Hans playing 'nursemaid to the small boy'. He was snatching a few minutes to reconnect with the diminutive Englishwoman who had clearly stolen his heart.

He was glad she had by now flown to warmer climes, but desperately sad that the miles separated them. Hans looked forward to Mildred gaining the acclaim he thought she richly deserved, yet was hesitant that in fame she would discard memories of him. Rather rashly, he committed to seeing her in Paris within two years:

> I've decided that long ago. But, should the plaudits of the multitudes and the meeting of so many nice people cause you to forget me just a little, I'll try not to mind. But remember this, when I do make my fortune, I shall not give you up and I'll be jealous too. Can't hardly realize you are gone, for even last night you were xxxxx [crossed out]. Cannot understand why I think of you so much. No other girl caused me to dream of

her night after night. God keep you, little one, until we meet again, Your Golden Butterfly.

This was quite an outpouring for a First World War warrior who would have been used to containing his emotions. That night he also began to draft the letter he sent to Ridley exculpating her for the accident at Medford.

The following day, the object of his affections faced an arduous flight of 550 miles to reach Midland in Texas. Again the wonders of the American landscape impressed her: today it was overflying the Rio Grande at El Paso at a chilly 6,000ft. A headwind slowed her progress; this was made evident because she was following the railroad going east, and the ever-impatient Mildred was annoyed she could not overtake a train, 'Of course the trains in America travel across the Plains at very high speed, sometimes seventy or eighty miles an hour.' The path of the railroad was shepherding her away from the highest peaks.

Mildred landed at Midland at 6 in the evening and the baggage aircraft arrived an hour later. Case then departed back to his home base in Washington State. Again following the railroad, the Bluebird non-express went to Dallas and from there, a long and boring journey over the wooded Ozarks and pig farms of Arkansas to St Louis. Just as in China, industrial pollution made it difficult to identify her destination. It was almost 6 in the evening when she at last saw, shimmering in the distance, the wide waters of the Mississippi River, 'What romance the name suggested'. After almost ten hours' flying that day, she slumped exhausted in her hotel bed.

The high point of her crossing of America was to be the visit to her mother's birthplace, but commercial expedience intervened. Standard Oil, who by now had become an important sponsor, asked her to detour north to Chicago. Afterwards, she clearly had no desire to return to the Windy City ('Hell with the lid off'). This far north it was numbingly cold in the cockpit, indeed well below freezing (-14° when she finally landed that night). Her mood was not lightened by having to circle for almost thirty minutes waiting for a man on Curtiss-Wright Field to wave a green flag at her, indicating she had permission to land in between the convoys of airliners. In her state of frozen fatigue, she almost dropped in the Bluebird from 20ft. The staff told her she should have been wearing a fur helmet – the belated advice fell on very cold ears.

That night Hans Looff wrote to his Little Bluebird again, 'You are on my mind constantly and it has turned out rather awkwardly.' The tired pilot had started talking in his sleep and Edna's suspicions were aroused! He asked Mildred to send her letters to him c/o the Boeing Company's airport at Seattle, as some colleague at Standard Oil was now spying on him. He related that Walter Case, Looff's replacement, had gone missing while flying the mails, and that he fully expected to be sent to search for him the following morning. This only made him more solicitous for Mildred's welfare:

> Be a good girl and don't take any more chances. Gee, that I'm happy that you really are getting recognition from the press now. Pluck, little girl, you deserve more than you will ever get no matter how wild they go over you. XXXX

The search for Case ended gloomily: he had died when he flew his large Boeing biplane into Bluff Mountain, while carrying the mails. The Golden Butterfly attended his funeral.

Then, as now, the airport at Chicago was very busy. Al Capone visited the airfield that night, 'Unfortunately I did not have the pleasure of meeting this great criminal, but [the following morning] I found written across the tail of the machine "Hurrah for Prohibition! Al Capone".' She called this, 'A trophy for England', but she was eager to leave the icy blasts of Lake Michigan behind. Indianapolis and then the orchestrated visit to New Albany, her mother's birthplace, beckoned.

Having bought some more cold-weather flying gear, Mildred was now better shielded from the Midwest winter; the umbrella of protection from Standard Oil also became even higher quality. From Chicago, her escort was the head of its aviation department, John P. Porter, in a Laird biplane. As they neared Indianapolis, Porter and Petre were met by a formation of five military aircraft, from the marvellously named Stout Field.

The press at New Albany had been excited about Mildred's arrival for some days. Arriving overhead Bowman Field at Louisville at the appointed lunchtime hour, her mother Jennie's house (The Manse, in New Albany, across the mile-wide river) was easily spotted as the locals had marked a white cross on its roof. There was also a typical crowd to greet her on the aerodrome. Thelma Durbin, the leader of the Girl Guide troop, stepped forward with a bouquet of American Beauty roses and three distant cousins were among the welcoming throng. Another large police cavalcade swept her down streets decked with American and British flags to meet New Albany's Mayor McLinn. Another slim grasp of British aristocratic nuances cannot disguise the civic pride and warmth of the welcome:

> Lady Bruce, you are at the gates of New Albany. We are proud to welcome you. We have never before had a great person who has ridden the air and encircled the earth to visit us, and we marvel at the spirit of love, and of courage, which has brought you to us. You have had honor and praise in

the great cities of the world. We give you honor, but give you also the kindly welcome of home folks, of friends, who knew your mother, and her people and who would be friendly to you. We have looked for your coming. We want you to be one of us whilst you stay.

The city of New Albany presents to you an air photograph of our city with your mother's birthplace marked. Take it to her and may it recall old memories for her and remind you of the little city which gave the mother, and with open arms receives the daughter.

Among the cables were, 'Congratulations from home and mother. Love Victor.'

Connections were made when she met an 85-year-old lady who used to play with her grandmother. The following day, she dropped the US flag on her mother's modest clapboard house, together with three bunches of flowers for the graves of her ancestors. Mayor McLinn had given her a letter to deliver to the US Ambassador in London, Charles G. Dawes, in which he referred to her as an 'ambassadress of goodwill'.[165] There was a widespread interest in the community and Mildred 'had a thrilling tale to tell of typhoons and jungles and adventures in strange corners of the earth ... but everyone, from savages up, was nice to me'.[166]

After the excitement of New Albany, Mildred was now looking forward to arriving in New York as a celebrity. She pointed the Bluebird eastwards for the modest 200-mile flight to Port Columbus. Charles Lindbergh had chosen the site of the town's airport only eighteen months earlier, so when she arrived the stonework of the sturdy art deco terminal building was gleaming. While staying in the town overnight she received a telegram from Glenn Martin's aircraft company suggesting she should fly to Baltimore before Washington, as there would be eighteen National Guard aircraft to provide a welcoming escort.

A morning flight took her to the Curtiss-Bettis Field at Pittsburgh, but after lunch the flight to Baltimore started badly. The geography was again far from benign, this time it was the Appalachian Mountains she had to vault. Firstly, one of her two escort aircraft had to return with engine problems. Minutes later, she noticed that some Columbus ne'er-do-well had unscrewed her St Christopher's badge affixed to the side of the Bluebird. This was unsettling. Then, more seriously, (she later claimed) her map slipped from her grasp and disappeared to the four winds. Finally, she also later asserted that her fuel gauge descended to the red, despite her having ordered 50 gallons at Columbus. With little fuel left Mildred had no option but to land in a field, whereupon the farmer gave her 9 gallons from his car and a bed for the night before heading for Baltimore.

The pilot who had escorted her much of the way, C.D. Brosman, gave a more plausible account to the press.[167] In rain and poor visibility, she had simply become hopelessly lost. Her radio did not provide any communication to allow an escort to guide her. The field near Tappahannock, Virginia, was a full 90 miles south of Baltimore, and 70 miles south-east of Washington, had that been her real destination. Mildred had made a monumental navigational error. Had she had more petrol, the Bluebird might have made its own watery grave in Chesapeake Bay or the Atlantic itself.[168]

The following day, after her involuntary farmhouse stay, Mildred spent an hour and a half wandering the polluted skies trying to locate Baltimore. Eventually she found the airfield at Middle River, but the Bluebird sank into thick mud up to its axles and barely stayed upright. However, on the morrow there was to be an even more serious lapse of decision-making ...

14

THE LAST LAP

The following morning the airfield was in no better state. A rational pilot would have waited for drier weather, but the Petre impetuosity, spurred by the arrangements for a reception in Washington and her New York arrival, impelled her to attempt a take-off from the same morass. She taxied out to the eastern end of the airfield where there was a sliver of concrete. The rest of the low-lying field was a 250-acre sea of mud. The January air was cold and damp, and Mildred, worried about nosing over, left the tail too low on the take-off run:

> Just as she was rising, I turned the plane a little off the run-way, to take advantage of a side wind. We rose, and I thought we were away, but then she suddenly dropped and I knew I had not enough flying speed yet. I tried to hold her off, with the consequence she just fell to the ground and over onto her back in the mud.

The aircraft nosed over, 'I was dazed and almost hysterical. I thought of my plane smashed to pieces, and only 200 miles from New York – my goal!'[169]

A journalist soon noticed the big gash to her head – she had broken her goggles as her head whiplashed forward – although he overlooked her bruised leg. Victor, therefore, heard at midnight via a melodramatic journalist that she was seriously injured and the aircraft 'wrecked beyond all repair'. The inconsolable pilot sat down in the mud, and for the first (recorded) time on this epic journey, wept. Both wings were seemingly irreparable, the propeller in shards, the rudder 'a tangled mess'.

But, on the other hand, she had had the good fortune to stage her biggest crash right outside an aircraft factory. Glenn Luther Martin, the pioneer and manufacturer, had relocated his factory to Baltimore and started building a new airfield only a couple of years earlier. Mr Martin himself told her he would stop by the following morning to see if he could help, but warned that the factory was already working round the clock meeting government orders.

A team with ropes pulled the crushed Bluebird back on to its skewed undercarriage, and a tractor with caterpillar tracks pulled her unceremoniously towards the factory. Muddy, and still for this episode in her ubiquitous thick sweater adorned with her Siamese and Japanese medals, Mildred could have passed for a Land Army girl, albeit an unusually decorated one.

Martin, like Mildred, neither smoked nor drank; unlike Mildred, he also never partied and never married (he lived with his mother, Minta, until well into his fifties). When he arrived in the morning, Mildred was in full damsel-in-distress mode, 'Do you think you could put it together again?'

'I suppose I will have to,' was his laconic reply. Preserving as much of the old fabric (with signatures) as possible, his workers began their urgent rebuilding task.

Once she had settled in to her room at the Lord Baltimore Hotel that night, Mildred wrote a letter to Victor explaining her circumstances, and wasted no time in shifting blame. 'The people here had no right to invite me to their landing ground as it was in a disgraceful condition ... condemned by the airline here as unsafe.' Rather ungratefully, she thought that Martin had been keen to have her land at his field in order to gain publicity.

The largest hotel in the state, the Lord Baltimore, was only two years old. Mildred was paying $3 a night for her stay, which turned out to be longer than she desired – it took the Martin workers ten days to restore the Bluebird's plumage. She visited the factory several times to oversee the work, looking more svelte now in crisp blouse and white slacks.

Her original intent had been to fly to Washington, but the crash had left no time for this. So it was by train that Mildred went to visit Sir Ronald Lindsay, the British Ambassador. The diplomat had previously served in Germany and Turkey, so they could compare notes about Turkish bureaucracy. Like Mildred's father, the lugubrious Lindsay had married an American. At this time, the Bruces were still harbouring a crazy notion of her flying down to Buenos Aires later in the year to coincide with a British trade exhibition there.[170] So, the merits of this were discussed with Sir Ronald.

On 30 January, Beth McQueen sent a letter to her new best friend:

Dearest Darling Mary [Mildred],
Thank God you were not seriously hurt. I am grateful. So near home too.
Well, do be extra careful, and carry out your hunches. You are a wonderful
flier and can beat the men, so do not be discouraged …

McQueen also reported she had written to a friend, John Huston Finlay,
who was associate editor at the *New York Times* to ensure that leading organ
did not overlook the arrival of this new international star.

Women aviators in the USA were already a well-organised bunch, and
they had taken Mildred under their wing. They ensured that she enjoyed
all the publicity that was her due, but the finale of her American odyssey
fizzled into another damp, fogbound end. At the conclusion of her 200-mile
flight to New York, she had been promised a twenty-five-aircraft welcome,
but the cloud was so low she could not find them, if indeed the pilots had
managed to take off. Eventually she located two military aircraft while
flying past the Statue of Liberty at only 100ft – if she reported her height
correctly she was 50ft below the lady's torch, '[in] consequence that I nearly
ran into a huge skyscraper by the docks'!

Despite this excitement, Mildred was very cold by the time the
Bluebird's wheels touched the turf of North Beach Airport (near the pre-
sent-day La Guardia). The anxiety of her stay at the Lord Baltimore faded
and once in New York the arduous part of her journey was over. Any
further flying would be in more familiar skies. So Mildred enjoyed the
glamour of the Big Apple, and would gladly have sunk into the luxury of
the Ritz-Carlton's sheets for a lot longer than the two days available, if her
ship had not beckoned.

The speed of New York's yellow cabs attracted this lady-in-a-hurry, and
the brand new Empire State Building also made a strong impression.[171]
Friends took the abstinent pilot to a speakeasy to complete the 1930s Big
Apple experience.

Meanwhile, Herbert Pratt was in town; as solicitous for her welfare as
ever, he ensured his company looked after all the logistics of boarding
arrangements for both pilot and aircraft. So, on a black February night,
Bluebird, wings folded, was trucked over the 59th Street Bridge to the
French Line's dock. Mildred and her aircraft sailed on the *Île de France* at
noon on 7 February. The ship, with salons by Le Bucheron, was the height
of art deco opulence and, at 791ft long, nearly twice the size of the liner
in which she had crossed the Pacific. It was perhaps understandable that
Mildred had used a non-British vessel (the *Empress of Japan*) to transport
Bluebird and herself across the Pacific from Japan to Canada. However,
given the intense competition in international passenger shipping in the

1930s, and Mildred's generally patriotic demeanour, it is somewhat surprising that she chose the *Île de France* to transport herself and her precious
cargo across the Atlantic. Perhaps she had been seduced by the reputation
of its décor …

Once in her cabin, her mind was looking west, rather than east, and
another telegram was dispatched to her Californian lover. A couple of days
later, Looff replied by letter:

> … shall always think of you as the genuine little lady that you are, and look
> back on those few days of worry as the finest experience of my life. Must
> try not to get sentimental because your husband might get jealous …!

He went on to relate the story of the death of Case and his funeral. Hans
was still plotting to meet his Bluebird again at Paris' Le Bourget aerodrome
in two years' time.

While Mildred had suffered her enforced sojourn in Baltimore, Victor had
been working hard behind the scenes to orchestrate the arrival at Croydon
that he felt his wife deserved, and that would help to launch her into the
orbit of famous aviatrix. Croydon Airport was at that time the default choice
in England for the landings for major global flights. At the end of January,
he visited officials at the Air Ministry in Gwydyr House in London. He
had badgered Francis Bertram CBE, the Deputy Director of Civil Aviation,
who in turn minuted, in true *Yes Minister* style, Frederick Montague, the
Undersecretary of State for Air, to lead the Croydon festivities:

> Mr. Bruce is desirous of arranging for her a welcome at Croydon on a
> fairly considerable scale … and that a great body of people would assem-
> ble at Croydon to greet her. In view of her accomplishment I think it
> would not be inappropriate if you could arrange to welcome her officially
> on her arrival at Croydon.

Cables flew to and from England to co-ordinate her arrival. On the *Île de
France*, there was no talk of dancing the night away to combat sea sickness,
no need to sweet-talk oil company magnates: instead, Mildred needed a
respite to recharge her batteries. On the ship she encountered an interesting
French aviation pioneer – Robert Esnault-Pelterie, an inveterate aircraft
designer who had invented the system of using a joystick to control the
machine. He had recently started investigating rocket propulsion.

On the sixth day of her crossing, Mildred was astonished on awakening
to find her husband, Victor, standing by her bedside. The thoroughbred of
a liner had docked briefly at Plymouth. As the ship eased back into the

Channel towards its final destination of France's major ocean terminal at Le Havre, the Bruces renewed their acquaintance with each other and discussed plans for the Croydon coronation. They were still contemplating her doing a flight to Buenos Aires to coincide with the British trade exhibition there and the Society of British Aircraft Companies was very much in favour.

Once docked at Le Havre, the Bruces were feted at dinner by the Aéro-Club de France – possibly not the most romantic way to celebrate their fifth wedding anniversary. Global pioneering was dear to the heart of the Normans, and only a few miles up the coast at Étretat four years earlier, two French knights of the air, Charles Nungesser and François Coli, were seen for the last time on their attempt to be the first to fly from Paris to the US. Their bodies were never found.

Taking the train to the capital with Victor, Mildred met her Paris match, so to speak. On 18 February, the Aéro-Club de France organised another dinner in her honour and her fellow VIP guest was Maryse Hilsz (a dour and dumpy Frenchwoman, but an Alsatian, hence the Germanic surname).[172] Hilsz had returned to Paris only eleven days earlier from an epic return flight to Saigon (capital of a French dependency, of course) in a small Morane-Saulnier AR35C monoplane. Her route covered much of the same hostile territory as Mildred's – Baghdad, Karachi, Calcutta, Rangoon and Bangkok, so there was much to discuss. While Hilsz lacked Mildred's star quality and easy charm, she did go on to have a sustained career of long-distance aerial adventures.

Also on the top table that night was 32-year-old Maryse Bastié, a sparkling, wide-eyed brunette, whose speciality at that time was endurance rather than distance. Five months earlier she had won 50,000 Francs in prize money after staying aloft for almost thirty-eight hours in her German-built Klemm L-25 monoplane.[173] Jacques-Louis Dumesnil, the very distinguished-looking Minister for Air in Pierre Laval's government, also attended the dinner – the French Establishment was taking these ladies seriously. Mildred's visit to Paris was partly in recognition of the medal that she had been awarded in French Indo-China, but we can assume it was also with an eye to heightening her profile in Europe for future flying endeavours.

The European winter was not being kind and it was snowing when Victor took his leave the following morning to catch the night boat to Southampton and finalise the Croydon reception. Some slack had been built into the schedule to ensure that Mildred arrived at Croydon at precisely noon on Friday. So, on Thursday, instead of flying directly from Le Havre to London's airport, she flew to Lympne on England's south coast.

The weather had one more final hand to deal Mildred and even she realised that it was 'very unsatisfactory'. Any sensible pilot would have advised her to tarry at Normandy's maritime hub, but the following day's appointment with celebrity was the siren call. So, one more time she took off into a damp wintry dawn – the clouds were low, and:

> ... it's impossible to see forward . The only line I can follow is the white foam on the coast. I can only tell my bearings by the time it is taking at all. And it is impossible to distinguish any landmarks today. I am flying low, about 20' above the water and keeping my eye on the white foam of the waves.

Crossing the yawning mouth of the Somme Estuary took an age and at that ridiculous height, concentration had to be intense. An hour later she was trying to fly round the snow showers and keep in touch with the rolling chalkland of the Pas-de-Calais landscape. Suddenly, 'a ghastly white cliff loomed up perilously near me – Cap Gris Nez!' She tried to divert to the small grass aerodrome at Saint-Inglevert, just inland, but its position, at more than 500ft above sea level, meant it was swathed in mist. Mildred spent the best part of an hour circling without success in a dangerous attempt to find it. Believing that conditions could hardly be worse in England, she resolved to set off across the Channel.

This meant a stressful ten minutes flying on instruments in cloud. After more than three hours' flying (when she should have landed safely at her English destination an hour earlier), the clouds parted to allow her the view she had been dreaming about for weeks – the White Cliffs of Dover, with Henry II's castle atop. Two minutes out from Lympne, Mildred's stiff upper lip softened a little, 'I wanted to cry and to laugh at the same time.'

The landing was an anti-climax – on a day when even the seagulls doubted the wisdom of flying, Lympne was tranquil. It had been a gruelling four-hour flight, in the worst weather a northern European winter can provide. With the exhaustion that comes from knowing that the travails are (almost) over, she dismounted from the Bluebird and walked over to the only person in sight – a mechanic. Demanding that he shake hands with her, she announced, 'I'm back!'

'From where?' was his underwhelmed reply.

'The world!', her headline-ready retort.

Mildred was soon in a taxi to the Red Lion Inn in Hythe down the road, where her first request was for a real English high tea, although it was barely lunchtime. The afternoon was spent fielding telephone calls and telegrams from friends and family.

At Lympne Aerodrome a bevy of celebrities assembled to form an aerial cavalcade to escort her to Croydon. Amy Johnson arrived in her Puss Moth; Winfred Spooner, as ever looking as though she had stepped from the pages of an Angela Brazil novel, landed in a Bluebird; a group of senior figures from the Blackburn Company also all arrived in Bluebirds. Led by Norman Blackburn, (who, by this time, shared the gaunt and haunted look of Victor), the group also included Squadron Leader Claude Ridley DSO (the man to whom Pickles had written from California), Flight Lieutenant N.H. Woodhead DSC and H.R. Field.[174]

Mildred had all but completed her circumnavigation. A neophyte when she had left Heston five months earlier, she had now joined the ranks of aviation superstars. The tyro airwoman had enjoyed more than her fair share of good luck – Mildred could have so easily met her end in desert, jungle or mountain. She had tempted fate by flying through some of the worst weather a pilot can endure – and ostensibly without any instrument training. But, luck aside, what had brought her back to English soil was her capacity to endure physical and mental hardship for hours on end – a skill honed on the roads and racing tracks of Europe. It was time to bathe in the celebrity she craved.

ARRIVAL AND ADULATION

For the final leg of her journey Mildred was lucky with the weather – earlier in the week Croydon Aerodrome had been beset with the same snow that had blighted her French stay.

As we have seen, the arrival in England had been stage managed. Victor had engaged Colonel Sanders as master of ceremonies. A director of Auto Auctions, Sanders was the actual salesman who had sold the Bluebird to Mildred. By 16 February, he had organised matters with Major Richard, the chief aerodrome officer at Croydon. Victor had issued 500–700 invitations and 400–500 people were expected to show up.[175] The invitations, as was the manner for celebratory arrivals, were 'stiffies' – formal printed cards as if for a reception or dinner:

> Messrs Auto Auctions Ltd and the Blackburn Aeroplane Co.
> Request the pleasure of your company
> At the Croydon Aerodrome
> At 12 noon on Friday 20th February 1931 to welcome
> The Honourable Mrs Victor Bruce
> On the completion of her 19,000 mile solo flight
> Round the world in a Blackburn 'Bluebird' Aeroplane
> The Honourable Mrs Victor Bruce
> Will be welcomed by the Under Secretary of State for Air

A troop or two of Boy Scouts were to 'assist the aerodrome staff in keeping visitors within bounds'. Sanders wrote to Frederick Montagu, Undersecretary of State for Air, leaning on him to lead the welcome party.

Amy Johnson's return to Croydon after her epic flight to Australia, less than a year earlier (even although it was by airliner), had attracted hordes of onlookers. There were 4,000 cars parked on roads next to the aerodrome and her route into London was lined with fans. As Martin Pugh wrote:

By following sport, cinema and politics, thousands of people who lived lives of hardship obtained a vicarious pleasure in linking themselves to the lives of successful, powerful and glamorous people, thereby mitigating any sense of alienation or antagonism they might otherwise have developed then.[176]

In 1930, aviators cast the same spell.

Croydon was somewhat quieter on 20 February. In the event, the crowd numbered only 100 or so, but *Flight* magazine noted that the quality of the audience compensated for its lack of quantity, 'Those who were [present] were thoroughly enthusiastic and fully realised the excellence of the flight which Mrs Bruce had made.'

As she flew over the Surrey landscape, Mildred's excitement rose:

… almost to nervousness. We flew slowly, for I had plenty of time for once in my life. At ten minutes to twelve I saw the Crystal Palace and almost at the same moment Croydon Aerodrome. I felt ill with excitement as I made a low circuit around the enormous field. My flight was over!

Mildred landed on the Surrey turf three minutes early: her round-the-world flight concluded at 11.57 a.m., five months after she had left Heston. *Flight* magazine reported approvingly, 'The whole welcome was carried through in a quiet and sensible manner and there was none of that hysterical public heroine worship.' Quality, not quantity, then – Mildred would probably have been quite content with hysterical heroine worship.

Many of the press reports recording Mildred's arrival that day note she was greeted by her husband and 10-year-old son. It is therefore strange that he appears in none of the press photos. Instead, Mildred is shown clutching a boy, admittedly bonny, with fetching blonde curls, but only around 2 years of age. His identity is a mystery, but one assumes he was a decoy – a very young child designed to give the impression that he was the son of Mildred and Victor? Lawrence Petre was there, and her dog Paddy completed the party to nuzzle his mistress.

Of course, the notable absentee was Sir Sefton Brancker. He very much liked to attend in person the arrival of notable flights to the UK, and Mildred would have adored his benediction, but he was lying with his fellow travellers in the graveyard of St Mary's, Cardington, 80 miles to the north.

As ever, Mildred was wearing the two decorations she had received on the journey – the Japanese one, and the Order of the Million Elephants and White Umbrella. Jesting to a reporter, 'I told them I could not afford the elephants but I would have the umbrella,' and she could not help reinforcing the globetrotting image, 'My husband has not had a dress-maker's bill recently. I am wearing a Hong Kong jumper, a Shanghai skirt, Vancouver shoes and hand-painted lingerie, the gift of Chinese ladies in Amoy.'[177]

Hardly needing the Boy Scouts to control it, the modest crowd assembled around the Bluebird. But despite the planning, the organisation seemed a little chaotic. Few could hear the welcome speech given by the portly Montague, 'The most striking feature of your accomplishment in the eyes of the people at home was its perfect unpretentious efficiency.' Noting her relative lack of experience before the flight, he continued:

A fact so striking must have an important bearing upon the develop-ment of air mindedness, and must do much to convince the public of the strides that are being made in air conquest as well as efficiency and reliability. Your journey also represents another triumph for British aircraft manufacturing skill and testifies to our Nation's technical development.

This was an era of fierce international competition in both aircraft design and establishing global communications routes, and Montague was rightly proud of her and Blackburn's achievement.

Other VIPs included Commander Perrin of the Royal Aero Club, J.H. Thomas, the government's colonial secretary, and the replacement for poor Brancker as Director of Civil Aviation, Lieutenant Colonel Francis Shelmerdine, only just returned from India to take up the post. This main party then repaired to the Aerodrome Hotel for some drinks. Relieved to be home at last, Mildred was too good an actress to show her disappointment in the scale of her welcome.

The major celebration of her success was a dinner held that night in her honour at the Mayfair Hotel, London. By a strange coincidence, her hero, Sir Malcolm Campbell, and his *Bluebird* were also being feted in the same hotel at another large dinner, anointing his recent breaking of the land-speed record in the USA.[178] Ungainly floral tributes in the shape of biplanes hung from the ceiling and the 100 or so guests at her event enjoyed a typical 1920s menu:

Smoked Salmon [strangely, *de Norvège* rather than *d'Écosse*]
Consommé Double Mayfair,

Suprême de Turbotin Ambassadeurs,
Poussin du Surrey Polonaise.

The evening was hosted by the British Aviation Hospitality Association and the Women's Automobile and Sports Association. Looking as though she could double as the prow of a Tudor warship, Viscountess Elibank, who was chairman of the former, proposed the loyal toast. She and another organiser, Lady Houston, had been at daggers drawn over petty politicking in the preceding days.

Colonel the Master of Sempill ('Sempill' to SIS/MI6, or 'Billy' to his few friends), in his capacity as chairman of the aviation section of the London Chamber of Commerce, proposed the toast to the latest aviation heroine. Donning his monocle, he underlined the scale of her achievement and also her successes on the racetrack – 'these alone testified to her staying powers, which were phenomenal'. He related the incident of her keeping the Baluchi tribesmen at bay with her alarm clock, and kept the audience at bay waving the very same clock. Sempill was purring with satisfaction at the impetus that Mildred had given to relations with the Japanese. A few years before, the Secret Intelligence Service (SIS) had been fretting that Sempill would replace the late Brancker as Director of Civil Aviation, and noted that 'the Air Ministry would view such an appointment with dismay'. The Air Ministry was therefore only somewhat put out when Sempill was elected president of the Royal Aeronautical Society in 1927.[179]

Tsuneo Matsudaira, the bloated Japanese Ambassador, spoke next, referring to the work done by Sempill for the Japanese Naval Service but obviously glossing over the secrets transferred. He concluded by saying that he 'felt sure that her flight had done a lot still further to cement the cordial relationship already existing between Great Britain and Japan'. Not so cordial, though, as to prevent the two countries waging war a decade later.

Winifred Spooner, one of the star pilots who had accompanied Mildred on the final leg to Croydon, proposed the toast to the chairman. Mildred, in her speech, paid testimony to the legion of helpers, not least Imperial Airways, whose engineers had performed countless hours of work on her craft at various stages in her journey, and the RAF, who had sent up many aircraft to look for her when overdue.

Most of the luminaries of British aviation were there to laud her: Sir Alan Cobham, Amy Johnson, manufacturers Whitney Straight, Sir Alliott Verdon-Roe, the de Havillands and Norman Blackburn. There was, of course, a good leavening of aristocrats: the Countess of Drogheda, Dowager Lady Swaythling (a friend of Sempill), Lady Maude Warrender, and others. Mildred's cousin and long-time supporter, Major Henry Petre (the old 'Petre the Monk') came with his wife, Kay Petre, who was about to start her own very successful racing career at Brooklands. W.O. Bentley, who had supplied cars to Mildred towards the end of her racing career, was another guest.

The following day, there was a more informal welcome at Heston Aerodrome organised by Auto Auctions and Airwork (which had bought the airfield). It was a chill morning – she alighted from the Bluebird dwarfed by her fur coat to be greeted by the looming hulk of Nigel Norman, the owner of Airwork, who was dressed in modish plus fours. Thirty pilots had flown in to acclaim her.

On 24 February there was yet another dinner, this time given by her London club, the New Burlington.

Summarising the flight in April, Mildred said:

> I had thrills and shocks. But what is the most important, I feel a different woman altogether from the one I was when I left. I think I have improved and become better. When you face danger, suffering and death, something changes in you and you view quite differently the things which seemed so important to you before – social matters, the commonplaces of everyday life, and so forth.
>
> But here I am; and if you ask me whether I would start my adventure all over again, I believe I would have to answer yes. Of course I shall now try to travel with my husband. And we shall very probably travel by air. But although there are many places I have recently visited, which I would much like to see again, if you ask me where I would like to live the rest of my life, I will say – in my home, in England. The world is small, and it is wonderful to know it and to roam about it. But home still remains home![180]

But, perhaps the best, if verbose, summary of the flight was made when it was only half completed. Snow, from the British Embassy in Tokyo, concluded:

> It is true that opinions were expressed that, in the successful termination of her flight to Tokyo, good luck had perhaps played a larger part than experience of flying or previous study or organisation. Any criticisms on this or other grounds, were, however, outweighed by the simplicity and lack of ostentation with which Mrs Bruce referred to her exploit, and her frank avowal on occasion that for her aviation was a means of livelihood: indeed her attitude was well suited to appeal to Japanese tastes, and the outstanding fact remains that thanks to her achievement, backed

by her unflinching energy in Tokyo, she conveyed a neat impression of British courage and British sportsmanship to hundreds in Japan who met her and the millions who were reached by the variegated tales of her adventures.[181]

It had become the fashion to display the aircraft used in epic journeys in prominent places. Years earlier, Gordon Selfridge had procured Louis Blériot's cross-Channel machine and had very recently beaten off intense competition to display Amy Johnson's Moth in his department store. The proud directors of Auto Auctions put Mildred's battered Bluebird on display in their showroom in Burlington Gardens, whence it had come. Then it spent a couple of weeks outside Charing Cross Station, where it brought joy to a Mrs Smith who spotted among all the signatures on the wings a message from her daughter who had greeted Mildred in Seattle, 'Good luck to all in the home country, Edith Ready, Seattle'. But by 17 March, *Bluebird* was being exhibited at the Brighton Aquarium – near to where years before she had crashed her brother's motorbike.

Mildred had long determined to capitalise on her celebrity in any way she could, having already proved her mettle as a public speaker in Vancouver and across the USA. After these initial speeches in her first week back home, *Flight* magazine described her as an 'extremely attractive and witty speaker'. Addressing a crowd held no fear for her – indeed it is sometimes difficult to discern what did frighten her. So, she signed up with a speaking agency and kick-started her lecture tour with a large gathering at London's Aeolian Hall on 17 March. Ten days later came a bitter/sweet award: the International League of Aviators gave Mildred second place as the world's Leading Woman Flyer for 1930 (in first place, inevitably, was Amy Johnson). Nonetheless, when Mildred's lecture tour took her to Amy's home town of Hull on 5 May, the welcome was very warm, 'She is the essence of femininity; she reveals a voice of Tallulah Bankhead huskiness.' Mildred in her speech was careful to express her pride in her aircraft, which had been manufactured in the town of Brough, a few miles to the west.

Mildred had done more than her bit to make flying accessible to women as well as men. However, misogyny was still rife in the industry. Captain Charles D. Barnard, a pioneer, air racer and latterly aerial chauffeur to the Duchess of Bedford, and therefore accustomed to strong-willed women, was touring the UK that spring, visiting 150 towns to offer a local *boy* one of 100 flying scholarships to learn to fly at a local aero club. As *The Vote* (a magazine allied with the Suffragette Movement) wryly noted:

Capt. Barnard seems not to know that last year Miss Amy Johnson flew alone to Australia, Miss Winifred Brown beat most of our flying aces in winning the King's Cup, and, quite recently, Mrs Victor Bruce successfully completed a pioneer flight to Japan, which placed her in the forefront among aviators of either sex!

A limp *Bluebird* was sent into retirement, and Mildred bought (or more probably was given) a new Bluebird, G-ABMI, and flew most days through the summer, often using it to take her to speaking engagements. Many of these lectures were hosted by women's organisations. For example, she spoke in Glasgow on 12 May under the auspices of the Society for Equal Citizenship and the Women's' Citizens Association, where she 'held a large audience breathless'.

The press were generally enthusiastic. In April, in Harrogate, 'she detailed many thrilling incidents, which kept her audiences deeply interested throughout'. As the British economy remained in the doldrums, Mildred made no attempt to disguise that her grasp for celebrity, and her doing such a rigorous series of speaking engagements, was to generate some income.

In her urge to surf the wave of publicity, Mildred had given herself no time to recuperate from the trip, nor indeed much time to relearn such mothering skills as she might once have possessed. Leaping straight into a lecture tour and flying herself around Britain was hardly sensible. By 25 May, the physical stress had caused her to fall ill with a high temperature and five days later she was admitted to a Weybridge nursing home with pleurisy. This knocked her out for only a month. Back at Croydon on 25 June and dressed more elegantly than last time, Mildred was not quite looking her normal confident self to welcome two diminutive Japanese competitors who were engaged in a madcap, Jules Verne-type round-the-world race using public transport.

A week later, she penned a rather pushy letter to the newly created Guild of Air Pilots asking to be considered for its Johnston Prize (created in memory of Squadron Leader Ernest Johnston, the first deputy Master of the Guild, who had lost his life in the R101 crash). This was obviously the first year it was to be awarded, the criterion being for the best feat of navigation by someone in a civilian capacity. In the event, the prize was justly awarded to Francis Chichester for his epic flights across the Tasman Sea in a Gipsy Moth.[182] In subsequent years it was awarded to Bert Hinkler, Jim Mollison, Edgar Percival and Jean Batten.

The illness meant Mildred did not fly again until 27 June, resuming her lectures four days later in Liverpool. All the while she had been speedily writing the account of her voyage. *The Bluebird's Flight* was published in

November that year. In his review in *Flight* magazine, Daedalus wrote, 'For those who have the pleasure of her friendship know that one of her assets is the manner in which she is always ready to laugh when the laugh is against her.'

Around this time, Victor was interviewed for a newspaper article which was entitled, 'What it Feels Like to be the Husband of a Famous Airwoman'! The words 'scorn' and 'cuckold' were not mentioned. What it really felt like was to be rejected. Soon after her return from the round-the-world flight she told him they were no longer suited.[183] This made it all the more commendable that Victor battled on in Mildred's company for several more years.

Perhaps it was as a fruitless attempt to engage with Mildred more closely, or perhaps merely a means to spend more time with her, but in 1931 Victor learned to fly. Although he did have some friends in the county from his motoring days, it is still somewhat strange that he chose to learn at the Blackpool Flying Club, rather than at Brooklands, on the doorstep of their Surrey home, 'Woodbines' (named after the leading cigarette brand of the time).

In June, she entered the most prestigious air race of the British aviation calendar – the King's Cup – but never made the start line. As the summer flying season engaged top gear, Mildred's celebrity status was not in doubt. On 22 July, she flew a Monospar again at the Household Brigade Flying Club's air display.

On 6 August she was back at Croydon, this time to welcome Jim Mollison on his arrival from breaking the Australia–England record in a DH.60G Gipsy Moth. After eight and a half days' flying, he arrived at a muddy Croydon in a state of near exhaustion – he had lost his flying goggles while over India and the subsequent four days in an open cockpit would have been excruciating. The ceremonies had more than an air of circus about them: the airport manager was knocked over by the Moth's tail as he was assisting it towards the apron; a kangaroo in boxing gloves, brought along for publicity purposes, was nearly decapitated by the propeller and tried to slug the tired Australian pilot. But the occasion did give Mildred a chance to be reunited with her former flying companion, Oscar Garden, now settled into a commercial career in England – he too was in the welcome party.

Pilots of greater standing, such as Mollison, clearly did not doubt Mildred's piloting skills, for he and Charles Scott invited her to join them in a formation flying display at an informal tea party at Hanworth, a few days later. After tea she took one of Mollison's uncles up for his first flight. As if to cement the notion that women were now capable of any male piloting feat, in September an 'All Woman' meeting was hosted at Northampton's Sywell Aerodrome. Mildred came second in the air race, clad in a rather lovely long, leather flying coat, her svelte appearance mitigated by a strange woollen cap.

By now, Great Britain had descended into total fiscal chaos. Sterling was under threat and drastic economies had to be made, but nine of the eleven Labour Cabinet members were threatening to resign over the suggested 10 per cent cut in unemployment benefits. Bankers were being accused of using the crisis to dictate economic policy. Those nine cabinet members *did* resign, and a coalition 'National' government was formed. The American banks made a loan to the UK conditional on a balanced budget. It all sounds horribly familiar ...

Meanwhile, Sempill was hedging his bets with the Axis Powers. In August, he appointed himself in charge of the customer aspects of a round-Britain tour by Germany's Graf Zeppelin airship. Thirty passengers were to pay £30 a ticket for this aerial tour of Britain's major cities. It doubled as an opportunity for German military reconnaissance, under the guidance of Dr Eckener, Germany's airship guru. Gales prevented a visit to Dublin and Scotland, but most of England's industrial cities were overflown. Sempill was again with his German friends in October when he joined the Graf Zeppelin on a voyage from its home base of Friedrichshafen to Brazil.

In September, half a million spectators lined the Hampshire and West Sussex coastline to watch the British win the Schneider Trophy for the fifth time and also beat the air-speed record. Thereafter, Britain held the trophy in perpetuity. Mildred flew on to Teignmouth for the town's annual 'air rally' and, although she did not take part in the racing, she was able to meet her traitorous friend Sempill at the dinner that night.

Later that month, Mildred started to try her hand at aerobatics at Hanworth, under the tutelage of Captain Schofield. She playfully told a newspaper journalist that 'the chief attraction aerobatics have for her is to enable her to keep her husband in order when an argument rises between them during the time that he is flying as her passenger'!

She was again in the VIP reception party to welcome Kingsford-Smith to British soil at Heston Aerodrome on 7 October. Shattered mentally, Smithy had failed to beat Mollison's record (for Australia–England), and like his fellow Australian, had now become chronically dependent on alcohol for these long flights.[184] He admitted to the welcoming crowd that he was due to see a 'nerve specialist' on the morrow, before doing any more flying.

Flight magazine reported the 1932 New Year's Eve celebrations at Hanworth's National Flying Services, where Mildred appears to have caused a stir:

> I was just talking about this, when there was a crash, and a figure in a messenger boy's uniform with a parachute trailing behind, slid across the floor. When the crowd had been pushed back, George was able to get his first view of Mrs Victor Bruce, the same, I told him, who made that very wonderful solo flight round the world (except for the Atlantic and Pacific) in a 'Bluebird'. She is always up to some prank, and her arrival was to signal the end of the old year. She brought with her a telegram from the inhabitants of Mars (very warlike and not a good omen – ED.), greeting all British pilots and the members of Hanworth Club. Later on – I mean early the next day – we had further taste of her versatility when she carried through a cabaret turn with Messrs. Geoffrey Dorman and R. Copeland. Her 'Hula Hula' dance, with nothing but a thatching of dried grass between her and us, was marvellous, and it was only my suggestion of a visit to the bar (kindly placed at our disposal through Lord Trenchard at such an early hour) which saved George from joining in. I thought Geoff looked a bit chilly without his skirt, for even his beloved messenger boy's cap was insufficient to hide his manly legs after 'Copey' had committed the drastic act of debagging , I mean deskirting him. Copeland has rare flair for the Ukelele, and I suppose he will use it to keep his brother pilots awake in the air. It would look well on the cover of a book, wouldn't it? – 'Us! Uke and Aircraft' or 'The Flying Minstrel Boy'! We had both had our fill of dancing by now, and after getting another laugh at the expense of Mrs Victor Bruce, who was this time 'taking off' Fred May in several of his songs, we braved the fog to London again.

Victor seems notable by his absence.

By now the economic climate had deteriorated further. Almost 1 million unemployed were having to register for transitional payments and were coming within the scope of the Means Test. So Mildred's thoughts were turning to making a career out of flying.

That month she was the first ever woman to do an instrument flying course; she chose Air Services Training, at Hamble airfield near Southampton.[185] If the weather conditions she encountered on her round-the-world flight were occasionally as bad as she had described, she had had the fates firmly on her side – most pilots of her experience, untutored in the dark arts of instrument flying, would have come to grief. The course was an overdue insurance policy to postpone her arrival at the Pearly Gates.

Mildred was due to lecture at the Royal Dublin Society in January, and set off in her Bluebird, but had to turn back over the Irish Sea due to bad weather. The lifeboat was called out, but she landed safely at Hooton on the Wirral. To her chagrin, the journey had to be completed by boat.

In March, she was signed off to do night flying by Flight Lieutenant J.B.W. Pugh, who was to receive an Air Force Cross three months later. Then, in May, Amelia Earhart hit the headlines with her solo flight across the Atlantic to Ireland in a Lockheed Vega. There were many festivities in London, and Mildred met the American aviatrix at a tea party hosted by Andrew Mellon, the US Ambassador, at his London home. Lady Bailey and Peggy Salaman were fellow guests (both best known for flights to South Africa).

On 22 May, Mildred was back at Hanworth Aerodrome with Shelmerdine (the Director of Civil Aviation) and many others to welcome Earhart after yet another flight across the Atlantic. But Mildred had by now planned her next attempt to remain in the headlines herself. Together with Victor, she intended to break the record for staying aloft – 'a month in the air' was the line fed to reporters. Madcap as this now seems, it followed naturally from her feats of endurance at Montlhéry, and it was also designed to test new techniques for in-flight refuelling. Clearly this would require a much bigger aircraft than she had ever flown.

In April, she had started flying down to Cowes regularly to have meetings with the management at Saunders-Roe.[186] Their imposing flying boats seemed just the ticket for the record attempt. The largest example, a three-engine Windhover, was available for rent, but it was owned by Gibraltar Airways. So, at the end of May she flew down there with Saro's chief test pilot, the 40-year-old Stuart Scott.

They were disappointed to learn that the aircraft had not flown for some months but after three days work it was 'running nicely'. They had a successful flight up the Spanish coast to Alicante. After some adjustments, they set out for England, but Scott lost an engine soon after take-off. He turned for the sea, but a second engine spluttered to a stop. They were at a height of only 100ft over unpromising terrain – a house surrounded by trees. In avoiding the former, Scott hit the latter.[187] Mildred was later very grateful that the Windhover was built so stoutly.[188]

It was time to start earning more serious money from her record-breaking. In July 1932 she and Victor founded Luxury Air Tours, as a commercial vehicle through which to funnel any income – its name indicating there was more than just an endurance flight in Mildred's mind. John Pugh held a few shares and, presumably for the sake of nostalgia, she gave one to her father.

Divisions in society were as sharp as they had been for a long time – the pilots were flying above the public in more sense than one for, on both sides of the Atlantic, life for much of the population remained grim. The US stock market continued to slide, reaching its lowest point in July 1932, by which time it had fallen by 89 per cent from its 1929 peak. The Great Depression was even deeper in the US than in Britain,[189] yet stars of the sky still reigned supreme: Amy Johnson was ranked by schoolgirl visitors to Madame Tussaud's Waxworks in London the second most popular figure they most wanted to be like when they grew up, behind Edith Cavell (the First World War nurse and heroine) but ahead of Joan of Arc.

Later in the year, Mildred gave a talk with lantern slides at Wethersfield Village Hall – not too distant from her ancestral lands at Ingatestone. The presentation quite overcame her host, A. W. Ruggles-Brise, who remarked she was the most wonderful woman he had ever met (history does not, however, record the views of his wife).

Victor later recounted a conversation he overheard in his London club, 'That's Victor Bruce. Would you let your wife fly around the world by herself? He must be a funny sort of chap.' When he recounted this to a journalist later, he added, '"Letting" my wife do anything is humorous. Her strongest characteristic is determination. The greater the opposition and hindrance, the greater the determination.'[190]

STARS IN THE SKY

Mildred had acquired the Windhover in July 1932, and renamed her *City of Portsmouth*. This was an amphibious aircraft, but Mildred had the undercarriage temporarily removed (presumably to save weight). The following month, she used it to attempt to break the world flight-refuelled endurance record of twenty-three days (then held by Americans).

Mildred was joined at Cowes by the lugubrious Pugh and Flight Sergeant W.R. McLeary – as flight engineer, he was destined to be very busy during these mammoth flights. Victor was a member of the crew of the tanker aircraft, which dangled an unwieldy hose down to the Windhover. This was a clapped-out Bristol Fighter of First World War vintage (G-ABXA) which she had bought in June. In earlier publicity Victor had been described as a member of the Windhover crew, with Mildred making somewhat ludicrous assertions about the detailed fitting out of the craft's interior so that she could be the perfect housewife for her husband and crew over the several weeks of the intended flight (it was sufficiently large to have several 'rooms'). The newsreel cameras were on hand to record the attempt, for which Mildred wore some very dashing pantaloons. (Doubtless during her preparations, she allowed herself a moment of jealousy that her rival, Amy Johnson, was enjoying a church wedding at St George's, Hanover Square, for her ill-fated marriage to Jim Mollison.)

In one practice refuelling session Mildred claimed to have received a goodly dousing of petrol. For the record attempt itself, the two lumbering aircraft departed the Windhover's home waters of the Solent, the former threading its way through a myriad of small boats, to fly mesmerising circles over the Ipswich area, within gliding distance of England's main seaplane base at Felixstowe. The Bristol Fighter unloaded 80 gallons of fuel five times every day to the Windhover below.

The third and final record attempt (the first two were aborted) started at just after noon on 9 August. It was truncated by a rising oil temperature. The crew had failed to modify the craft so that filters of the outboard engines could be changed in the air.[191] The flight's aftermath was soured with acrimony: the Royal Aero Club, which ratifies record attempts, took a dim view of Mildred discarding the barograph – the ultimate proof of height and time aloft. In a petulant conversation with a journalist, she explained that the crew had had to discard 300lb of equipment, and the 18lb barograph was one of the items to be jettisoned. 'If the Royal Aero Club or the British public do not wish to believe us, they are welcome to their records.' The fifty-four-hour flight cost her £7,000, and there was a 40 per cent risk of losing their lives, she added, 'Flying Officer Pugh in his capacity as observer, was on his honour as a gentleman to state the truth. He had no financial interest in the flight, and his word must be taken.'[192]

The crew were left with breaking just the British endurance record, set three years earlier, by three and a half hours. A day or two later, Mildred was staying in an Ipswich hotel, still sore at her failure. A hotel resident spoke to her of the flight 'in a humiliating way', so with some encouragement from 'friends from the aerodrome' she 'hit him hard, several times, so hard, in fact, that I hurt my hand'.

The aviation press gave their habitual praise, 'She has always proved herself to be full of real courage and energy. And whenever she has been beaten she has proved herself a thorough sportsman.'[193] In later years, Mildred laid bare her motives for this project, 'I wouldn't have done if there was no publicity.' But the *Daily Sketch* paid her handsomely and 'I made my fortune'. In her view, it was therefore a complete success.

On 1 September 1932, she gained her 'B' licence, enabling her to carry passengers and freight for commercial purposes, and later in the month took Flight Lieutenant Pugh in her Bristol Fighter to an 'All Women's Flying Meeting'. It is difficult to conceive that the debonair Pugh was dressed in drag, while she, on the other hand, was wearing her favourite light leather flying jacket.

In November 1932, she bought a Fairey Fox (G-EBWI) for £12 10s from a scrap dealer, and later a Miles Satyr – a rare single-seater, which was good for aerobatics. On the basis of 'if you can't beat them, join them', Victor learned to fly that autumn at Blackpool – well removed from their Surrey home (which was rather oddly named after a leading cigarette brand of the time, 'Woodbines'). Why he chose to learn to fly so far from home is a mystery. He never showed any great enthusiasm for aviation thereafter.

To close the year, Mildred participated in a Boxing Day Air Rally at Feltham Aerodrome (now the site of Heathrow). There was pylon racing in ultralight 6hp machines, but sadly Mildred was disqualified from her heat due to flying the wrong side of a pylon. The meeting was, however, enlivened by an aircraft vs horse race. Giving the horse half a lap start, Flight Lieutenant Stainforth (of Schneider Trophy fame) succeeded in beating none other than Colonel Sempill on his horse 'Ebor' by 'about a nose'!

As the New Year dawned, motorsport had yet to lose all its allure for this inveterate record-breaker. In March Mildred started the 1,000-mile RAC Hastings Rally from Bath in a Jowett Ten. The previous day she had flown her 500hp Fairey Fox for the first time (it had clearly taken a while to be restored to flying condition), 'and now I am down to ten [horsepower]'. She pointed out to journalists that this was her return to motorsport after learning to fly. By Mildred's standards this was but modest exaggeration: the Fox she had bought, in theory, could look to no more than 450hp. The rally had a large entry – 357 cars – but Mildred triumphed, being the first of sixty-two lady entrants. It had been a test of endurance, with many competitors falling asleep at the wheel. This played to her strengths and Mildred came in ahead of such luminaries as Mrs Tommy Wisdom and Miss Fay Taylour.

Clearly this cemented her relationship with the Bradford-based Jowett business. In April they provided her steed for yet another record attempt: the seventy-two-hour record, which they battered at Montlhéry again. She and Victor managed 2,733 miles, aided by a very dangerous Heath Robinson set-up – the Jowett towed a trailer containing 100 gallons of extra fuel (the refuelling was carried out at walking pace). There was little time to bask in the glow of journalists' praise, however, for she flew back to Britain to participate in a British Hospitals Air Pageants' (BHAP) event at Maidstone. The car was driven back to Bradford to be welcomed by the city's lord mayor. This was to be Victor and Mildred's last venture together.

The BHAP had been set up in April 1933 by Mildred's good friend Pauline Gower (who, a few years later, was to become the inspirational founder of the Air Transport Auxiliary). It was a fast-paced but light-hearted existence – by September, Gower had given more than 4,000 aerial baptisms in more than 200 hours of flying.

The BHAP circus arrived at Gloucester on 7 May, with fifteen of the best-known pilots in the country. Apart from Mildred and Pauline, these included Charles Scott and Mildred's new colleague, Pugh. Within the space of two weeks, Gloucester had hosted an air rally (organised by Cotswold Aero Club), Sir Alan Cobham's Great Air Pageant, and the BHAP. Sky fever had taken hold, and towns such as Gloucester were desperate to establish municipal aerodromes.

Like similar aerial circuses, the public could have rides in open-cockpit aerobatic aircraft or, if they were more cautious, flights in cabined machines such as the De Havilland Dragon. There was plenty of 'stunt' flying (of which Pugh was the main exponent) and carousing. Ostensibly the BHAP concept was a charitable one, but the motives of Mildred and her colleagues were more commercial. They wanted to have their flying funded and to progress their celebrity and aviation careers. BHAP received only 10 per cent of the gate money and a third of programme sales.

However, Pugh was flying his aerobatics in between the more mundane work of flying for Mildred's Commercial Air Hire Company from Croydon (which had yet to be incorporated). On 8 May, he was missing for several hours after doing the morning newspaper run to Paris. He had been forced to ditch in the Channel – the first of several accidents while in her employ.

The dramatic tone of Mildred's activities did not relent. In July, the BHAP circus had moved to Ford Aerodrome in Sussex. After doing his 'Fox Dive' (250 knots down to 50ft), Pugh zoomed skyward before manoeuvring to land. As he did so, a petrol pipe split, and the Fox caught fire. Pugh's decision-making was hampered by concern for his passengers – two elderly ladies. He executed a violent side-slip to lose height as quickly as possible, and had to ease himself from his seat to avoid the flames. This made control a little harder, and after a hasty landing in the nearest field, the machine overturned. Thankfully, Pugh could extricate the two elderly neighbours, Mrs Davies and Mrs Doherty, before they were all incinerated; the former suffered a broken arm. But an hour later, Pugh was back in the air, although he was to be criticised by the Inspector of Accidents for his handling of the aircraft.[194]

Despite this proof of the danger of fire, less than a month later the circus had moved to Derby, where hot summer temperatures caused some of the pilots to fly in 'bathing costumes or other very light attire'!

Come October, Charles Ulm, the Australian pilot, made a new Australia record, with a total time of under seven days. When told of this, Mildred revealed her own plans:

Now I should like to see him back in four and a half days. I would like to go in for the race in 1934 [the first London–Sydney Air Race]. I have been building a machine in readiness for it, and I hope to have a shot at the record.

There is no evidence she was building such a machine.

On 1 July there was a dinner at Croydon given by Air Union, the French company that had given Mildred the contract for her Paris newspaper run, to introduce officially its new trimotor aircraft, the Golden Clipper. Of the more than 200 guests, some were given flights over London in the evening. Among them was the clerk to Surbiton Council, and Reverend Featherstone, the rector of Hook. Around this time, Mildred was flying a lot from the small airfield at Hook. She subsequently recorded several flights in a Golden Clipper in her logbook.

A month later, Mildred was reported as contemplating entering a Miles Hawk in the London–Sydney Air Race scheduled for October the following year. This was to be the most high-profile aviation competition for quite some time, and was to attract entrants from around the globe. The successful aircraft in that race were hot ships that required a crew of two, but there was never any mention of Mildred joining forces with anyone else. Mildred now did not want to share any limelight that came her way.

On 14 October 1933, Germany walked out of a disarmament conference of the League of Nations in Geneva.

Mildred's cousin, Major Henry Petre ('Petre the Great'), remained keen on flying. In December 1933 he bought a Puss Moth (its registration G-AAVB would presumably have made Victor covetous), which he kept until it was impounded in 1941.

Mildred was still lecturing around the country in 1934, albeit less frequently, but her thoughts were turning further to commerce. Victor was still living in Esher, which was very handy for Brooklands, and to a lesser degree the airfields at Heston and Hanworth, which had developed into busy commercial fields. However, Croydon had already risen to pre-eminence as the centre of the UK's airline industry – it was the Heathrow of its day. Mildred wanted to be at the centre of the action. As she moved from the relatively frivolous trials of air-to-air refuelling and joyriding, towards mainstream passenger and freight transport, she wisely chose to locate her embryonic empire at Croydon. She moved out of the marital home – for Mole Cottage, in Cobham.

In June, she incorporated Air Dispatch Ltd, with an office address at Croydon. As well as the air ambulance activity, which she had been doing for some while, Air Dispatch was the umbrella for some other ideas: Inner Circle Air Lines, 'Cherbourg Rapide', 'Le Touquet Express' and the 'Paris Dawn Express'. The last was her morning newspaper run, which she had operated under contract from Air France from 20 June. The aircraft had to arrive at Le Bourget before 7.30 a.m. and carry at least 650kg of papers for 6d a kilo. Mildred ceased the service on 14 August 1939. Inner Circle was a sort of aerial Circle Line around London's airfields, charging 6s 6d single and 10s 6d return between Croydon and Heston.

Her chief pilot, Flight Lieutenant J.B.W. Pugh, left Commercial Air Hire in November 1935 to join Spartan Air Lines, but her recently recruited pilot, Eric Noddings, effectively replaced him as chief pilot. They overlapped a little, since in July 1935 both were doing paper runs.

Croydon was more than Britain's chief airport; for the many pilots and other staff who worked there it was also their social hub. The pilots liked to meet in the buffet in the main reception hall of the air terminal to drink when their working day had been completed. Visitors also liked to go there, some in the expectation that they might recognise famous airmen whose adventurous lifestyle had been reported in the popular newspapers. Woods Humphrey (Imperial Airways' MD) was uneasy about the impression that their cheerful carousing might give to nervous passengers. Imperial Airways' superintendent, Major H.G. Brackley, gave an order to the company's pilots that the buffet was out of bounds; 'this was greatly resented'. Fortunately, the Aerodrome Hotel was next door, so its management created a bar for the exclusive use of pilots and senior staff. This wood-panelled room was decorated with caricatures of the leading pilots by the talented artist Charles Dickson. While, by 1934, the airport had grown used to welcoming the world's leading women pilots at the end of their record attempts, those congregated in the Pilots' Bar were much less accustomed to welcoming into their throng female aviation entrepreneurs such as Mildred.

Flight Lieutenant Eric Noddings, on the other hand, slipped easily into this milieu. Gaining his RAF wings in 1930, he was posted to the prestigious No. 1 Squadron in 1931 to fly the Siskin fighter at Tangmere. A year later, promoted to flying officer, he had a somewhat less exciting tour on the Station Flight at RAF Duxford, where Pugh had been a more senior colleague, flying the Bulldog and Atlas. He started his last tour in February 1934 with mundane work on the Anti-Aircraft Co-operation flight at RAF Biggin Hill (commanded by his old 1 Squadron boss), but left the service in September 1934, remaining in the Reserves as a flying officer.

In an uncertain job market, he immediately used the skills he had acquired in the air to qualify as a GPO wireless operator, as a fall-back career option. But, when he received a job offer from Mildred, he had no hesitation in remaining in the Home Counties, leaving his 23-year-old wife, Ada, and young daughter, Theodora, in Cambridge. He moved into the Aerodrome Hotel and soon also into Mildred's affections. Like Looff before, he found the peripatetic lifestyle of a commercial pilot in the 1930s a perfect cover to mask an affair.

The transport of gold bullion between London and European banks was big business at Croydon. Like bees to a honeypot, this attracted unsavoury characters. In 1935, £21,000 of bullion disappeared from the airport's strong room – Cecil Swanland, 'of no fixed abode', was jailed for the crime. Mildred could sniff the profit in these gold contracts. After a rival at Croydon lost a load of bullion when it broke through the floor of a Dragon, Mildred successfully pitched for the business in her metal-floored Avro. She would claim later that she personally picked up the bullion from a London bank in her AC coupé, accompanied by a young traffic clerk.

Having amassed a reasonable amount of funds from her lecturing, writing and sponsorship deals, Mildred held 31 per cent of the shares in Luxury Air Tours. Noddings had 20 per cent and was appointed to the board in November 1935. So, together the couple held a controlling interest. Viscount Scarsdale and N.M. Poole were the other shareholders and directors.

Scarsdale was appointed joint managing director. He was 6th Baron and 2nd Viscount, with his seat at Kedleston Hall. While having a nobleman on the board was a positive move in those times, it is likely that he also contributed some capital. Mildred would have known Scarsdale from two different worlds. First, like her, he was a member of the Ancient Monuments Society, which, despite its name, had been founded only a decade earlier – old buildings, and Kedleston in particular, were Scarsdale's passion. Second, Mildred knew Lord Curzon, later Earl Howe, who was Scarsdale's cousin. He was at the pinnacle of British motor racing. He raced Bugattis and Bentleys, and indeed had raced a Bugatti in the 1930 Double-Twelve meeting against the Bruces. He went on to co-found the British Racing Drivers Club and had made Mildred a life member after her Montlhéry record. Curzon's expensive lifestyle had been funded by his successive marriages to very wealthy American heiresses.

Commercial Air Hire was incorporated a couple of months later, with a similar board, save that Poole was replaced by Sir Maurice Bonham Carter. The attraction of 'Bongie' Bonham Carter to Mildred was that he was married to the daughter of Herbert Asquith, the former Liberal prime minister. The two other shareholders were of note: General Aircraft, a company that much later was to be bought by Blackburn, the manufacturer of her Bluebird, and one 'D.M. Sieff', who invested more than £7,000. This was possibly Daphne Madge Sieff, who had married the Hon. Michael Sieff, the son of one of the founders of Marks & Spencer. By 1937 one 'I.M. Sieff' had loaned a further £1,000 to Commercial Air Hire.

Mildred's parents had spent rather separate existences for some while, Jenny in the company of the bottle, Laurence in the company of God knows whom. By November, their separation had been formalised. Louis, Mildred's older brother, had disappeared from the planet. In reality, in 1928 he had embarked on the P&O line's SS *Baradine* for Cape Town. Once in South Africa, he withdrew into an alcoholic haze and any thoughts of resurrecting his supposed previous career as insurance agent were abandoned. However, in 1933, he renounced the demon drink. His mental state was still such that he never posted the long letter he wrote to Mildred alerting her to this volte-face.

However, a year later, just as she was making final preparations for yet another record flight, she would have been most surprised to receive a missive from Louis in Cape Town. He was obviously out of touch with developments in England, as he earnestly invited Mildred and Victor to visit him 'for a few months' (using the Imperial Airways Trans Africa route). He was obviously also feeling either guilty about his lack of communications or homesick, as he requested Mildred to send photos, having asked his father ('Dada') to do the same. As the family splintered further, Louis was belatedly trying to paper over the cracks. He was to die in South Africa only nine years later, at the relatively early age of 51.

The fractures in Mildred's relationship with Victor were widening. It is doubly surprising, therefore, that in 1933 she changed the name of her son, Tony. He had been registered at birth as Anthony Billy Stephen Petre Easter (with Mildred declaring herself unlawfully as Mildred Easter!). Yet, in March she changed his name by deed poll to Anthony Petre Easter-Bruce. Further muddying the waters, when he eventually signed up for the army in 1939 he enlisted as Anthony Petre Stephen Easter-Bruce.

Ever keen to embrace technological innovation, Mildred had set her sights on a new form of aerial transport – the autogyro. This was a hybrid between an aeroplane and a helicopter (the latter had yet to be developed, of course). The attraction of an autogyro was that it could land and take off from very small spaces, but it required different piloting skills. Mildred's innate ability made short order of this and she acquired Cierva C30a G-ACVX in July 1934. Dressed in a white leather flying helmet, beautiful tight-fitting leather flying jacket and checked tweed skirt, on a damp November dawn (25 November 1934) at just after 7 a.m., she lifted off from Lympne in Kent bound for the Cape. After a brief stop at Le Bourget (Paris), she reached Dijon, ears ringing, at 5 p.m. – the long day's flying showing she had lost none of her stamina. Victor was handling the press back in Surrey. However, his wife was not alone on this venture: Flight Lieutenant Pugh was captaining her Dragon, to handle radio communications and presumably to carry her wardrobe. The plan was to fly down the western coast of Africa, skirting the Sahara.

On 27 November, a deputation from the Parliamentary Air Committee, including Sir Philip Sassoon, visited the prime minister to lobby for more investment in route networks and aviation infrastructure. They would have been pleased by Mildred's pioneering work. However, that day Mildred had aborted the Cape trip, having smashed a rotor blade when landing at Nîmes near the French coast. She had told Reuters that after she landed a gust of wind overturned the machine. Plausible? Autogyros are considered to be easier to handle in strong winds than conventional aircraft. However, this early Cierva model was tall and gangly, and its centre of gravity may not have been best placed to counteract a sudden gust. The autogyro was to be shipped back to the UK from Marseilles. It is unlikely to have flown again, being struck off the register in 1937.

Mildred was appointed to the advisory board of Mutual Finance, an ambitious small bank, in December 1934, with a view to introducing aircraft financing business. It was a potentially lucrative deal for her, with remuneration of 1 per cent of the department's turnover and a minimum annual guaranteed £50. The directors were also seeking to appoint Sempill to the same role. She was later to operate a couple of De Havilland Dragons on hire purchase from Mutual Finance.

The Paris runs continued, and Noddings had to make a forced landing in a Picardy field when his Dragon (G-ACCR) encountered a heavy snowstorm early on the morning of 27 February 1935. The aircraft had iced up and his engines had failed. A couple of months later, Pugh yet again had to take an unplanned bath in the Channel. On 10 May 1935, he had to attempt a water landing in the Spartan (G-ABTY) while doing the early morning paper run. Pugh had suffered engine failure with all the symptoms of fuel starvation, although subsequent checks showed the fuel cocks had been on and the tanks half full. He and his radio operator, H.F. Burgess, were picked up by the *Ave Maria*, a French trawler, off the coast at Le Tréport. On learning of the disaster, Mildred dispatched a Flight Lieutenant Hattersley in a Dragon to offer assistance. Hattersley could only bring the damp duo back to Croydon.

Life for an embryonic aviation business was hand to mouth, even at Croydon, the epicentre of the nation's aerial networks. Entrepreneurs had to seize opportunities where they could. And all the while, the European political scene was tottering.

Mildred guarded her public reputation fiercely – the half-truths with which she garlanded some of her achievements pay tribute to that. So, readers may not have been totally surprised to open the paper on 14 January 1936 to read that Mildred had initiated a libel action against Odhams Press and then taken it to the Appeal Court. An article in *The People* the previous

September had alluded to a famous (but anonymous) British airwoman being behind a scheme to smuggle aircraft to Abyssinia for conversion to bombers, in contravention of a British trade embargo with that country. Mildred's ego could conceive that it related to no one but her. It was a messy court case, but Mildred eventually won damages of £525 – the benefit being much reduced by the fees of her top-class solicitors and barristers.

17

MILDRED, THE ENTREPRENEUR

The year 1936 turned out to be one of the most disturbing and turbulent of the decade for Great Britain. It started with the death of King George V:

> Old men in country houses hear clocks ticking
> Over thick carpets with a deadened force;
> Old men who never cheated, never doubted,
> Communicated monthly, sit and stare
> At the new suburb stretched beyond the run-way
> Where a young man lands hatless from the air.
>
> John Betjeman, 'Death of King George V', 1937[195]

The appetite for technological advances was unabated. Mildred's hero Malcolm Campbell's *Bluebird* machine was exhibited at the Bentalls department store in Kingston after breaking the land-speed record the previous autumn. At Easter, Amy Johnson opened the first ever Butlins holiday camp at Skegness. (This brought holidays to the masses: the weekly cost was only £3 per person for full board, including all entertainment.)

Until now, Mildred's aviation businesses had enjoyed a relatively good safety record by the standards of the times, but 1936 was to change all that, with two fatal crashes whose aftermath would occupy her time for many months afterwards. As Great Britain sluggishly began to improve its defences, Mildred had obtained a contract to fly her Dragons for Army co-operation work (she was later to incorporate another company, Anglo-European Airways Ltd, specifically for this kind of business). This task required circling southern England, typically at 8,000ft, to give practise to the newly formed searchlight units – resulting in tedious flying, but a steady income.

The Dragons were equipped as passenger aircraft so the pilots would invite friends to join them for these otherwise boring night flights. On the evening of 26 March, 32-year-old Captain Francis Birmingham invited along his younger brother, Brendan. Also on board was a colleague at Commercial Air Hire, 19-year-old radio operator Robert 'Snowy' Burgess. Snowy was well-liked at Croydon and had brought along his new fiancée, Daisy Marsh, aged just 17, for one of her first experiences of flight. She worked for a cleaning firm just across the Purley Way from the airfield and had met Snowy at the Aerodrome Hotel. Mr Norman Burton completed the team as a mechanic.

The Dragon (G-ACAP) was engaged in the normal work as a searchlight target over Cowes and Portsmouth, but all perished when it crashed near Lyndhurst in the New Forest at 8.20 p.m. Funeral arrangements, inquests and Air Ministry investigators swamped the Commercial Air Hire offices. Mildred received a flood of letters of sympathy, and sent Eric Noddings to the crash site to assist the Air Ministry men. He concluded, 'There was no portion of the aircraft or engines worth salvaging.'

Captain Birmingham left two orphaned children and a widow who was to pursue Commercial Air Hire for compensation.

Then, on 16 May, Captain Ellis Hill, formerly with Imperial Airways, died shortly after taking off from Croydon in Mildred's Monospar ST4 (G-ADLM) – he appears to have departed with the fuel cocks closed, leading to an inevitable crash on playing fields the other side of the Purley Way. A very basic error for an experienced pilot.

That year, Mildred merged most of her commercial activities into Air Dispatch, and became even more ambitious in expanding her route network. The company started flights from Croydon to Plymouth, via Portsmouth, Bournemouth and Torquay (these days, only Bournemouth retains an airfield at all!).

In August, Mildred had yet another brush with death, and it was all her own fault. She had made a 5s bet with Pugh about who could do the shortest landing when arriving at Stafford for a BHAP event. While on final approach to the common in her Miles Satyr (considerably faster than most of the craft she had flown, and very conspicuous in a distinctive red and white chequerboard colour scheme), she noticed too late an array of telegraph wires in her path. That their poles were hidden behind houses was her excuse. Too late to deviate up or down, she hoped she might pass through them, but the relatively lightweight Satyr was simply arrested in mid-air and propelled by the recoil backwards into the field. Although Mildred was again miraculously unhurt, the Satyr was more seriously wounded. In *Nine Lives* she consoled herself with the thought that she had won the bet, but the accident was doubly unfortunate as the Satyr was uninsured!

In July 1936, the Berlin Olympic Games underlined, even to those of limited vision, the aspirations of Nazi Germany, but hostilities had already erupted in Spain and the protagonists realised the need for aircraft. The British Government, like most in Europe, was very unwilling to be seen to be providing arms to either side in the conflict. So securing such equipment required great subterfuge on the part of the Spaniards and the bulk came from the USSR, Germany and Italy.

Crilly Airways (later bought by the first British Airways) sold its four Fokker F.XII airliners to Spain as soon as the war started. After it recruited Polish pilots for the task, it cleared customs at Gatwick for the export of the aircraft to Poland, although at least one crashed in France on its way to Spain.[196]

In the hothouse and village atmosphere of Croydon's airport, the aspiring airline tycoons knew most of the adventures of their rivals. Mildred would have heard very quickly of the part that Captain Olley (of Olley's Air Service) had already played in this war.

On 8 July, Captain Cecil Webb was called to Captain Olley's office and introduced to Señor Luis Bolin, a right-wing Spanish journalist. Olley explained that Bolin was asking for a pilot to carry out a top-secret assignment: the ferrying of a 'Riff' leader (i.e. one of the leaders of a guerrilla group operating in the Rif Mountains) to Morocco to 'help start a revolution'. The passengers from Croydon, in Webb's Dragon Rapide (G-ACYR), were Bolin, Major Pollard and two girls (whose role was merely 'cover'). Via Bordeaux, Lisbon and Las Palmas, they made it to Morocco. Pollard and the girls had been jettisoned en route.[197] The VIP passenger – the Riff leader – turned out to be none other than General Franco. He was taken to Casablanca and Tetuan from Las Palmas (where he was in semi-exile) for some important plotting and politicking, and indeed to be acknowledged as the new leader of Spain.

Through the summer, Mildred's Dragons were detained three times by the authorities at Croydon (prior to embarking ostensibly on the daily paper run) on suspicion that she was seeking to export them illicitly to Spain. Ever the one for the *mot juste*, Mildred fed the press:

It is a ridiculous piece of muddle. These 'grounding orders' are interfering with our services. It is simply scandalous that this should happen to a commercial company. Hundreds of English visitors to Monte Carlo and the South of France will not get their English papers today through our plane being grounded.

But three Dragons departed from Croydon in early August; two of these belonged to Mildred. In later years, she was keen to stress that these were her ambulance aircraft and could not have been used for any warlike purpose. It is a posture which would not have withstood even a trainee barrister: an ambulance can soon be converted into a transport or reconnaissance aircraft, or even a bomber. Disingenuously she claimed that she ceased such sales as soon as an embargo was imposed.[198]

Mildred's businesses had been enduring a tougher time of late and Commercial Air Hire was still making losses. So, when a stranger arrived bearing unspeakable amounts of cash, he was given an instant and intent hearing. Any ethical doubts in Mildred's mind were overcome by the sight of £10,000 (in £1,000 notes!) with which the mystery buyer appeared in her Croydon office. She drove immediately to her bank in nearby Whaddon, where the manager was most surprised to receive her sudden windfall – cash flow had been looking rather dire at that moment.

One of the two Dragons being sold was G-ACDL, which was flown to Barcelona by Flying Officer G.W. Haigh, RAFVR. Given its destination was Barcelona, one can presume it was bought by the Republican side. While Mildred viewed the decision to sell as purely a commercial one, it is doubtful whether she discussed it in advance with any of her family, as back in Britain the war had created divided opinions among Catholics. The official 'Bishop's Fund', Woodruffe (the editor of the Catholic magazine, *The Tablet*), and Cardinal Hinsley were all for the Nationalist campaign, but many Catholic church groups worked for the Republicans. The 1930s was an era like few others in British history, which forced clerics of all persuasions to think critically about their appropriate response to political options.

The British Government was in an unenviable position; as *Flight* magazine rightly observed, 'Although these civil machines are sold by private enterprise, the impression in Spain and elsewhere will simply be that this country as a whole is supporting one side or the other – with consequent repercussions.'[199] On 8 August, the French Government had stopped arms sales to the Republican side.

Mildred's manipulation of the press continued, every impounded aircraft representing a considerable loss of income. On 11 September the Board of Trade relented and she was allowed to fly her Dragons without restriction in the UK, but overseas flights were limited to Paris Le Bourget and Le Touquet – an increasingly irascible Mildred found this difficult to tolerate.

Ethnic and class tensions peaked on 4 October 1936 with riots in Cable Street (in London's East End) in which Oswald Mosley was the central figure. But, as winter took hold, one of the Britain's biggest tragedies for decades occurred – London's Crystal Palace burned down. A *Daily Mail* journalist hurriedly hired an aircraft from Croydon to report on it, although the flames could be seen all over the capital. Sempill was later unsurprisingly to advocate that the site be turned into an aerodrome 'with a great tower topped by an illuminated globe "which would symbolise the Empire on which the sun never sets"'.[200] One cannot be sure whether he was referring to the British Empire or that of the Rising Sun …

Mildred reinvested the proceeds of the sales of the Dragons to Spain in the purchase of two De Havilland Dragon Rapide twin-engine biplanes (an evolution of the Dragon), and an Avro 642, which carried sixteen passengers and was deployed on the Paris route. To stimulate this trade, she employed one of the first stewardesses – 'a very attractive blonde' named Daphne Vickers.

In another effort to boost traffic, Mildred had engineered an association with North Eastern Airways. Air Dispatch was to reschedule its Paris flights so that passengers on North Eastern Airways' Scottish flights could connect with her own at Croydon. This enabled a Scotsman to fly to Paris in only six hours. The service was inaugurated in October – just in time to catch dismal and disruptive Scottish autumnal weather.

However, disaster was never far away. A couple of days earlier, Air Dispatch lost one of its wireless operators, A.H. Morgan, who was killed when an Airspeed Envoy piloted by Ken Waller crashed in Kenya during a race from Portsmouth to Johannesburg.

Business was becoming increasingly varied: one day Pugh would be bringing more than 400 brace of grouse down to Heston; on the next flight Noddings would be bringing a sick child back from Lausanne. But Air Dispatch received very favourable publicity in October when it answered a plea for help from Miss Sonja Henjie, the Norwegian Olympic figure-skater and film star, who needed to be in Paris by that evening and all the scheduled services were full. Noddings took her in Dragon G-ACCR, reaching the capital at 10.30 p.m.

In 1937, 22 January was a thoroughly miserable day – a strong southerly gale was blowing over the Channel with plenty of rain over the English coast. Nonetheless, two Air Dispatch aircraft left Croydon before dawn for another newspaper run to Paris. Halfway across the Channel the first Dragon, piloted by Captain D.P. Boitel-Gill, suffered an engine failure. He only scraped back to Lympne, a few miles from the coast, by ordering his wireless operator to dump the half-ton load of newspapers into the sea. Charles Scott departed from Croydon at 10 a.m. with a relief load of newspapers, but could find no trace en route of the other Air Dispatch aircraft, Mr Jones-Evans' Dragon (G-ACCR).

Mildred found time to be a witness in front of the government's Committee of Inquiry into Civil Aviation. As part of its belated preparations for a war, the British Government had been examining how the burgeoning civil aviation industry could be used to the nation's advantage in wartime. Government strategy had hitherto been to focus on supporting Imperial Airways in its expansion of air routes to the corners of the Empire. Lord Cadman's committee reported in March 1938; its major conclusion was a desire that civil aviation should be self-supporting and, to this end, it recommended that no two British airlines should compete on the same route. Imperial Airways should concentrate on its long-haul routes, and it should co-operate with the new British Airways on shorter ones. Imperial Airways had been blighted by poor industrial relations – a result of management's imperious attitude to its pilots. Cadman's committee led to the formation of the British Overseas Airways Corporation, which was to supplant Imperial Airways after the outbreak of war.

Mildred received a portentous letter that month from the Department of Civil Aviation at the Air Ministry, asking her to set out the proposed size and details of her fleet twelve months hence. No doubt a similar letter was sent to her rivals. Whitehall was preparing its corral.

By 1937, the British car industry was producing more than half a million vehicles a year. Women drivers were now commonplace. However, there were undercurrents of social unrest and on 1 May there was a busmen's strike, ahead of the coronation of Bertie eleven days later.

At the end of May there was an international handicap race from London to the Isle of Man. Sadly, one S. W. Sparkes and his passenger perished in a crash just after he had taken off from Hanworth. (Sparkes had been the pilot of the Bristol Fighter during Mildred's endurance flights.)

In the summer, Mildred and her colleagues were distracted by further court appearances. Unusually for her, this time she was appearing as a witness for the prosecution. Commercial Air Hire had been used by a reprobate named Daniel Corrigan to bring a few people into and out of the UK other than through official customs aerodromes.

In July, Mildred formally walked out on Victor – he forlornly wrote in his diary, 'Jane [his pet name for Mildred] left me today.'[201] A few months later, she wrote to Victor, 'I have had nearly 10 months to think things over, and feel it is for the best that I should not return.'[202]

By 1938 Mildred and Eric Noddings were living together, at Leys Cottage in Chipstead, only 6 miles south of Croydon Aerodrome on the North Downs. At the speed Mildred drove, it would have been a very swift commuting journey along some pleasant country lanes. However, in formal documents Eric maintained the fiction that he was still living at the Aerodrome Hotel at Croydon.

The profitability of Mildred's businesses was improving, although she was using much of the surplus cash flow to repay the loans from Sieff. Her business life was increasingly reflecting her personal life, and when she incorporated yet another business, Dawn Express Ltd, she and Noddings were the only (and equal) shareholders and directors.

The night-time nature of the Army Co-operation work meant that she had plenty of daytime hours to spare. She re-ignited her childhood love of horses, this time with very adequate funds to do justice to her passion. Initially she bought a pony to practise jumping in the field behind her Chipstead home. Then, at Easter 1938, she started a riding school, renting stables from Lady Moberley. As her competence rose quickly, she bumped into the three Carter brothers, one of whom, Len, persuaded her to buy an imposing grey called 'Grand Manner'. It was billed as a 'supreme' jumper, and had already been entered for the *Daily Mail* Gold Cup at the International Horse of the Year Show at Olympia in only two days' time. Mildred paid the £200 asking price and took over the entry. It was nearly midnight when the diminutive Mildred astride the very Grand Manner was called to the ring. He raced around the figure-of-eight course, clearing most of the jumps with ease, collecting just half a fault. Sadly, Colonel Llewellyn (founder of a great show-jumping dynasty) later recorded a completely clear round. Nonetheless, Mildred had come second in her first very major competition.

Meanwhile, Sempill's true racing colours were becoming more evident. He had become one of two founder directors of the Anglo-German Club – designed to provide a haven for Germans in London, and foster relations between the two countries. In November 1938, he lunched with Geoffrey Dorman, an unsavoury character who edited *Action*, the magazine of Mosley's British Union of Fascists, expressing his 'strong support for the movement'.[203]

The Air Ministry's efforts to harness the power of civil aviation were stepping up a gear. Mildred received a letter outlining the terms of a new contract for Army Co-operation work: these were rather generous – £16 10s per flying hour for the first 7,350, and £4 10s per hour for all ferrying work and Army Co-operation in excess of 7,350 hours. It looked like Mildred was going to have a good war. This was to take up almost all of her capacity (she claimed to the Ministry that she had had to buy in extra craft to fulfil the contract): twenty-one aircraft were required for two hours a day on six days a week, and two hours a night on five days a week.

In August 1939, a tragic event unfolded at Croydon. An agitated young man arrived at the airfield and marched up to the offices of Surrey Flying Services, asking to be taken up in an open-cockpit machine. He was told to go away and apply for flying lessons in the normal way. He then seemed to walk deliberately into the revolving propeller of an Air Dispatch machine and was killed instantly. He was an officer in the Lancers, who had just been called up.

That month, Mildred came third in the Open Hacks class at the Westerham Horse Show and above this Kent village, Biggin Hill's fighter squadrons were in ever more urgent practise. But the outbreak of war meant that she and Eric had to leave their first extra-marital home at Chipstead. A few months earlier, Eric had made a momentous decision – on 28 March 1939 he filed a new will in which he gave his entire estate to Mildred; somewhat drastic for an airman with a young child.

18

THE RESTLESS SOUL

As the summer rolled by, international passenger numbers at Croydon escalated. By the end of August, they had tripled to 1,500 a day as Britons sought to escape the dark clouds over Europe. The bell tolled for Britain's airlines two days before the outbreak of war. On 1 September 1939, the Air Navigation (Restriction in Time of War) Order was enacted and Mildred was no longer in charge of her commercial fate. Owners of companies such as Air Dispatch had been given sealed orders from the Air Ministry, to be opened on receipt of a sequence of three coded messages. These would activate dormant contracts and redeploy the airlines' machines.

Early on the morning of 1 September, the German Army had invaded Poland (without declaring war) and later that day the British Government announced a general mobilisation of its armed forces. For the airlines, the final message was received late in the evening of 1 September.

The following morning, Mildred ordered that all her machines be towed out on to the Croydon apron. They departed in haste for their new base at Cardiff, leaving Croydon Aerodrome to become RAF Croydon – one of 11 Group's fighter stations protecting the capital.

A day after war was declared, Mildred's fleet became very busy ranging from south Wales across the Midlands and southern England, with some flights to northern France in support of the British Expeditionary Force. Much of the materiel her craft transported there was to be abandoned months later on the dunes of Dunkirk. She reported that Charles Scott (then one of her pilots) returned to Cardiff one day, 'saying "France has fallen. The roads are full of nuns winding up their puttees." "What do you mean?" we asked. "German soldiers, disguised, blowing up bridges".'[204]

With her aircraft now in the hands of the RAF, Mildred needed to find another source of employment for her staff (if they were not to be conscripted), and another source of income. Just in time she managed to secure a contract to repair aircraft wings – clearly work of sufficient national importance to stave off the government nabbing her workforce. From having had to deal with the layers of bureaucracy at the Air Ministry, she now had to bite her lip in dealings with the Ministry of Aircraft Production. Capacity at her Cardiff factory was ramped up by increasing her workforce to 400 and working eighty-hour weeks.

The 1936 divorce of Wallis Simpson, in order to marry the king, had thrown the spotlight on the country's divorce laws. A.P. Herbert launched a Private Member's Bill in the Commons in November 1936 in an effort to modernise them. This was 'vociferously opposed' by the Mothers' Union, which eschewed divorcees as members and remained hostile, even then, to all forms of birth control. Yet women were far from supine – in the first half of the 1930s they filed more than 50 per cent of all divorce petitions.

In Mildred's case, it was her husband who started the process. A modest, gentle man, Victor had refused to cite anybody. He petitioned Mildred in December 1940 on grounds of desertion, as soon as it was legally possible for him to do so. Desertion was true – she had left him in July 1937 – but he was keen to follow this route as this would absolve either party from having to attend court. The decree nisi was granted on 5 December. A newspaper reported that the marriage had been happy for only its first two years, and they had drifted apart as she had pursued her interests in motor racing and flying. When she had returned from the round-the-world flight, she had told him that they were unsuited. Relations between them, however, remained cordial.

Having left Croydon, Mildred and Eric had obviously vacated Leys Cottage, her house at Chipstead, and at the outbreak of war she had rented Tanglewood, an imposing house in the northern Cardiff suburb of Lisvane. During his employment with Mildred, Eric had remained on the RAF's Volunteer Reserve list and he was therefore called up as soon as war was declared. The Air Ministry wisely decided his experience could be best put to use in the instruction of others. So, he was posted to 6 Elementary Flying Training School at Sywell, just outside Northampton.

Still only 33, Eric must surely have felt frustrated plodding around the Sywell circuit in a Tiger Moth demonstrating that no rust had encrusted his original RAF flying training. Some of those with whom he had originally joined the service would by now be commanding their own squadrons. He found the parting from Mildred and the living arrangements both very trying, 'I don't like this instructor at all and am getting very liverish … the room and the clothing are all very damp.' Just one of many souls parted from their loved ones, he wrote, 'I miss you terribly dear, and wish this silly war would come to an end soon … My own little darling lovebird, I'm longing to be with you again. So roll on the weekend!' He was trying to persuade her to meet up somewhere nearer to Sywell than Cardiff!

After his Sywell course, Eric travelled widely around the country, writing expressions of love from a variety of places, including the Angel Hotel at Cambridge, when he was presumably paying a fleeting visit to his daughter Theodora, and his ex-wife, Ada.[205]

Cash flows at Air Dispatch were healthy, and Mildred needed a more central base to facilitate seeing Eric in his brief periods off duty, so she bought Down Farm at Westonbirt in Gloucestershire, together with its 500 or so acres, and had her stable of showjumpers moved there. However, that rural idyll was disrupted by a man from her least favourite part of Whitehall. The joyless Air Ministry chap gaily reckoned that she would have no need for grazing for her string of horses, as she would soon be eating them. It is difficult to conceive of a remark she would find more offensive. Further, '[part of] your land will make a good satellite aerodrome'. He was wrong about the former, but was to be proved prescient about the latter.

While Eric was busy doing his bit for Britain, Sempill was busy scurrying around on behalf of the Japanese. He had been warned by MI6 and the Air Ministry of his responsibilities under the Official Secrets Act as long ago as 1926. Through the pre-war period, he was a close associate of some of the most senior figures on the extreme right, notably Captain Archibald Ramsey, MP for Peebles and one of the principal organisers of the pro-Fascist Right Club.

After the outbreak of war, Sempill had returned to service as a temporary commander in the Royal Naval Volunteer Reserve and was given a job in the Department of Air Materiel, and soon put in charge of investigating air accidents.[206]

On 27 September 1940, Japan signed the Tripartite Act with Italy and Germany. It can be no coincidence that on that day the Lords of the Admiralty instructed Sempill 'not to have contact with the Japanese or with anyone who is likely to make use of information for the benefit of the Japanese' – which he promised to do, with the very significant caveat that it only prevented him discussing any matter to do with the services. Six months later, MI6 put a telephone tap on Sempill's line (again) and 'it was immediately apparent that he had not severed his connections with these people'.[207]

Sempill willingly submerged himself in the *Asaka Maru* affair. This was an armed merchant ship dispatched from Japan in January 1941 to pick up 3,000 tons of German weapons and stores from the port of Bilbao. The British Government agonised over whether to destroy the ship or its cargo, or even to search it. With a reticence that now seems unworldly, it was unwilling to disturb the relations between the two countries. The Japanese Government, via the spymasters in its London embassy, found it was very useful to be able to tap Sempill for knowledge of the British Government's intentions. On 1 April, Sempill was so eager to help he phoned the ambassador.[208]

'Vee Vee' Vivian, vice chief of the SIS (MI6) was very exercised. One of his senior staff, with typical Whitehall understatement, wrote that month:

> Sempill is certainly an unsatisfactory person. There seems little doubt that he was receiving a reduced salary of £200 a year from the Japanese at the time when he told the Board of the Admiralty that all payment had ceased … There is the uncomfortable fact that he is £13,000 overdrawn.

There was also some indication that he had failed to break his consultancy for the Mitsubishi Corporation (which was, of course, effectively under the control of the Japanese Government), which he had been enjoying since 1925. The Admiralty's Directorate of Naval Intelligence seemed loathe to deal with this reptile in their midst. However, someone in Whitehall, possibly the Cabinet Office, thought Sempill's continued contact with the Japanese, while in a senior naval position, should be brought to the attention of the prime minister. Churchill was outraged.[209] In September he minuted:

> At any moment we may be at war with Japan, and here are all these Englishmen, two of whom I know personally [one was Sempill], moving around and collecting information and sending it to the Japanese Embassy. I cannot believe that the Master of Sempill and Commander MacGrath, have any idea of what their position would be on the morrow of a Japanese declaration of war. Immediate internment would be least of their troubles. None of them must have access to any Government department.

With a characteristically Winstonian flourish, he concluded, wishing for 'the effectual closing down of the activities of this English nebula'. A month later he decided, 'it was intolerable that Lord Sempill should be employed in these circumstances'.

A lot of very senior time became occupied in dealing with Sempill – Viscount Swinton, Admiral Sir William Whitworth (the Second Sea Lord), not to mention that of the prime minister. The latter decided that Sempill must be banished to some sinecure in northern Scotland, far from his Japanese friends. 'Clear him out whilst time remains,' was Winston's pithy instruction.

In September, it was felt that 'a peremptory dismissal at this moment might have immediate and undesirable repercussions in Tokyo where the Japanese were tending to a fresh reduction of contacts between their officials and ours'. This sort of pusillanimous behaviour makes the collapse of British forces in Singapore all the more plausible. Like a naughty schoolboy, Sempill was summoned to another meeting with a senior prefect, this time the Fifth Sea Lord.

On 7 December there were the dreadful events at Pearl Harbor, where tragedy could have been averted had US intelligence been more thorough and co-ordinated. The US and Great Britain declared war on Japan the following day.

As the war dragged on, Sempill became involved with a variety of fascist and far-right organisations, and became interested in the topic of economic reform. By the end of 1943 he wished to go on a 'lecture tour' of Canada. His having already secured the sponsorship of the Canadian Army made it very difficult for the British authorities to prevent his departure, loathe though they were to have cannons as loose as Sempill firing off across the North Atlantic. He arrived in New York on 19 December, and soon made his way to Ottawa.

As usual, he tried to insinuate himself into the corridors of power and claimed he was co-ordinating supplies for the YMCA, Salvation Army and Knights of Columbus (a Catholic charity). The latter soon became 'utterly disgusted with him'. Despite this failure, Sempill wished to stay in Canada for another three months.[210] He was following his own agenda and not helping the charities with whom he claimed to be working. The agenda appeared to be to find out as much as possible about Canadian aircraft production. He secured a platform with the Board of Trade, whom he lectured about his financial theories of social credit and, soon after, the Alberta Legislative Assembly allowed him a seat on the floor of the house for its opening. In his letter of thanks to the Speaker, Sempill took the opportunity to lecture him on his ideas for 'new financial techniques'. It is not thought that Sempill had had any formal training in economics – when the letter was read out in the house, it aroused the ire of the Opposition.

Rather foolishly, B Department of Counter-Intelligence in London had failed to warn their counterparts in Canada until after Sempill had been in Canada for a few weeks. He had used his title to meet all sorts of senior Canadian military figures and most of the Cabinet. Cyril B. Mills (of MI5, and son of Bertram Mills, the famous circus owner) went out to Canada to fight a rearguard action to try to have Sempill recalled to the UK, but by mid-March Sempill had moved on to Newfoundland to vent his economic views on fresh audiences. (He claimed to be a 'baronet' of Nova Scotia). Due to an administrative slip-up by the Canadian passport authorities, it is thought he then went on to bore audiences in New England.

Mills had been keeping Guy Liddell, director of B Department, up to speed and Liddell noted in his diary, 'The trouble with Sempill now is that he is grossly indiscreet,' as indeed was his new wife, Lady Cecilia, who had been blurting to near strangers that she knew (through her own naval role) all about the impending invasion of Europe.

The following month, Whitehall's Joint Intelligence Staff completed a study of the Japanese operations in Malaya in 1941, which had, of course, led to the disastrous fall of Singapore. It concluded that the Japanese' detailed knowledge of Britain's aircraft fleet in the theatre, and its naval assets, had come from a well-placed source in London.[211] The finger pointed at Sempill. There was blood on his hands.

MORE PAIN FOR MILDRED: AN EVENTFUL WAR

As 1941 started the war news remained gloomy, not least because Amy Johnson, still very much a national heroine, had drowned in the Thames Estuary on 5 January after ditching during an ATA ferry flight in very poor weather. It is thought the destroyer sent to pluck her from the water ran over the drowning pilot.

Mildred was now certain she wanted Eric as her life partner. The day after Amy's death, she wrote to her solicitors to see if the divorce process could be hastened. The decree nisi was in her desk, but she wanted the decree absolute as soon as possible so that she and Eric could marry. Her solicitor told her that only Victor, as the petitioner, could apply to the court for more urgency, and that the King's Proctor would fully investigate the matter. The costs would be at least 20 guineas. 'It is an unusual course to take, and I think it is doubtful in the circumstances whether the court would agree to shorten the period.'[212]

Some months earlier she had already given Eric a love token superlative in its magnificence – a Rolls-Royce Phantom III, an extremely distinguished conveyance for a humble flight lieutenant! Eric by now was instructing at No.9 Flying Training School at RAF Hullavington in Wiltshire on the Miles Master I advanced trainer aircraft. Towards the end of their ten-week course, students at the school progressed to combat-fatigued Hurricane fighters. With more than 3,000 flying hours, Noddings had considerably more experience than most of his fellow instructors, who typically had only recently come through the training system themselves, but because of frequent bombing by German raiders, which particularly disrupted its night flying programme, the flying school had opened a relief landing ground. By an extraordinary stroke of fate, this was on the land spied by the Ministry man a few months earlier – at the more remote location of Babdown Farm, on Mildred's Down Farm estate. The first aircraft to hop over Mildred's hedge were Hawker Harts and Audaxes, one evening in late July 1940. Unlucky airmen had to lay out a landing path with 'gooseneck' flares every night. Barely a week after this had started, a lone German bomber bid a hearty '*wilkommen*' with some high-explosive bombs.[213]

By this stage of the war, many families' domestic arrangements had been split asunder, but Mildred and Eric were blessed since Eric's new base was less than a mile from Down Farm, where Mildred now spent most of her time, so that she could see Eric when his duty permitted. Their domestic life was much more normal than for most aircrew in the air force, and Eric would have been grateful to escape the primitive conditions at Babdown: there was only one Nissen hut there, with a coal stove, glowing red hot in winter, around which the men would huddle for their night flying supper. If back at Hullavington on their rare days off, men would hasten to Chippenham's Old Bakehouse Café (where no ration coupons were needed) for a 3*s* 6*d* mixed grill.

Babdown received a second visit by the Luftwaffe on 26 March 1941. From the low cloud base emerged a bomber whose front gunner sprayed his wares over the airfield, but no damage was done. Four weeks later, on 22 April 1941, as twilight approached, two aircraftmen were detailed as usual to set up the flarepath, its smoke then wafting back down the runway. The duty pilot, together with his signaller and a runner, were huddled in the comparative warmth of the control van.

Noddings had been detailed to take a student on a night flight from Babdown. It was after midnight when he and the 23-year-old Leading Aircraftsman James Day mounted Miles Master T8468. They were to do circuits – giving Day practice at night landings, so to speak. At the end of the grass runway Day, in the front cockpit, sat staring at the inky black-ness and then his instruments. The duty signaller gave a green light to the shadow of the Master. With engine RPM set to 2,750, Day advanced the throttle to 5in of boost and the aircraft sped forward. Once he sensed it had reached flying speed he pulled back the stick as for any take-off, but the Master reached a height of 100ft before stalling and spearing into the earth. It burst into flames in Long Covert – a wood only half a mile south-west of the landing ground. Noddings and Day were consumed by flames, and it fell to their colleagues to pull their charred corpses on to an ambulance.[214] Did Mildred draw aside her blackout curtains in the drawing room that night to see the inferno only a couple of miles to the north-west?

John R. Davies, a fellow instructor recalled, 'His aircraft flew straight into the ground and he was killed, with his pupil, in a flaming crash. It was thought that he was doing a practise overshoot and that his pupil lifted the flaps by mistake.'[215] This was not what the official RAF enquiry concluded. The spate of training accidents in the wartime RAF was continuous, and investigations were typically more cursory than in peacetime – the flying training schools were focused on sustaining their tempo of output. But any lessons had to be drawn as quickly as possible, and there was a relatively full inquiry into this crash. Why had Noddings met his maker?

The Master had a small design flaw that was easy to overlook, but which assumed great importance in night flying. If the two lights that illuminated the trim control box were turned up to maximum intensity, the pilot was dazzled by reflections in the Perspex cockpit canopy. If he reduced the intensity of the lights, then the settings of the rudder and elevator trims could not be seen.

The Master had been loaded with seven ballast weights in its tail (as was needed when only one pilot was aboard), instead of the prescribed single weight. In the blackness of an April night, both Noddings and Day must have overlooked this in their pre-flight inspection. But this fatefully meant that the centre of gravity of the aircraft was near or beyond its rear limit. Further, Day had wound the elevator trim right back. With the cockpit lights dimmed, Noddings had failed to notice his pupil's error.[216] These two fundamental mistakes sealed their fate as soon as the Master rose into the air. Afterwards, senior officers reiterated standing instructions about the use of ballast weights and ordered modifications to the Master's cockpit lighting.

Eric's burned and mangled remains were taken back to his parents in Hartlepool for burial. Mildred was given probate of his estate, to ponder what might have been. Eric's widow remained in Cambridge, together with their daughter, Theodora. As mentioned earlier, Eric had rather oddly made no provision for his daughter in his 1939 will, in which he left his entire but modest estate to his mistress. So, although under no obligation to do so, a year after Eric's death Mildred settled a deed on the 7-year-old girl, giving her an income of £42 a year until the age of 18.[217]

In a further bitter twist of fate, Mildred's decree absolute arrived too late, and its posting on 16 June 1941 only served to remind her of the sudden vacuum in her life. However, Victor wasted no time in ceding bachelordom – he married Peggy Beechey, three days later in Esher. They had met in a Devon pub where he was staying while competing in a hill climb. She had been acting as chauffeur for a Norfolk colonel and it was love at first sight. (Peggy thereafter called him Michael, because she did not like the name Victor!)[218]

In consequence, Peggy became the new Hon. Mrs Victor Bruce. However, Mildred did not relinquish her old name – it had become her brand, and one to which she was very much attached. In later years, Peggy's family were understandably miffed at Mildred's intransigence on this matter. Victor and Peggy went on to have three children, the first of whom, Margaret Jill Bruce, was born in January 1943.

A practical consequence of Eric's demise was that Mildred had to find a new managing director for several of her companies. Son Tony had joined the Royal Army Service Corps (like his stepfather in the Great War), but was to receive an emergency commission in the Intelligence Corps in January 1945. Now Mildred made him MD of Air Despatch at the tender age of 21. This must have been a merely titular role, for he was to remain in the army until after war's end.

As the war progressed, so did the capability of her companies, which moved on to the repair of complete aircraft. However, 1943 was not to be a year for sentiment, at least for Mildred. Her mother died in a Surrey nursing home, a lonely dipsomaniac. Tidying up her estate, Mildred consigned to Christie's the centrepiece of her mother's jewellery collection – the magnificent diamond necklace that Lawrence had given Jennie on their engagement. The star piece in Christie's auction on 20 October, it was sold to Jerwoods, a London jeweller, raising the astonishing total of £12,000. 'Enough to buy a house,' in the words of a Christie's expert – and that is probably what Mildred did, for she was now taking advantage of wartime crises and financial distress to assemble an impressive property portfolio.[219] She considered buying a house in Bishops Avenue, Hampstead – then a refuge of plutocrats (with now a spicing of oligarchs).

In 1944, two months before D-Day, Lawrence ('Dada') died in Malmesbury hospital, aged 79. A year on, while Churchill was meeting Roosevelt and Stalin at Yalta, Mildred bought a 3-year-old racehorse, 'Birthlaw', after it won a selling race at Cheltenham – this was one of the first races when racing resumed after its cessation in 1939. Its 500 guineas cost was evidently a sound investment since she had to wait barely a week before Birthlaw won its first race in her colours. It went on to further success, winning, for example, the Newnham Handicap chase at Cheltenham for her a year later. However racing, for Mildred, was not always quite so rewarding, and in 1946, Golden City, her 6-year-old colt, had to be destroyed after an accident. The insurance claim kept her occupied for weeks afterwards.

Meanwhile, politicians had turned to the challenges of post-victory national reconstruction. The public mood had shifted against Sir Winston Churchill, the inspiring wartime prime minister. Even before the end of the war in Europe, Whitehall had published its blueprint for post-war civil aviation. This stipulated that all the 'independent' airlines existing before the declaration of war could only resume work as charter and air taxi operators. The only airlines to be licensed to operate domestic scheduled services would be the state-owned British Airways (the successor to Imperial Airways, which had ceased trading at the outbreak of war). This remarkably socialist act understandably incensed Mildred and what one might loosely call the 'Croydon coterie'. After considerable research and effort, she drafted a lengthy letter to the Air Ministry outlining her stiff opposition to this creation of a state monopoly.

It was presumably this frame of mind that caused Mildred to enter the fray to stand in the forthcoming general election as an independent candidate for the nearby constituency of Stroud. Ironically, the incumbent MP was a Flight Lieutenant Perkins, who was Undersecretary of State at the Ministry for Civil Aviation. She must have been supremely confident that she could do better, or at least better represent the interests of the private airlines.

However, only two weeks later she had a change of heart, and withdrew her candidacy:

> I am convinced now more important than ever for us all to rally together in a united effort to return our great war leader, Mr. Churchill, and his followers to power so that they may carry through the plans which they have formulated for our post war future and security without molestation. There are already three candidates in the field in Stroud, and by withdrawing at this stage I do so in the hope that the Stroud electorate will rally together once again, and cast their votes in favour of the Churchill supporter, Flt Lt Perkins.[220]

Perkins lost to the Labour candidate by less than 1,000 votes, and Churchill was cast into the wilderness.

Before the war's end Mildred had found a diversion in riding and driving her horses. She had entered a variety of shows in West Country towns and villages that were as quiet as one could find in wartime Britain. Perhaps she only recorded her successes, but there were several: for example, she won first prize in the Class 9 ('Best Hackney') at the Highworth & District British Legion Show in August 1944. One imagines the field was slender. Soon after VE Day, she came first in the Private Driving Turnout at Churchdown, near Badminton.

With Britain now again at peace, she acquired a townhouse in London (58 Queensway) from her father's estate. In September, she visited Montreux and stayed at the Palace Hotel to wait for Tony who was being demobbed.

Her younger brother, Roderick, had by now become a tenant of hers at 42 Runnymede Road, Egham, where he was well tended.

But peacetime had brought a commercial vacuum for her business empire, and when Tony returned from the army, son and mother shifted the group from aircraft work to the manufacture of bus bodies, initially for Cardiff Corporation although, in the event, this diversification was stymied by a national shortage of aluminium. By the end of October, she was advertising the sale of the remainder of her Down Farm estate, comprising 274 acres. The house and 200 acres had already been sold by private treaty. In the mood to tie up the loose ends in her life, she sailed with Tony to Cape Town, South Africa, on SS *Umtali*, presumably to see her brother, Louis.

In wartime Cardiff, Mildred had met another entrepreneur, Raymond Boulton, who hailed from a West Country glove-manufacturing family. He was to become Mildred's last lover. He persuaded her to buy Holman Byfield, a rival glove-manufacturing business. With any airline business snatched from her hands by the government, and bus manufacturing (Air Dispatch had now been renamed Bruce Coach Works Ltd, under Tony's hands) in rapid decline, she needed something to keep her still-agile mind busy. The new business was based in the army town of Warminster in Wiltshire, so she added to her property empire with a house there.

Raymond proved very louche by the standards of her previous partners. His influence, and the economic dereliction of post-War Britain, gave Mildred perhaps her least happy years in business. Enjoyment came from retail therapy, particularly in furnishing her main London residences. In 1950, she settled in Bradford on Avon, Wiltshire, and the Avon Valley became her hinterland. Her neighbours there were aware of her rich history, and she played the part of a wealthy middle-aged lady with aplomb, collecting her pension each week at the sub-post office on the Trowbridge Road dressed in her large fur coat. She still kept a stable of her best cars – and drove them appropriately, of course.

20

EPILOGUE

After the war Mildred's first love, Stephen Easter (described 'of a somewhat retiring disposition'), busied himself as chairman of Worthing Rural District Council. When his cuckolded wife Alice died, he presented a window in her memory to their church at Rustington. However, within six months of her death he had married again, to Claire Fluckinger, a Swiss citizen, and they decamped to her country. He died in Hilterfingen in May 1952. His son with Mildred, Tony, had remained in touch with his father until the end. Both he and Mildred benefited from Stephen's will.

★★★

Sempill, who became increasingly batty in his later years (his letters to the *Times* and the *Financial Times* increased to one per fortnight), died in 1965 at the age of 72. The absence of his economic foresight was not missed by the nation.

★★★

While many of his piloting colleagues in north-west USA perished doing their job in the 1930s, Hans Looff was a survivor. He returned to Grant's Pass, Josephine County, Oregon, and died in October 1969 at the age of 76.

★★★

Victor was pushed out of Holroyd & Bruce by his nephew, Lord Rosebery. He died just before Christmas in 1978.

★★★

In April 1974, Mildred, aged 78, took out her 1937 Rolls-Royce Phantom III (with a Hooper Sedanca body) from her garage at Bradford on Avon. This was the very same machine that she had given to Eric before the war – an object that stirred her emotions.

Some months previously, she had attended a vintage race meeting at Silverstone. 'Had I sat sedately in the stands, of course, I would have kept myself out of trouble, but once I saw those cars in action I simply had to get a closer look. So off I went in the general direction of the pits.' There, she met John Waddell, head of Ford PR. His team was aware of her motorsport pedigree, in particular Peter Wardle:

> He was about half a century younger than I was, but I soon found we had quite a lot in common, particularly the Montlhéry circuit outside Paris. Peter had driven there, too, a couple of score years later, of course. Together we talked each other round the circuit almost yard by yard. It took me right back, I can tell you, and I soon gathered that the old place had not changed very much. I remember Peter saying to me, 'There's a huge bump high up on the banking at one point.'
>
> I knew all about the bump, and I told him how during the 15,000-mile record, Victor turned over on the ice-bound track because of that bump and some wheelspin, and how he was buried under the car and escaped unhurt. For quite a while we exchanged our Montlhéry bump experiences; but as we talked my eyes kept straying to his Formula Atlantic car.[221] It looked such a thoroughbred. Peter noticed my interest and, to my surprise and delight, he asked me whether I would like to try it for size, which really was a compliment, because no driver likes strangers climbing in and out of his machine just before a race. In I climbed and took hold of the little steering wheel – so different from the large ones I had known long ago. As I climbed out of the car, I said to Peter, 'I really must have another go on a track some day.'

Stuart McCrudden, the head of motorsport press for Ford Europe, over-heard this and suggested she come down to Thruxton to test drive the new Ford Capri Ghia, 'The thought of driving on a track again was pure joy for me, and of course I agreed.'[222]

So, in April she set off for Thruxton in her Rolls-Royce and thundered past McCrudden on the A303 on the way to the circuit! Once there, after a lap with McCrudden (who later wrote the foreword for her *Nine Lives*), it was her turn at the wheel:

> Stuart explained that, under the rules of the track, I must wear a crash helmet and he produced one. I told him I never used such contraptions in my day and I put it on back to front. I never wore any special kit. I was never keen on overalls or slacks, but always drove in a blouse, tailored skirt and a string of pearls.
>
> I was going pretty fast when I reached the first corner and I clung closely to the edge, but as I neared the end of the corner, the car tried to take charge. I quickly changed down at about 70 into third gear and managed to right the car and avoid the rough where so many drivers end up. Then one more corner and the finishing straight. I had no wish to break the Capri but did want to get the maximum speed out of her. So I asked Stuart to call out my speed after I reached 90, as I wished to concentrate totally on driving the car.

He was very happy to do this as it meant she could remain focused on the track! She was desperate to break the 100mph barrier – in what was a totally standard road car, apart from four-point harnesses:

> I heard him say, 'Ninety … ninety-five … a hundred … hundred and five … hundred and ten … Better brake now …' I did. [In the opinion of the Ford team 110mph was right on the limit of the Capri's capabilities.]
>
> One or two of the track officials were admiring my Rolls. So I invited them to have a spin round the track. I managed to squeeze in five — three journalists and two track officials. This wonderful car managed to top 90mph on the track and they all enjoyed the experience.[223]

After all that, the champagne was opened and there were toasts to all and sundry. Mildred even had a sip – she had forsworn her total abstinence a few years earlier.

Three years later came her last flight; she was treated to some mild aerobatics in a de Havilland Chipmunk. Not a bad day out for a lady of a certain vintage!

The last car Mildred purchased was a Morris 1100. Car aficionados will agree this is suitably staid for an old lady by now in her eighties. However, Mildred had ordered it to have a conversion by Downton, the Wiltshire tuning firm renowned for creating the 'hottest' British engines.[224] This fast lady was still keen to show a clean pair of heels to any upstart on the lanes of Wiltshire and Avon! Coincidentally, Victor's last car was an Austin 1100.

In 1990 a filmmaker, Gabrielle Bown, directed a programme about sportswomen of the 1920s, entitled *Adventurous Eves*. She interviewed Mildred shortly before her death. In their conversation, like some declining Hollywood star, Mildred knocked six years off her age, and rather meanly she made no mention of Victor when reflecting on the glories of her motorsport career.

Mildred's endurance finally faltered and she finished her last lap on 21 May 1990 in Camden. She was cremated at Golders Green Cemetery, where a plaque was later unveiled in her memory. In her will she left £168,394 and the estate was resolved with dispatch, probate being granted by September.

Tony only outlived his mother by seven years, dying in 1997. Her first grandson, Philip, had been born in 1949 in Cardiff but died in 1993 of Aids. Her second grandson, Michael, born in London in 1953, reversed his great-grandmother's direction and married in the USA, never having shown much interest in his grandmother's exploits.

Victor's grandson, Michael Grimmond, showed that motoring skills remained in the genes, managing to finish the 2016 Monte Carlo Classique Run (from John O'Groats) in a 1927 AC Six – a fitting tribute to his grandfather.

Mildred in the Rear-View Mirror

Focus, determination and stamina: these are undoubtedly qualities Mildred possessed in spades. She was one of those figureheads of the 1920s and '30s who advanced the cause of women in Great Britain. It is clear from her prolific writing (for women) on motoring that she wanted equality of opportunity. And she veered towards record-breaking so as to pit her skills directly against the men.

Mildred developed an unusual amount of mechanical knowledge from an early age, and this helped her when she progressed to aviation. Whether at the wheel or stick, she was a 'sympathetic pair of hands'. However, it is difficult to avoid the conclusion that the success of her round-the-world flight owed a large amount to luck (as well as the great efforts of an army of supporters and civil servants).

If Mildred had worn an eyepatch and had a skull and crossbones pattern on her scarf, it would not have looked out of place, for she was a buccaneering type who had thrived in pre-war aviation at Heston and Croydon.

However, when the fetters were tightened, she was not at all comfortable, and while the Second World War brought extreme personal tragedy for her, she would also rather have been running her airlines than a warplane repair business.

Mildred's exploits speak for themselves and, from a twenty-first-century standpoint, it is slightly surprising that she felt the need to inject the elements of fantasy and hyperbole to which she was prone. She was an early adopter of the need for the oxygen of publicity to attract sponsorship and thereby income. Mildred had no need of a Max Clifford type to stoke that interest. Possibly helped by her mother's genes, it came naturally to Mildred.

The focus of her charm, and the force of her personality, lit fires in (predominantly male) souls around the world. I would have loved to have met her, and I do believe you would too …

For those who have the pleasure of her friendship know that one of her assets is the manner in which she is always ready to laugh when the laugh is against her.[225]

APPENDIX 1

MILDRED'S MOTOR-RACING CAREER

1926

        Skegness Motor Races   AC   3rd, Class 10

                                        1st, Class 14 (h'cap)

        Boulogne Speed Trials   AC

1927

        Monte Carlo Rally   Winner, *Coupe des Dames* (6th overall)

        AC Six four-seater fabric saloon with gurney nutting body

        (regestration PF 6465)

Brooklands

21 May   MIdd'x Cty AC Jnr Short H'cap   AC 3rd of 4   (Brooklands Archives (BA))

2 Jul   Surbiton MC Allcomers' H'cap   2ltr AC Winner (of 6)   (BA)

10 Sep   Boulogne Motor Week   AC Aceca (4th)   (TNA)

1928

        Monte Carlo Rally (from Stockholm) Arrol-Aster   (Motor Sport (MS))

                5th overall

Brooklands

21 Jun   BARC Ladies H'cap Sweepstakes   AC 2ltr   (BA)

30 Jun   Midd'x Short H'cap Open   AC 2ltr 2nd   (BA)

Midd'x Long H'cap   np
Midd'x 50-mile H'cap Open   np
Midd'x 50-mile H'cap Grand Prix Open   np
Milan to Munich Alpine Trial   AC (special medal)   (Nine Lives)

1929

Monte Carlo Rally (from Berlin) Arroll-Aster   (MS)
      One of 24 finishers from 64 starters

1930

Monte Carlo Rally (from Sundervall)   Hillman Straight 8   (MS)
      21st of 87 finishers

Brooklands
19 May   JCC Double 12hr Race (with VB)   2ltr Alvis Silver Eagle   (BA)
      13th overall, 3rd in Class

1931
Brooklands
17 Oct   BARC Ladies H'cap 6.5 miles   1.5ltr Aston Martin   (BA)

APPENDIX 2

THE HISTORY OF THE BLACKBURN BLUEBIRD

The Bluebird was designed for the famous Light Aeroplane Competition at Lympne in 1924 (the rushed development meant it failed to make the competition). Its evolution was hampered by its small three-cylinder radial engine. By 1926 it had a five-cylinder 60hp Genet engine but could only manage a maximum of 75mph; however, on 18 September that year a Bluebird so equipped did win the Grosvenor Cup at a speed of 85mph.

In 1927 Blackburn started serious production of the machine, and acquitted itself well at the Easter meeting at Bournemouth (winning the top three prizes). Being both aerobatic and having side-by-side seating were key to its popularity. Being all-metal also distinguished it from most of its competition, notably de Havilland's products. An extensive sales tour was undertaken that November. In 1928 it was re-engined with a more powerful ADC Cirrus II engine and Colonel Sempill undertook a 3,000-mile 'holiday tour' of Great Britain and Ireland in August in a float-equipped model (having started out from being moored outside the Houses of Parliament!). Sempill continued to be involved in promoting the machine in 1929, in which year Blackburn Aircraft ceded its marketing to Auto Auctions.

Controls were by push rod rather than the more normal (for this style of aircraft) wire. This would have given a much more precise feel to the handling. Its useful load in normal circumstances was 580lb – with 22 gallons of fuel, this meant that two passengers and their luggage (in a separate compartment behind the cockpit) could total no more than 380lb.

Mildred's G-ABDS was a Bluebird Mk IV, fitted with a Gipsy II engine, producing 120hp. It had a normal maximum gross weight of 1,680lb, increased by special dispensation for the round-the-world flight, as described in the text. Its list price was £675, so Mildred had a bargain if she paid only £550.

NOTES AND REFERENCES

Chapter 1

1   Interview in *Airways* magazine, January 1931.
2   *Australia & Back*, Cobham, p.44.
3   Dudgeon, p.15.
4   *Britain and the Persian Gulf*, Briton Cooper Busch, p.45.
5   *The Bluebird's Flight (BF)*, Mrs Victor Bruce, p.48.
6   Letter to Captain Norman Blackburn, dated 10 October 1930.
7   Ibid.
8   *BF*, p.54. Time of departure from Bushire – Reuters reported it as 0550 (*Dublin Evening Herald*, 6 October 1930), which would have been sensible so as to avoid the heat of the day and associated turbulence.
9   Quoted in *We Danced all Night*, Pugh, p.339. The crash at Kuhmabarak: Mildred's reporting is inconsistent with third-party evidence and her own logbook. She frequently refers (e.g. in *Nine Lives* and a letter to Norman Blackburn from Jask, dated 1 October 1930) to being stranded in the desert with the Belushis for three days. She also says it took the messenger forty-eight hours of 'marching' and crossing 'seven shark-infested creeks' to reach the telegraph station. The facts are that her logbook records her unscheduled arrival in the desert at Kuhmabarak on Monday, 6 October, and take-off for Jask only two days later, on the Wednesday. The report of the British Mission/Telegraph Department states that they received the message from the messenger at 7.30 p.m. on Monday, 6th. It seems she spent no more than two days and two nights in the desert.
10   *Nine Lives (NL)*, Mrs Victor Bruce, p.115.
11   *Amy Johnson*, Constance Babington Smith.
12   *Airways*, January 1931.

Chapter 2

13   *The Rise of the Plutocrats*, Camplin, p.15.

14   Camplin, p.19.

15   Tony Pastor: He had started his career in circuses, initially with P.T. Barnum, and by 1860 he had evolved into a comic singer in variety revues. The talent came from his father, who had supplemented the family income with some singing in the evenings after he left his barbers shop. Tony's bawdy songs were aimed firmly at male New Yorkers.

    However, after Pastor had built up his own chain of theatres in New York, he decided to promote an 'acceptable' form of vaudeville there. He created a 'Grand Double Company', and claimed that his vaudeville theatre was the only one to enjoy 'élite patronage'. He pitched to a distinctly middle-class audience, and succeeded in attracting ladies on uptown shopping excursions, for example. In 1881, his New Fourteenth Street Theatre claimed it would be 'catering to the ladies, and presenting for the amusement of the cultivated and aesthetic Pure Music and Comedy, Burlesque, and Farce'.

    He kept a close watch on the material staged, and towards the end of that decade banned the sale of alcohol across his theatres. His empire soon extended to touring companies. Legends such as Buster Keaton and Sophie Tucker started out their careers on his stages. Unlike many of his peers, he continued to tread his own boards and so probably enjoyed better relationships with his actors. Somewhat florid, with a striking moustache not unlike that of Louis Blériot, the French pilot pioneer, he cut quite a figure.

16   Jennie's theatre career: She is strangely absent from chronicles of the US and London stages of the time – e.g. *The Cambridge History of American Theatre*, ed. Wilmeth & Bigsby, 1999; *Notable Names in the American Theatre*, James & White, 1976; nor *The London Stage 1890–1899* and *A Calendar of Plays & Players*, J.P. Wearing, Scarecrow, 1976.

17   The full description of the necklace in the Christie's catalogue (when it was later sold by Mildred – see Chapter 19) runs, 'A superb diamond necklace, composed of 53 graduated circular-cut diamonds, of fine colour and brilliancy, with a diamond 4 stone clasp. It supports a fine circular centre cut diamond within a border of small diamonds and outer border of ten larger circular-cut diamonds, with diamond points.' The auctioneer noted that the pendant could be worn singly as a clip brooch.

18   *More Equal than Others*, Montagu, p.168.

19   *The Decline and Fall of the British Aristocracy*, Cannadine, p.347.

20   *NL*, p.23.

21   Roderick Petre, Mildred's younger brother, was educationally subnormal, and in adult life appears to have done little other than sell newspapers. Coptfold, with all its 346 acres, vinery, tennis courts and cricket pitch, was eventually sold to the Upton family in 1906. The Petres' building itself lasted no more than a century, and New Coptfold Hall was built in 2002. In 1901, Petre's tenant at Coptfold was the extravagantly named William Dallas Ochterlony Greig, a goalkeeper of all things, in residence with his widowed sister. Greig had distinguished himself as a goalkeeper for the Wanderers by being the only keeper to let in sixteen goals in the first round of the FA Cup, yet still win the competition the following year.

22   Camplin, p.29.

23   Land sales post-First World War: Montagu asserts a quarter of the land in England
     changed hands in the four years after the First World War.
24   Thorndon Hall was designed by James Paine and built by the Petre family in 1767,
     with gardens by a certain Capability Brown. The estate was later enhanced by the
     8th Baron, a keen botanist and garden designer, who planted 40,000 American
     trees.

Chapter 3

25   *NL*, p.25.
26   Brooklands interview.
27   Women speeding – in this crime the French had a lead. Anne de Mortemart,
     Duchess of Uzès, was caught roaring at more than 12kph in the Bois de Boulogne
     on 9 June 1898, only two months after passing her test.
28   *We Danced all Night*, Pugh, p.111.
29   Bestic article, Brooklands archives.
30   The Australian Central Flying School at Point Cook was named after John Cook,
     a mate aboard HMS *Rattlesnake*, which undertook surveys in the area in 1836.
31   Petre the Great's death: Mr Handasyde attended the inquest and appears to have
     been very concerned that there should be no suggestion of structural failure in his
     machine. My conclusion is that Petre was very rash to continue this journey in
     such high winds.

Chapter 4

32   *We Danced all Night*, Pugh, p.126.
33   Pugh, p.134.
34   *The Decline and Fall of the British Aristocracy*, Cannadine, p.75.
35   Pugh, p.132.
36   *After the Victorians*, Wilson, p.248.
37   Shoreham Aerodrome – for a list of the units based at Shoreham during the First
     World War, I suggest *Action Stations Vol. 9*, Patrick Stephens, 1985.
38   *Testament of Youth*, Brittain, p.559.
39   Brooklands interview.
40   *NL*, p.34.
41   Her first car: some sources indicate that in 1919 Lawrence indulged his daughter
     with her first car, a Vauxhall 30/98, which she later claimed was 'the fastest car of
     its day' (Bestic). If so, this was a rare and glorious car for a young girl – Lawrence
     clearly remained under the spell of his daughter, and as an absent father, carried
     a degree of guilt. Other sources indicate the car was the gift of Easter. The *Nine
     Lives* story, which ignores the Vauxhall altogether, is used in the main text.

Chapter 5

42   Boddy, *The History of Brooklands*, p.4.
43   Quoted in *We Danced all Night*, Pugh, p.241.

44   Pugh, p.246.
45   Pugh, p.253.
46   Pugh, p.254.
47   Pugh, p.259.
48   *Catholic Who's Who*, 1929.

Chapter 6

49   *The Decline and Fall of the British Aristocracy*, Cannadine, p.577.
50   Cannadine, p.380.
51   *A History of the Monte Carlo Rally*, Frostick, p.17; *Monte Carlo Rally: The Golden Age*, Robson, p.20.

Chapter 7

52   Victor's diary.
53   1926 Monte: Robson implies that Mildred acquired the car, rather than borrowed a works example. She acquired a 'Weymann-bodied AC Six saloon which Gurney Nutting had built to her exact requirements'.
54   Marriage: she later told a reporter that they were married in 'a little church on the hill [above Monaco]' (unknown paper in Brooklands archive). The photo of the wedding party exiting the ceremony suggests it was at the *Mairie* or the British Consul's office, and indeed that is where her later divorce papers stated the location.
55   Brooklands interview.
56   *The Twenties*, Montgomery, p.166.
57   Montgomery, p.169.
58   *Nine Thousand Miles in Eight Weeks* (NTM), Mrs Victor Bruce, p.20.
50   Brooklands Interview.
60   *Who Do You Think You Are* magazine, October 2012, p.76.
61   *NTM*, p.31.
62   *Country Life*, 5 February 1927; and *NTM*, p.33. The car for the 9,000-mile trip – in an appendix to *Nine Thousand Miles*, Victor summarises their car thus, 'It was an absolutely normal S.F. Edge 6 cylinder AC chassis, with special lightweight fabric saloon body. The engine was 15.9hp, 1991cc, with overhead camshaft and overhead valves.'
63   *Monte Carlo Rally: The Golden Age*, Robson, p26.
64   *A History of the Monte Carlo Rally*, Frostick, p.17.
65   *NTM*, p.41.
66   *NTM*, p.54.
67   'Today in Italy – Motoring realities in the Land of Romance', Mildred Bruce, *The Motor*, 14 June 1927.
68   *NTM*, p.62.
69   *NTM*, p.80.
70   *NTM*, p.237.
71   *Dictionary of National Biography*.

Chapter 8

72 *Fifty Years of Brooklands*, Gardiner, p.496.

73 *Bentley Drivers Club Magazine*, August 1990.

74 *Times Law Reports*, July 1927.

75 Sir Chartres Biron was later to gain some sort of fame by banning Radclyffe Hall's paean to lesbianism, *The Well of Loneliness*. Radclyffe's first name was actually Margaret, but she was always known as 'John'. The editor of the *Sunday Express* laid his views out plainly, he would 'rather give a girl a phial of Prussic Acid than this novel'.

76 *Autocar* interview.

77 15,000-mile attempt: In *Nine Lives*, Mildred says it started at 7 p.m. on Friday, 9 December; in the *Times* report of 14 December, it started at 10.28 a.m.

78 Brooklands interview.

79 *Sunday Express*, 18 December 1927.

80 *Times*, 20 March 1928.

81 *New Statesman*, 24 December 1927.

82 Letter to Lord Knowledge, 20 December 1927.

83 *Monte Carlo Rally: The Golden Age*, Robson, p.30.

84 *Heavenly Adventurer*, Collier, p.11.

85 *Titbits*, 14 July 1928.

86 The Arrol-Aster contract was at a salary of £300 p.a. plus up to £300 for expenses.

87 1929 Monte Carlo Rally: competitors could choose their starting point from a list of sixty towns, and at a time of their choosing, observed by their national motoring association. They had to pass several controls en route, and average between 30 and 40kph, with a speed of more than 43kph leading to disqualification. Prizegiving, 27 January.

88 Letter, 22 March 1929, Wiltshire County Records.

89 According to her Brooklands interview.

90 Letter to Ben Jowett, 22 May 1929, Wiltshire County Records.

91 1929 record: YV7263, the 4.5-litre Bentley, four seat Le Mans Sports chassis CH.KM 3077, was built in 1928, and had an illustrious racing history in Grand Prix and at Le Mans, in the hands of Captain Sir Henry (Tim) Birkin. It still exists.

92 Brooklands interview.

93 *Bentley Drivers Club Magazine*, p.248.

94 *Illustrated London News*, 22 June 1929.

95 *Wings*, 13 June 1929.

96 Quoted by David Baines, *Daily Telegraph*, 15 November 2003.

97 Sir George Beharrell: there must have been some chemistry between them because in 1937 he became chairman of Imperial Airways – and therefore in charge of what became Mildred's major competitor.

98 Cross-Channel attempt: *Mosquito* was built by Percy See, a Fareham boatbuilder noted for his innovation of light craft. In the Second World War he went on to design and build the canoes used by the Royal Marines in the raid that earned them the name of 'Cockleshell Heroes'.

99   One source says she had problems with her steering gear on the return, not making it back to Dover until 4 p.m. Another source and *Nine Lives* say she did the return journey in 107 minutes.

100 The crash in the Double-Twelve Race had repercussions that have lasted to the present day. Regulations were changed, with medicals for drivers being instituted, for example. A spectator sued the Brooklands organisers (Hall vs BARC); although he was unsuccessful in his suit, this led to all tickets for British motoring events ever after stating 'motor sport can be dangerous'.

Chapter 9

101 Why learn to fly? She claimed in *Adventurous Eves* that if she did not learn to fly, 'I'll be so old-fashioned no one will want to talk to me.'

102 Bert Hinkler's flight England–Australia: fifteen and a half days in an Avro Avian. At the dinner, Sir Charles Wakefield presented Hinkler with a platinum and diamond brooch showing a kangaroo leaping from Britain to Australia! Sir Sefton Brancker proposed the toast to Hinkler.

103 *National Flying Services Annual*, 1929.

104 Victor Bruce's private testimony.

105 Where did she learn to fly? In the *Adventurous Eves* interview she continued to claim she only had six lessons before her round-the-world flight, and these were all at Heston.

106 George Lowdell went on to become chief test pilot at Vickers Aviation, at Brooklands.

107 Victor Bruce's private testimony.

108 Air Ministry notes of initial meeting.

109 *The Bystander*, 15 April 1931.

110 *European Skyways*, Thomas, p.57.

111 *Flight*, 27 March 1931.

112 The Bluebird's weight: G-ABDS was certificated on 26 September 1930 for an all up weight of 1,950lb. This compares with a normal maximum permitted weight for the Bluebird IV (with any of the five engine options) of 1,750lb. It carried a 'special' category certificate of airworthiness, presumably on account of this uplift in weight.

113 *BF* (this is another fiction: she was to lose a Burberry coat to a brigand at Kuhmabarak, yet later said she even had a spare).

114 Cluett, *Croydon Airport 1928–1939*, p.159.

Chapter 10

115 *Nottinghamshire Guardian*, September 1930.

116 *Straits Times* interview, 4 April 1931.

117 Writing in January 1931, in *Airways* magazine, she described the technical problem as an oil (not fuel) leak.

118 *European Skyways*, Thomas, p.192.

119 *Heavenly Adventurer*, Collier, p.223.

120 *Sir Sefton Brancker*, Macmillan, p.413.

121 Brancker's journey to Cardington: the obituary of Jessie Blackburn (in the
    Independent newspaper) avers that she took Brancker to Cardington from Brough
    (or her home in Leeds), and that Jessie heard of his death on her journey back
    up north. This story was confirmed to me by Professor Robert Blackburn, Jessie's
    grandson. I have chosen to describe the version given in Macmillan's biography of
    Brancker.

122 Macmillan, p.414.

123 Macmillan, p.403.

124 RAF Shaibah became a major internment camp in the recent Gulf Wars.

125 *My Flying Life*, Kingsford-Smith, p.125.

Chapter 11

126 *Shopping, Seduction and Mr Selfridge*, Woodhead, p.230.

127 Cluett, *Croydon Airport 1928–1939*, p.26.

128 The other Bluebird present was G-AAIR (in which Mildred had flown).

129 Seventy-one years later, I was flying this part of her route on my way to Australia.
    Despite being in an enclosed modern aircraft flying at 8,000ft, we could smell
    Karachi 20 miles away. For Mildred, flying much lower and in an open-cockpit
    biplane, the city must have announced itself even more pungently.

130 Queen's Royal Surrey Regiment records.

131 Asian journeys: there are significant divergences between her logbook, and her two
    published books. Her logbook records a direct flight from Jodhpur to Allahabad
    lasting nine hours. *BF* refers to an intermediate stop at Delhi. Her logbook also
    records a direct flight from Calcutta to Rangoon of nine hours and fifty minutes
    (and 810 miles – surely beyond her range). *BF* records a stop at Akyab (this route
    measures approx. 704 miles on my map), making, she claims, almost twelve hours'
    flying in a day.

132 *Australia & Back*, Cobham, p.52.

133 *BF*, p.88.

134 Here, again, my 2001 Air Race route coincided with Mildred's. She would
    have felt relief at leaving behind her the squalor and corruption of the Indian
    subcontinent, but would have been apprehensive at heading for the more remote,
    and less well-known Burma. In our case, we were apprehensive at arriving in a
    country with no record of welcoming tourists, and placing ourselves at the mercy
    of the military regime.

135 Rangoon: Mildred and Oscar were among the first pilots to land at Rangoon's
    new aerodrome. On our Australian air race, we too arrived at Rangoon (by then
    temporarily renamed Yangon) late in the day, just in time to attend a reception
    with the Minister of Aviation – who was unsurprisingly one of the colonels.
    Another guest, a local businessman, was very off-message and whispered to me
    some home truths about how the colonels' regime really worked. Like Mildred, I
    faced an early start the next morning.

136 Cobham, p.64.

137 More discrepancies: in *NL* she talks of Bangkok to Korat being 500 miles, and
    in *BF* refers to it being a four-hour leg. In fact, it is only 75 statute miles. Her
    logbook records five hours/400 miles from Bangkok to Lahone (wherever that

is), and a further four hours/400 miles thence to Hanoi. From Korat to Nakhon Panom is approx. 285 miles and another 260 miles from there to Hanoi. In *BF*, Mildred records those two legs as 680 nautical miles.

138 *On Intelligence*, Hughes-Wilson, p.318; and The National Archives, Sempill file.

Chapter 12

139 Brooklands interview.
140 Lakhon stay: these inconsistencies continue. In *NL*, she describes going to mass on the fifth day of her stay at Lakhon, a Sunday. Yet according to her logbook she arrived on Saturday, 1 November and left on Thursday, 6 November.
141 *John O'London Weekly*, 19 December 1931.
142 *NL*, p.122.
143 How high did she fly? In *NL*, she overflew the Annamite Mountains at 'nearly thirteen thousand feet, the highest the Bluebird could go'. I would personally be surprised if the fully loaded Bluebird could have made it to that altitude. In none of Blackburn's specifications is a service ceiling noted. Jackson quotes 15,000ft for a Cirrus III-engine Bluebird. Mildred's machine was, of course, usually flying well over the normal maximum permitted weight. Given that the leg to Hanoi was anticipated to take at least four hours, she would have wanted as much fuel as possible, however, she reports in *NL* that the governor could only give her 30 of the 50 gallons of fuel she was requesting. So, she would have theoretically been 144lb below her own max permitted weight for this reason. She logged this flight in her logbook as four hours. Yet, in *NL* she describes herself as still flying above cloud after four and a quarter hours.
144 *BF*, p.123.
145 At that time a pilot in the Royal Navy. *Aviation Memoirs*, Cathcart-Jones, p.116.
146 Armistice Day: this is taken from *BF*. In *NL*, she gives a completely different account, saying she went to an Armistice Day service in Hong Kong before she took off!
147 Foochow: again, a difference in her tales. In *NL*, she claims that the Petrol Company's manager told her about the war and she therefore demanded an audience with the admiral.
148 Brooklands interview.
149 Seoul: the timings in *NL* and *BF* do not ring true. She claims that she had not seen land after seven hours, yet it is only 279 miles from Shanghai to Ross Island (which, in *BF*, she says she gained after eight hours, making a ground speed of only 35mph); Mokpo on the mainland is a further 90 miles, and Seoul 189 miles beyond that. She records 'two hours flying over land' before arriving at Seoul. This is far too rapid for the headwind she must have encountered on the oversea leg. The logbook records an unusually precise eight hours and fifty-eight minutes for the total leg.
150 The National Archives, Sempill file.
151 The National Archives, Mildred file.
152 *Japan Times*, 5 December 1930.
153 8 December 1930 – The National Archives, Mildred file.

154 Logbook accuracy: when she arrived in Tokyo her logbook recorded a cumulative
    total of 13,465 miles. The Royal Aero Club, for their records, noted a distance of
    10,330 miles.

Chapter 13

155 This is not mentioned in *BF*.
156 *Las Vegas Daily Optic*, 13 December 1930.
157 *Vancouver Daily Province*, 17 December 1930.
158 The broken exhaust: Mildred had told the Mitsubishi engineers at Tachikawa that
    she was going to have the engine replaced in Vancouver (there is no evidence
    that she subsequently did); accordingly, they were asked to inspect and repair only
    the airframe. In Tokyo, she was introduced by Nagakawa of Mitsubishi to a Mr
    Thomas McRae Jnr, an engineer of the Curtiss Aeroplane Company, and she asked
    him if his company would help her in Vancouver, to which he assented.
159 Sidney Pickles was an Englishman who had formerly worked for Blackburn
    Aircraft as a test pilot. He was now chief flying instructor of the local flying club
    in Vancouver; he designed the new exhaust pipe that was fitted by Yarrows.
160 *BF*, p.183.
161 Interview – *Airways* magazine, April 1931.
162 When did she leave San Francisco? 11 January in *NL*; 12 January in *BF* and 14
    January in logbook!
163 *BF*, p.227.
164 *BF*, p.235.
165 Ambassador Charles Dawes had served with the American Expeditionary Force
    in Europe in the First World War, and was later vice president of the USA under
    Calvin Coolidge, with whom he had a fractious relationship.
166 *Indianapolis Star*, 24 January 1931.
167 *Pittsburgh Post-Gazette*, 26 January.
168 From New Albany/Louisville her journey is less easy to track. She recorded in her
    logbook the following:
       26/1 Louisville–Virginia: 4 hours 30, 380 miles.
       27/1 Virginia–Baltimore: 2 hours, 160 miles.
       5/2 Baltimore–New York: 2 hours, 160 miles.
    These dates are wrong, and the journeys misleading. *BF* mentions Columbus
    (Ohio), where she stayed overnight then Washington, but no mention of Virginia.
    NL merely talks about Baltimore and NY. *Pittsburgh Post-Gazette* reported on
    26 January that she forced landed in Tappahannock 'yesterday'. *Chicago News* also
    reported she landed at Columbus on the 25th.

Chapter 14

169 *BF*, p.252.
170 The National Archives, Mildred file.
171 The Empire State Building was still three months away from its official opening
    when Mildred claimed to have had a tour, escorted by a member of the New

York Flying Club. This also renders unbelievable her assertion that she had flown around it several times on her arrival flight, watching spectators waving at her.

172 *High-Flying Women*, Pelletier, pp.98 & 106.

173 Hilsz and Bastié both went on to have distinguished careers, particularly the latter. In 1936, she established a new record for crossing the South Atlantic and continued her epic voyages until the outbreak of the Second World War, when she volunteered for the Croix Rouge, and then the French Women's Air Force Auxiliaries, when they were mobilised. She was the first woman to be made a commander of the Légion d'Honneur in 1947.

174 The welcoming party at Lympne and Croydon:

   Norman Blackburn – my grandmother's favourite among the four brothers.

   Squadron Leader Ridley – a much decorated First World War veteran who was in charge of Blackburn's relationship with Auto Auctions.

   Flight Lieutenant Woodhead DFC – the test pilot of the Bluebird, and presently chief flying instructor of one of the Blackburn-owned RAF flying schools.

   H.R. Field – the owner of three Bluebird machines.

Chapter 15

175 The National Archives: AVIA 2/498.

176 *We Danced all Night*, Pugh, p.94.

177 *Sydney Morning Herald*, 23 January 1931.

178 Sir Malcolm Campbell – fifteen days earlier he had broken his own record of three years' standing, achieving 246.09mph at Daytona Beach, in the USA.

179 The National Archives, Sempill file, note 649.

180 *Straits Times*, 4 April 1931.

181 The National Archives, Mildred file.

182 Francis Chichester described his feats in a subsequent autobiography, *The Lonely Sea and the Sky* – well worth a read.

183 *Empire News*, 8 December 1940.

184 *The Argus*, 9 October 1931.

185 Instrument flying course: this is not recorded in her logbook. But she did beat Amy Johnson by more than a year in doing one – Amy underwent her course in August 1932.

186 SARO: Sir Henry Segrave in 1929 became Technical Advisor to the Aircraft Corporation Ltd (AC), which owned shares in Saunders-Roe, the original company behind the Segrave Meteor (which was more properly called the Saro Segrave Meteor). AC subsequently developed links with Blackburn Aircraft.

187 The Windhover crash was later attributed to dirt in the fuel lines.

188 Her logbook for this period would again appear probably to have been written up later, and in error, as it indicates she was flying from early 1931 in G-ABVG, a Bluebird Mk IV, whereas G-ABVG was the Miles Satyr she later acquired, which was not registered to her (as Luxury Air Tours) until 21 April 1933. Her logbook does not mention the second Bluebird she acquired, G-ABMI, until July 1931, whereas it is likely that it was this machine she used as soon as G-ABDS was pensioned off as a display piece, immediately after her round-the-world flight.

189 *Fifty Years of Brooklands*, Gardiner, pp.18–19.

190 *Bentley Drivers Club Magazine*, p.249.

Chapter 16

191 Refuelling: she originally intended to make the attempt in a Monospar, an aircraft
with which she was familiar, but technical reasons prevented this and she was
forced to acquire the Windhover. Had the team's preparations been more thorough
they would have rerouted the oil pipes into the fuselage so that oil and filters
could be replaced at will.

192 The Saro Windhover A21/2, the first and only production example, was completed
in July 1931. After modifications (the addition of an auxiliary winglet over
engines to improve air flow and lift), it was sold to Francis as G-ABJP, who sold
it on in September to Gibraltar Airways for the Gibraltar–Tangier route. Mildred
and colleagues acquired it in July 1932, and renamed it City of Portsmouth
(presumably for sponsorship reasons) and its undercarriage was temporarily
removed. Mildred disposed of it in May 1935 to Jersey Airways, it being taken out
of service in 1938.

Its wheel and ground landing gear were removed to save weight. It had a fuel
capacity of 180 gallons, with an estimated consumption of no more than 15
gallons per hour. The team received sponsorship (£121) from their fuel supplier,
Trinidad Leaseholds Ltd.

The first record attempt was dogged by radio failure after the ingress of water
during take-off and propellers which were unsuitable for the machine's overloaded
state. The second attempt on 5 August failed due to a recurrence of radio
problems, fuel supply issues and fog around the Isle of Wight that prejudiced the
refuelling operation. They landed at 6 a.m. on 6 August (letter from G. Abell, late
Major RAF).

The accompanying smaller aircraft was described as a Gipsy Moth, not a
Comper Swift, in *Nine Lives*. Abell clearly states several times it was a Swift. In his
letter to the RAC, Jolly, the Ipswich manager, also noted that the propeller of the
centre engine had been rubbing against a loose pin in the cowling, and was within
minutes of failure by the time they landed. A narrow escape.

193 *The Aeroplane*, 17 August 1932.

194 Fairey Fox crash: the accident investigation revealed the fire was caused by a
fatigue fracture of the annular connection at the outlet of the petrol pump, with
the escaping fuel being ignited by a flame from one of the stub exhaust pipes. The
fatigue fracture was probably because of undue force being used on the union nut
at the annular connection. The pilot was criticised by the Inspector of Accidents
for not promptly closing the petrol cock, which would have allowed him to retain
full control of G-ACAS as the fire died out. (Source: http://sussexhistoryforum.
co.uk/index.php?topic=2594.0;wap2)

Chapter 17

195 *Fifty Years of Brooklands*, Gardiner, p.371.
196 Cluett, *Croydon Airport 1928–1939*, p.68.
197 Cluett, *Croydon Airport 1928–1939*, p.177ff.
198 *Derby Evening Telegraph* & *Nottingham Evening Post*, 9 September 1936.
199 20 August 1936.

200 Gardiner, p.477 (reprinted by permission of HarperCollins Ltd).
201 Victor Bruce in divorce report.
202 *Empire News*, 8 December 1940.
203 The National Archives, Sempill file (HO 45/17538).

Chapter 18

204 *NL*, p.181 – possible Mildred exaggeration. I am not sure the *Wehrmacht* actually wore puttees!
205 Eric's marital state: the deed in which Mildred granted an income to Theodora Noddings (dated 30 May 1942) refers to Eric as being 'formerly married' to Ada, implying they were divorced by the time of his death. I have not found any other evidence that this was the case.
206 Sempill and the Japanese: all from Sempill's file in the The National Archives.
207 Hughes-Wilson, p.318.
208 *Asaka Maru* Affair – this must still be very sensitive as some parts of the file have been well 'filleted'.
209 The National Archives, Sempill file, WSC minute M 909/1.
210 Secret cipher telegram, 1940A in The National Archives, Sempill file.
211 *Intelligence and the War Against Japan*, Richard J. Aldrich, Cambridge UP, 2000.

Chapter 19

212 Letter from Kenneth Brown Baker, 13 January 1941, Wiltshire County Records.
213 *Action Stations, Vol. 5*, Chris Ashworth, PSL, 1990.
214 Air Ministry Form 1180.
215 John Davies – correspondence with the author.
216 The National Archives – AVIA 5/20 W1008.
217 Wiltshire County Records – deed dated 13 April 1942.
218 Author's interview with Wendy Grimmond.
219 Christie's representative, conversation with author.
220 *Gloucestershire Echo*, 30 May 1945.

Chapter 20

221 Warr was racing an STP Surtees car in the John Player Formula Atlantic series.
222 *Daily Telegraph* 15 November 2003, by David Baines, who appears to have lifted most of this from the introduction of *Nine Lives*.
223 *NL*, p.13.
224 Author's conversation with Spencer Elton, whose father sold it to her.
225 Review of *BF* by 'Daedalus' in *Flight*, 13 November 1931.

SOURCES

The Hon. Mrs Victor Bruce's Books

The Bluebird's Flight (Chapman & Hall, 1931).
Nine Lives Plus (Pelham, 1977).
Nine Thousand Miles in Eight Weeks (Heath Cranton, 1927).
The Peregrinations of Penelope (Heath Cranton, 1930).

Other Books

A History of Britain (Vol 1), Simon Schama (BBC Books, 2000).
A History of the Monte Carlo Rally, Michael Frostick (Hamish Hamilton, 1963).
A Time to Fly, Sir Alan Cobham (Shepheard Walwyn, 1978).
After the Victorians, A.N. Wilson (Arrow, 2006).
Amy Johnson, Constance Babington-Smith (Wm Collins, 1967).
Amy Johnson: Enigma in the Sky, David Luff (Airlife, 2002).
Arms for Spain, Gerald Howson (John Murray, 1998).
Australia and Back, Sir Alan Cobham (A&C Black, 1927).
Aviation Memoirs, Owen Cathcart-Jones (Hutchinson, 1934).
Blackburn Aircraft since 1909, A.J. Jackson (Putnam, 1968).
Britain and the Persian Gulf 1894–1914, Briton Cooper Busch (University of California Press, 1967).
Brooklands: Cradle of British Motor Racing and Aviation, Nicholas Lancaster (Shire Library, 2009).
Croydon Airport 1928–1939: The Great Days, Douglas Cluett, Joanna Nash, Bob Learmonth (London Borough of Sutton Libraries and Arts Services).
European Skyways, Lowell Thomas (Heinemann, 1928).
Fifty Years of Brooklands, Charles Gardner (Heinemann, 1956).
Happy to Fly, Ann Welch (John Murray, 1983).

Heavenly Adventurer: Sefton Brancker & the Dawn of British Aviation, Basil Collier (Secker & Warburg, 1959).

Hidden Victory: The Battle of Habbaniya, May 1941, Air Vice Marshal A.G. Dudgeon (Tempus, 2000).

High-Flying Women: A World History of Women Pilots, Alain Pelletier (Haynes, 2012).

Miles Aircraft Since 1925, Don Brown (Putnam, 1970).

Monte Carlo Rally: The Golden Age, Graham Robson (Herridge & Sons, 2007).

Montlhéry: The Story of the Paris Autodrome, William Boddy (Cassell (now Orion Publishing Group), 1961). All attempts to trace the current copyright holder have been unsuccessful.

More Equal than Others: The Changing Fortunes of British and European Aristocracies, Lord Montagu of Beaulieu (Michael Joseph, 1970).

My Flying Life, Sir Charles Kingsford-Smith (Aviation Book Club, 1939).

On Intelligence, John Hughes-Wilson (Constable, 2016).

Peeresses of the Stage, Cranstoun Metcalfe (Andrew Melrose, 1913).

Playboy of the Air, Jim Mollison (Michael Joseph, 1937).

Shopping, Seduction & Mr Selfridge, Lindy Woodhead (Profile, 2007).

Sir Sefton Brancker, Norman Macmillan (Heinemann, 1935).

Sky Roads of the World, Amy Johnson (W&R Chambers, 1939).

Spitfire Women of World War II, Giles Whittell (Harper Perennial, 2007/8).

Testament of Youth, Vera Brittain (Virago, 2008). Quotations from Vera Brittain are included by permission of Mark Bostridge and T.J. Brittain-Catlin, literary executors for the estate of Vera Brittain, 1970.

The Challenging Sky: The Life of Sir Alliott Verdon-Roe, L.J. Ludovici (Herbert Jenkins, 1956).

The Decline & Fall of the British Aristocracy, David Cannadine (Anchor, 1990).

The First, the Fastest, and the Famous: A Cavalcade of Croydon Airport Events & Celebrities, Douglas Cluett (London Borough of Sutton Libraries & Arts Services, 1985).

The Gaiety Years, Alan Hyman (Cassell, 1975).

The History of Brooklands, William Boddy (Grenville Publishing, 1957).

The Rise of the Plutocrats: Wealth and Power in Edwardian England, Jamie Camplin (Constable, 1978).

The Scandal of the Season, Sophie Gee (Chatto & Windus, 2007).

The Third Route, Philip Sassoon (Heinemann, 1929).

The Thirties, Juliet Gardiner (HarperPress, 2011).

The Twenties, John Montgomery (Allen & Unwin, 1970).

We Danced All Night: A Social History of Britain Between the Wars, Martin Pugh (Bodley Head, 2008).

Wings over Brooklands, Howard Johnson (Whittet Books, 1981).

Women of the Air, Judy Lomax (John Murray, 1986).

Women with Wings, Pauline Gower (John Long, 1938).

Archives

Blackburn Aircraft Company archives at BAe Systems.
Brooklands Museum archives.
Hon. Mrs Victor Bruce – private collection.
Hon. Mrs Victor Bruce commercial archives – Wiltshire County Records Office.
The National Archives, Kew.

Interviews and Private Correspondence

Wendy Grimmond.
Flying Officer John Davies.
Stuart McCrudden.

The destination for history
www.thehistorypress.co.uk